SWAHILI
FOR THE
BROKEN-HEARTED

Cape Town to Cairo by any
means possible

D0012352

PETER MOORE

BANTAM BOOKS

LONDON · NEW YORK · TORONTO · SYDNEY · AUCKLAND

SWAHILI FOR THE BROKEN-HEARTED
A BANTAM BOOK : 0 553 81452 4

First publication in Great Britain
Originally published in Australia and New Zealand by Bantam,
a divsion of Random House Australia (Pty) Ltd in 2002

PRINTING HISTORY
Bantam edition published 2003

1 3 5 7 9 10 8 6 4 2

The Swahili sayings at the beginning of each chapter are from *Swahili Sayings 1* by
S. S. Farsi, reproduced by the kind permission of the Kenya Literature Bureau,
Nairobi, Kenya.

The right of Peter Moore to be identified as the author of this work has
been asserted in accordance with sections 77 and 78 of the Copyright Designs
and Patents Act 1988.

Set in 11/15pt Minion by
Midland Typestters, Victoria, Australia.

Bantam Books are published by Transworld Publishers,
61–63 Uxbridge Road, London W5 5SA,
a division of The Random House Group Ltd,
in Australia by Random House Australia (Pty) Ltd,
20 Alfred Street, Milsons Point, Sydney, NSW 2061, Australia,
in New Zealand by Random House New Zealand Ltd,
18 Poland Road, Glenfield, Auckland 10, New Zealand
and in South Africa by Random House (Pty) Ltd,
Endulini, 5a Jubilee Road, Parktown 2193, South Africa.

Text design by ignition brands

Printed and bound in Great Britain by
Clays Ltd, St Ives plc.

Peter Moore is an itinerant hobo who is lucky enough to be able to support his insatiable travel habit through writing. In doing so he has become the voice of alternative travel both in Australia and the UK. He writes a regular travel feature for *TNT* magazine and has knocked out travel articles for the *Sydney Morning Herald*, the *Times* in London, the *Sun Herald* and the *Australian*. His website continues to pull in the hits and awards. In his travels, Peter has survived a shipwreck in the Maldives, a gas heater explosion in Istanbul, student riots in Addis Ababa and the continuing free fall of the Australian dollar. He survived a confrontation with the legendary Big Nambas tribe in Vanuatu and rates his first encounter with an Asian-style toilet as one of his life's defining moments. At last count he had visited 92 countries but, sadly, still has to doss on friends' sofas whenever he is in London. When he is not lugging his senselessly overweight backpack through Third-World countries, Peter can be found at home in Sydney watching *Neighbours*. Sad really.

No Shitting in the Toilet:

'Moore has a parched dry wit, the solid brass *cojones* of a true traveller and a rare eye for the madness of the wider world'
John Birmingham

'The cheeky, anecdote-packed book – a spin-off from an Internet site Moore created in 1995 – was born when he became aware that traditional guide books failed to accurately describe "what it's like to be in these absurd situations and still end up loving it"'
Who Weekly, 'Inside Scoop'

'Peter Moore's travel guide may well be the most useful of its genre a traveller – novice or seasoned – could select . . . Whether you're actually going anywhere or just thinking about it, this book is a hoot'
Queensland Times

The Wrong Way Home:

'Peter Moore is the genuine article, a traveller's traveller . . . Thoroughly enjoyable . . . Inspirational stuff'
FHM

'Moore's a sharp observer of the bizarre . . . Read, enjoy, escape'
Maxim

Also by Peter Moore

NO SHITTING IN THE TOILET
THE WRONG WAY HOME
THE FULL MONTEZUMA

and published by Bantam Books

CONTENTS

ACKNOWLEDGMENTS

This book is the result of more than just one man and his laptop. On the home front, thanks for all the love and support from my family: Lorraine and Phil Petersen, Les and Judy Moore, my sisters, Lesley-Ann, Vanessa and Melinda, and all the kids – Kai, James, Harrison, Amanda, Taylor and Jessica. Also a special thanks to Andrew Hawkins and Carolyn Crowther for advice, Kilkennys and the occasional grilled tuna steak.

On the road, cheers to Graeme 'Thommo' Thomson from Worldwide Adventure Travel for keeping me entertained in Nairobi and showing me Geoff Crowther's special seat at Buffalo Bill's, and to Clive Moore and Leanne Guild for easing me into my African adventure (although it was largely thanks to their hospitality and generosity that this grand adventure very nearly didn't ever get out of Cape Town). Also, Aneleh Midgely and her daughter Jackie for showing me parts of Cape Town I wouldn't have seen otherwise, and Craig and Sarah Quiding for doing the same in Jo'burg.

Acknowledgments

Thanks as well to Paul and Marjo Heskens for getting me out of the Tropical Hotel in Addis Ababa, and Paul Vettorazzo for all the beers and laughs from Zimbabwe to Kenya (although I was disappointed that after hours of careful explanation I still couldn't convert his love of ice hockey into a deep and abiding appreciation of cricket). A special mention to Academy Award–nominated director Caroline Link, too, for giving me my big break in the motion picture industry. The fact that I have not gone on to great things since is not her fault.

Of course, I couldn't lead this fabulous life without the hard work and dedication of all the folk at my publishers, especially Heather Curdie and Jude McGee at Random House Australia and Simon Taylor, Richard MacDonald and Garry Perry at Transworld UK. A very special thanks to Sally Wray, the most amazing publicist any author could ask for, and Brad Rose, a friendly face whenever I fly into Heathrow.

And finally, I'd like to say a big thanks to Michelle, Alby Mangles's South African love interest in *World Safari III*. It was the sight of her parent's hacienda-style villa in South Africa when Alby came a-calling to ask for her hand in marriage that made me think of going to South Africa in the first place.

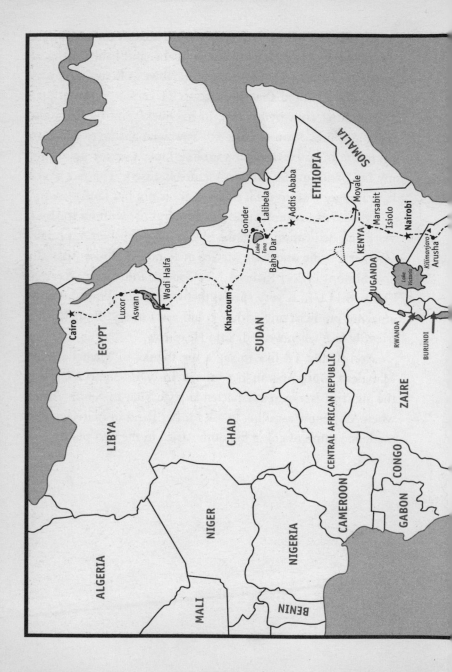

To the desire of my heart

PROLOGUE

Baada ya dhiki, faraja.
After hardship comes relief.

Back in 1999 I wrote a book called *The Full Montezuma* about travelling around Central America with my girlfriend. I called her the GND, short for the Girl Next Door, because she was my neighbour before we left. Six months after we got back we broke up.

I won't go into details other than to say it was entirely my fault. The GND discovered that the things she had written off as travelling idiosyncrasies were in fact full-blown personality disorders and in the short space of a year she went from being the Girl Next Door to the Girl Indoors to the Girl A Couple Of Suburbs Away.

I'm not a big fan of breaking up. No matter how hard you try to keep it civil and friendly, it always ends in tears. A friend

1

of mine says that you should treat a break up the way you'd treat a Bandaid – yank it free in one sharp pull. While I'm not comfortable comparing what the GND and I had with a soggy sticking plaster, he may have a point. My attempt to ease out of the relationship was about as successful as trying to pull off a Bandaid slowly – more pain and over a longer period.

Not that I got any support from my friends. They all loved the GND and thought I was mad for breaking up with her. And the GND's family and friends – who, she delighted in assuring me, had never liked me anyway – acted as though I had gone and joined the Taliban. People I had laughed and joked with over Christmas dinner were now cursing me and, I suspect, reporting me to the appropriate authorities.

Things got *really* awkward one morning when I ran into the GND's sister-in-law. I was on my way to the local store to get a litre of milk and she was standing at the traffic lights on the opposite side of the road. During the entire time the GND and I were together I had only met this woman at parties and family gatherings. I didn't know whether to wave and pretend everything was normal or to ignore her and hope she didn't see me. In the end I did the friendly thing and waved. She snarled at me and walked off in the opposite direction.

I know that doesn't sound like much of an imposition. It wasn't like she pulled out a knife and threatened to neuter me. But it happened in my suburb, on my street, in my space. If I didn't act quickly I'd be forced to face the consequences of what had happened every day of the week. I decided to do what any maladjusted commitment phobe would do. I decided to run away to Africa.

The idea certainly had appeal. Unless I was mistaken, none

of the GND's family or friends, or indeed the GND herself, were planning an African safari any time soon. I would be able to stand on a vast open savanna somewhere until it all blew over, staring off into the middle distance at wildebeests gathering around a waterhole. Or at worst, find a certain anonymity in the crowded buses and bustling villages of the more populated parts of the continent. And if per chance an acquaintance of the GND's popped up, I was sure I could hide behind a mud hut until they passed.

My research showed that I was not alone in taking what I had begun calling 'The Africa Option'. In the late 19th century the continent had been crawling with young men escaping angry fiancees and their shotgun-wielding fathers. I imagined David Livingstone of 'Dr Livingstone, I presume' fame setting off to Africa from Scotland to escape an unhappy marriage. Or Cecil Rhodes, the guy who dreamed of building a railway from Cape Town to Cairo, leaving Oxford in a cloud of recrimination involving the daughter of a local clergyman. I even read somewhere too that my hero, Australian filmmaker and adventurer Alby Mangels, began his travels by leaving his bride at the altar in the small Murray River town of Murray Bridge.

The more I thought about it, travelling from one end of Africa to the other with the wind blowing in my hair and the strains of 'Born Free' playing on a constant loop in my mind seemed the most natural thing for a recently single fellow to do.

It would also give me the chance to tie up a few loose ends. When you break up with someone you feel as though it's an opportunity, if only brief, to do stuff that you always meant to do before you got yourself tied up in a relationship. For most guys those loose ends are a red sports car and a leggy blonde.

For me it was dealing with some unfinished business in Africa.

I'd been to Africa before. But I had only been south as far as Tanzania, so I hadn't seen Table Mountain in South Africa or Victoria Falls in Zimbabwe. Nor had I visited Malawi, one of the friendliest countries on the continent.

I wanted to climb Mount Kilimanjaro. I'd climbed Mount Kenya on my last visit and it was only a couple of hundred metres shorter. But it bugged me that I hadn't climbed the highest mountain in Africa, despite the fact that by all accounts Mount Kenya is the more difficult climb.

I also wanted to visit St George's church, one of the famous chapels hewn from rock in Lalibela, Ethiopia. The first time I saw a picture of it was in Jerusalem. I'd been wandering around the Church of the Crucifix and inexplicably found myself on the roof. It wasn't your normal church roof – it wasn't pitched, nor were there shingles or gargoyles. In fact, it was flat, with a number of small dwellings on top. A group of Ethiopian monks lived in one of them and they invited me into the small stone structure for a cup of coffee.

I have to admit, back then I didn't even know there were Christians in Ethiopia, let alone a form of the religion that was older than that practised in the West, with churches that pre-dated those in Europe. Of course it helped that these men were exotic too. They had coffee-coloured skin and grey beards and wore thick black robes and crucifixes more ornate and beautiful than any others I had seen. I probably would have wanted to go to Ethiopia even if I hadn't spotted the old Ethiopian tourist bureau poster of St George's church above their beds. The image of a church three storeys high, carved into solid rock, just kind of sealed it.

I had my reasons for wanting to finish in Cairo too. My grandfather had been stationed there briefly during World War II. He was a pilot with the RAF, and as the Allies' fortunes waxed and waned they were moved from one country to another. First they were trained in Canada, then brought to the Middle East. Eventually he would end up in Asia, shot down over Burma, dying before ever seeing my mother, who was born after he left for the war.

One of my favourite photos of him when I was a kid showed him standing in front of the Sphinx. He must have been hot – he was in his woollen uniform – but he is smiling, not quite believing that he's in Egypt, standing in front of the wonders of antiquity. It was that photo that had first stirred within me the urge to travel. Now that my grandmother was poorly – she had just had a stroke – I felt an urge to reconnect with that memory of her husband, my grandfather, before she died.

Having said that, going to Africa was not a decision I was ever going to take lightly. A visit to the Dark Continent meant getting vaccinations – lots of them. And if there's one thing I hate more than breaking up, it's getting needles. I have a real problem with the concept of puncturing skin on purpose. I would quite happily suffer everything that a disease can throw at me rather than go through the few moments of discomfort that a preventative vaccination brings.

I guess my phobia started at age five when my mother took me to Dr Austin to get my triple antigen booster. Dr Austin was a feeble old man with a hunch and a white coat that was disturbingly stained. My mother had taken me to his surgery under the guise of having him look at a sniffle I had. After a brief pretence of checking my tonsils and looking in my ears,

Dr Austin shuffled across to his desk as if to write out a prescription. But when he turned, it wasn't a scrap of paper covered in illegible handwriting he was holding. It was a syringe.

To my young mind it played out like a scene from a horror movie. The syringe looked enormous, casting a long and menacing shadow on the back wall of the surgery, and vaccine squirted out the top as Dr Austin tested the plunger. And although my mother denies it to this day, I swear he cackled as he advanced towards me. I waited until he reached out to grab my arm before jumping off the bed and bolting back into the waiting room. In the melee that followed my mother ended up on the floor in an undignified position and Dr Austin accidentally jabbed himself in the arm. I never did get my triple antigen shot, but I'd like to think that Dr Austin missed out on catching diphtheria when it was going around later that year.

I've never been much good at getting injections since and have spent most of my adult life avoiding them. Unfortunately, if I wanted to lose myself in Africa I would have to. Africa is where most diseases get their start in life. The continent acts as a kind of development academy for virulent infections. They practise wiping out entire communities there before venturing out into the big wide world. Even old favourites like anthrax, eradicated everywhere else in the world, keep making more comebacks in Africa than old pub rock bands from the eighties do in Australia.

I decided to put myself in the hands of an expert. That expert was Dr Chu at the Travellers' Medical and Vaccination Centre.

Alarmingly, Dr Chu looked like a younger version of Dr Austin, albeit a little less hunched. Unlike Dr Austin, Dr Chu made no pretence of hiding the tortures that lay ahead. 'Hepatitis A, B, C, D, and E,' he mumbled as he got the vials of serum out of a small bar fridge and arranged them in a neat line in front of me. 'Rabies, that's a course of three . . . yellow fever, you'll need that. Tanzania won't let you in unless you have had that . . . Japanese encephalitis . . . meningitis . . . TB *and* tetanus . . . and, finally, typhoid.'

When he looked up he found me now flat on my back on the consulting bed, my hand pressed to my damp forehead.

'Yes, yes, good idea,' he said, not noticing how pale I'd become. 'Make yourself comfortable. This is going to take a while.'

He wasn't lying. The sun was much lower in the sky when he turned to give me the tablet for polio.

The polio vaccination had been the undoing of my mate Sean. He had visited the same medical centre before going to Africa years ago. After taking all his shots like a trooper, Sean fainted when the doctor announced that the polio vaccine went under the tongue. Poor bastard hadn't realised it was a pill – after so many jabs he assumed it was another needle.

I didn't faint, but at the end of it all my yellow vaccination card had more stamps in it than a library copy of *Lady Chatterley's Lover*.

While I rubbed my arm, silently mouthing 'Oowww!' Dr Chu propped me up and talked about malaria. It was the biggest killer in Africa, he assured me, knocking off close to two million people a year. 'It's rife anywhere north of KwaZulu Natal,' he said. 'And most of the mozzies are immune to chloroquine and paludrine. I'd suggest Larium. There are some side effects but it seems to be the only prophylactic that works.'

The potential side effects included nausea, dizziness, anxiety and the possibility of psychotic episodes. But Dr Chu assured me that only 1 per cent of people using Larium suffered those. As long as I wasn't harbouring any mental illnesses, the worst I could expect was vivid erotic dreams the evenings after I took one. Just what a recently single chap needs!

Then Dr Chu explained other diseases I should be wary of, afflictions rife in Africa that you couldn't get vaccinations for. There was leishmaniasis, causing skin ulcers that never healed, filariasis, the principal cause of elephantiasis, breakbone fever, the ebola virus – the list seemed endless. Then he warned me about intestinal worms that burrowed into your feet as you walked along a beach, tsetse flies that infected you with sleeping sickness and insects that laid eggs under your skin to provide a source of protein for the youngsters when they hatched. It sounded like I was heading off to the set of *Alien*, not a continent only 14 hours away by plane.

'Oh, and one more thing!' Dr Chu called after me as I hobbled out the door, my buttocks clenched involuntarily from all the jabs. 'Be careful of bilharzia. It's in most of the lakes and rivers over there and if you get it, there's nothing you can do. The least you can expect is liver cirrhosis and kidney failure. Your liver and spleen could enlarge abnormally too.'

Cheers, Doc. As alarming as the prospect of a major organ exploding was, it really was the least of my worries. My plan to travel from Cape Town to Cairo along the east coast of Africa would be a path littered with other, more serious problems.

Every country enroute was in a state of political agitation. In Zimbabwe war veterans were repatriating farms, mostly at the sharp end of a machete. In Kenya, opposition to President

Moi's rule was growing more vocal and violent each day. Eritrea and Ethiopia had just concluded a brutal war, but the cease fire was on shaky ground. No one knew what was happening in Sudan or if they were issuing visas. Even in Lesotho, a tiny landlocked country that was sleepy to the point of being comatose, there had recently been a coup attempt that had seen most of the capital, Maseru, go up in flames.

Crime was also a major concern. With so much poverty in Africa, a backpacker, even one as destitute as myself, was regarded as a walking ATM. In South Africa, the most politically stable country I would travel through, more law enforcement officers are killed, more women raped and more cars carjacked than anywhere else in the world. There are over 60 attempted murders a day, homes have panic buttons above the toilets and BMWs are fitted with flame throwers to scorch would-be carjackers. The week before I was due to arrive in South Africa a newspaper reported that a backpacker hostel in Johannesburg had been robbed at gunpoint and the female guests raped.

As sobering as all that was, the biggest danger to my life was my decision to do the trip by public transport. In a continent where famine and disease are commonplace road accidents are by far the biggest killer. In the previous two years alone traffic fatalities in Africa had risen by 300 per cent. Fuelled by bad roads, poorly maintained cars and alcoholic drivers (a recent UN report discovered that 94 per cent of traffic accidents in Africa were alcohol related) the roads of Africa are a killing field. In South Africa over 11,000 people die in motor vehicle accidents each year. By those statistics, I was 1000 times more likely to end up wrapped around a telegraph pole than trampled by a hippo, the biggest killer in the natural kingdom. And that was before I got out of Cape Town.

The foolhardy nature of what I was attempting wasn't lost on my travel agent. 'I hope you've got good travel insurance,' she said when I picked up my ticket to Cape Town. 'One of my clients just got airlifted out of Zululand after her bus went over a ravine. Looks like she may never be able to walk again.'

I think it was about then that I began to suspect that being snubbed by the ex-girlfriend's family at traffic lights wasn't so much of an imposition after all.

Chapter 1

CAPE TOWN, SOUTH AFRICA

Mwenda mbio hujikwaa dole.

A person in too much of a hurry stubs his toe.

I knew I had been in Cape Town too long when people started asking *me* why the freeway overpass near the waterfront had never been finished. It stopped abruptly, just at the bottom of the City Bowl, as the city and inner suburbs are known, and didn't start again for another kilometre or so. It left an unsightly and dangerous drop of 30 metres at both ends, and for some reason I had taken a vague interest in why. Now – sadly – when visitors asked hostel managers about it, they were sent to me. In just ten days I had become the backpacker community's leading expert on Cape Town's unfinished freeways.

There were several theories. Some said it was because the city ran out of money before the freeway was finished. Others, in hushed tones because it reflected badly on South African engineering, spoke of a miscalculation that meant the two ends would never meet up. My favourite theory was that the overpass had been abandoned because it would have blocked the view of Table Mountain enjoyed by old retired seamen in the Salvation Army Hostel. But the really disturbing thing wasn't that there were so many different theories about the two ugly bookends of concrete and exposed metal reinforcement. It was that I knew them.

In retrospect, my decision to start my grand African adventure in Cape Town had not been a smart one. It is a stunning city of white beaches and tall leggy blondes bearing an uncanny resemblance to Charlize Theron. Beer is cheap and good and the parlous state of the rand meant that I could feast on rump steak as thick as a phone book for less than four bucks. Table Mountain provides a dramatic landmark – no matter where I went in the city it brooded, craggy and flat-topped, just to the south, or peeked out seductively from behind a building. And everywhere the good folk of Cape Town go about their business with an assurance that comes from living in one of the most beautiful cities in the world.

Nor did it help that I was dossing with Clive and Leanne in their flat in Gardens, a pretty suburb nestled at the base of Table Mountain. Clive and Leanne ran the southern Africa division of Worldwide Adventure Tours, an overland trucking company that specialised in taking travellers to Zimbabwe through Namibia and Botswana. Leanne, a determined blonde from Perth, made sure travellers got on the trucks. Clive, an English mechanic with a ginger beard that was a touch demonic, made sure the trucks were capable of making it there and back.

Clive and Leanne hardly knew me – it was a friend-of-a-friend doss – but that hadn't stopped them from telling me I could stay as long as I wanted. I had my own room (no long-term couch-related injuries). I had an immediate and lively social circle (they introduced me to their friends). I had unfettered use of a television and a sound system (including a selection of half-decent CDs). And the fridge was full of beer (including half a dozen bottles of prized Primus lager from the former Zaire). If I wasn't in dosser heaven, I was only a couple of clouds off.

It didn't take long for a daily routine to form. When Clive and Leanne left for work in the morning I'd still be in bed. And when they came home they'd find me sitting on the sofa, drinking beer and watching TV soaps.

I'd like to think that I was fixated on soap opera because I was still in a funk over the split with the GND. I was finding consolation in the trials and tribulations of people with big hair and shiny teeth, convincing myself that in comparison my own problems were insignificant. Sure, I'd broken up with the GND, but at least I hadn't found her in bed with her half-brother who was secretly also my own father.

It was a local soap, 'Isidingo', that really had me hooked. Evocatively subtitled, 'The Need', it chronicled the lives and loves of a mining town called Horizon Deep. Cast along demographic lines to reflect the new 'rainbow nation' it was South Africa's most popular television show.

'You're not watching that crap are you?' Clive would ask when he came home.

I'd nod, eager not to be distracted from the latest carryings-on between Maggie Webster, an attractive 25-year-old with a bit of a weight problem, and Constable Leon du Plessis, the solid and incorruptible local policeman.

'You know it's a real place, don't you?' he said. 'I pass the sign every time I go to Harare.'

I said that was all well and good, but if he didn't mind, they were just about to take a group of visiting VIPs on a tour of the mine. And if the dramatic promos that had been showing all week were anything to go by, there was going to be a major explosion that some characters *would not survive*!

'You really ought to get out more,' said Clive, only half joking. 'You're beginning to scare me.'

That was a little unfair. My stay in Cape Town hadn't been all bizarre love triangles and Windhoek Lagers on a comfy couch. I had left the house. A number of times. It was just that they were short trips so I'd get back in time for my shows. It was unfortunate, too, that the time Clive and Leanne walked in after a hard day's work at the office coincided with the prime soapy slot.

For example: I'd caught the Rotair cable car to the top of Table Mountain and marvelled at the spectacular view over the city to Signal Hill and towards Table Bay. Onboard entertainment was provided by a large Afrikaner who couldn't come to terms with the rotating floor, designed to spin slowly so that everyone could enjoy the view. He insisted on holding onto the rail no matter how many times it dragged him to the floor.

Then there was my day trip to the Cape of Good Hope Nature Reserve. Here I wandered along the sandstone cliffs, among the proteas and past the pounding surf, before spending an hour or so in the carpark watching a pack of baboons competing to see who could put the biggest dint in the roofs of the cars parked there. I finished the day at Hout Bay, eating fresh fish in a cafe overlooking the fish markets and the sheer slopes of Chapman's Peak.

Another day I visited the seaside town of Muizenberg to see the brightly coloured bathing sheds. I ate my lunch beside them and enjoyed a lively conversation with a coloured woman who told me a story about being busted by police while she was naked. 'I hope they like blue movies!' she kept muttering. Apparently the whole raid had been videotaped.

At other times you'd find me down at the Victoria and Albert Waterfront, wandering through the smart shops and restaurants, trying hard to convince myself that I wasn't back home at Darling Harbour in Sydney. Most days I'd sit on the docks, flicking food at the seagulls or watching them harass the Mandela huggers, as Clive called them, all clutching their battered copies of *Long Walk to Freedom* as they boarded boats for Robben Island.

I shouldn't have been surprised to find it difficult to leave Cape Town. It has always been a town that seduces visitors to stay a little bit longer than they had planned. In the days when Dutch trading vessels passed by on their way around the Cape of Good Hope, it was a refreshment station for the ships of the Dutch East Indies Company. It was an amiable halfway point where captains could stock up on fresh provisions before heading off for the Far East again.

That it was also known as the 'Tavern of the Seas' indicates the kind of 'refreshment' the sailors were indulging in. To them Cape Town was a place to have a few ales and wink at some wenches before hitting the lonely seas again. I suspect that, like me, a lot of those sailors would have quite happily stayed in Cape Town. But at least they had made a start on their journeys. I hadn't even begun my grand adventure to Cairo yet.

Before I left Cape Town though I wanted to visit a township. Not because I thought the shanty towns out on Cape Flats were the 'real' Cape Town (I've never understood how one facet of a city could be any more 'real' than another). But more out of interest in how things have changed since apartheid unravelled in the early nineties.

Cape Town's black and coloured populations had been moved to Cape Flats, 25 kilometres from the city centre, by the white government back in the eighties in an attempt to 'clean up' an area called District Six. It had been a vibrant district, close to the centre of town, where people from all over South Africa came to live and work at the harbour and in the factories nearby. But District Six was bulldozed and now its former inhabitants are forced to travel to work each day on buses or trains or in taxis and then return at night to makeshift huts in shanty towns like Khayelitsha, Nyanga and Guguletu. In Khayelitsha alone, 1.3 million people are squeezed into 12.2 square kilometres filled with the huts, humpies and lean-tos you see in a World Vision ad.

I had first spotted Khayelitsha on my way into the centre of Cape Town from the airport. From a speeding car it looked like an indiscriminate pile of corrugated iron, plastic and cardboard. It was only when I saw small children playing among the rubble that I realised the place may be inhabited. Then I noticed power lines and tall, slender poles topped with searchlights. Clive told me the lights had been used to illuminate the area when the army came in to flush out ANC rebels in the old days of apartheid.

Of course, the ANC were running the country now. Nelson Mandela was swept to power in the first free elections in 1994, and his successor, Thabo Mbeki, managed to hang on during the last election in 1999. But affordable housing continues to be a problem. Joint ventures between the government and private sector had seen some success – the townships are dotted with tiny two-bedroom homes gaily painted in yellows, reds and blues, which were built cheaply and sold to the very poor at heavily subsidised rates. In fact, since 1994 well over a million of such houses have been built, over 150,000 around Cape Town alone. That most township dwellers are still living in such deplorable conditions indicates the vast scale of the problem.

I'd read in the weekend paper about a woman in Khayelitsha who had turned her shack into a down-at-heel bed and breakfast and decided a visit would be the best way for me to experience township life. Her name was Vicki and when I called the number listed in the article she gave me her address and instructions on how to get there.

Clive was not impressed by my plan to visit Khayelitsha. Like most people living in South Africa his experience of township dwellers was limited to the annoying car space jockeys who roamed the popular thoroughfares like Long Street and Loop Street on foot, looking for empty parking spots that they'd claim as their own. He'd read articles in the newspapers about the high levels of violence and poverty in the townships and considered them hotbeds of crime. When he discovered I planned to stay overnight, he was flabbergasted. 'It's a different world out there, mate,' he said. 'You'll get necklaced!'

Necklacing had been quite a common feature of life in the townships. Any white person found wandering around a township – or any local suspected of consorting with the authorities – had a tyre put around their neck, which was then doused with petrol and set alight.

Clive was even less impressed when I told him that I intended to catch a minivan, or taxi, as the locals preferred to call them. 'Taxi!' he spluttered. 'Do you want me to arrange your funeral now or should I wait until your body turns up in a ditch somewhere?'

Taxis in South Africa don't have the best of reputations. They are poorly maintained and often crash. I had visited a web site about Khayelitsha (even shanty towns have their own web sites these days) and it confirmed that they were death traps. It also hinted that bald tyres and dodgy brakes would be the least of my worries. 'Sometimes the drivers do not wash,' it warned. 'They just get up and smell awful. Sometimes, they are drunk.'

There was also an ongoing dispute over routes between the taxi drivers and the Golden Arrow Bus Company. The dispute had recently escalated into violence and the local papers were calling it a war. Passengers were being shot and bus drivers were wearing flak jackets, so I guess it was war. But I wanted to visit Khayelitsha and there was no other way of getting out there.

The minivan I caught to Khayelitsha came with standard side and forward safety cushioning in the form of African mammas heading back to their township homes after working in the city. They wore the uniforms of the cafes and super-markets that employed them and sat chatting and gossiping with their friends. When I clambered in they shut up immediately and stared at me, stunned. 'What you doing going to Khayelitsha?' asked one after an interminable amount of time. 'Don't you know it's *dangerous*?'

I must have looked startled because she laughed and the other women in the van laughed that big infectious African laugh too. With that laugh the ice was broken. I spent the rest of the journey fielding questions about where I was from and where I was going and trying to convince them that not having any children did not necessarily mean I was impotent.

I steered the conversation towards more comfortable ground by showing the women the address for Vicki's B and B. They passed it among themselves and debated just exactly where I should get off. The consensus was that I should get off at the market in Section C and ask for directions from there. Daphne, a cute check-out girl who worked at the Spar supermarket at Sea Front, said she'd help me.

The other women tittered among themselves. 'You be careful, girl,' one teased. 'He be after your black bootie!'

Daphne and I both blushed, causing more laughter.

I never got to prove that my intentions towards Daphne were (nearly) entirely honourable. When we arrived at the market area of Section C, one of the other passengers, a drunk woman called Ruth, claimed she knew exactly where Vicki's house was and insisted on being the one to take me there. She was wiry and muscly and gave me a look that said she was in no mood to be argued with.

The rattling sliding door on the van took an age to open, but when it did it did so with a loud scraping noise that made sure everyone within 200 metres was looking at me. Young guys slouched drinking beer looked up from their card games, the corner of their mouths curling menacingly. Women buying vegetables from stalls gaped at me open-mouthed, one of them letting the potato she was about to buy fall from her hand and drop to the ground. A guy boiling sheep heads in a 44-gallon drum gave me the kind of look that suggested he was sizing up my head for tastiness and nutritional value. I knew in an instant that I was somewhere I shouldn't be. And my life was in the hands of a woman who had spent the day necking a bottle of moonshine.

'Come, we'll ring that woman from the public phone,' Ruth slurred, dragging me towards a group of the most dangerous-looking guys.

The public phone was in a 'telephone centre' – a shipping container filled with half a dozen phones and a fax too. All the businesses were conducted in old shipping containers – barber shops, shoe repairs, telephone centres – arranged in a line like the shops on a high street back home. I tried Vicki's number. There was no answer.

'Don't worry. You can come back to my mother's house. She has her own phone.'

My first inclination was to wave down the first minivan and pay the driver whatever he wanted to take me back into Cape Town. My second was to get Ruth to ask one of the more kindly looking folk for directions to Vicki's house. But before I could suggest this, Ruth was out of the telephone centre and striding back through the markets towards the main road.

I stopped for a moment to consider abandoning Ruth and trying to find Vicki's house on my own. It couldn't be that hard. But then I felt the hostile stares from the bored young men and started after her again, lucky not to lose her when she dived between two shacks and darted along a tiny dusty path.

Ruth wove a circuitous but assured path through tumble-down shacks and rubbish piles. We passed some children who stopped playing when they saw me, the smallest of them bursting into tears. I tried waving but that only seemed to make matters worse.

We had just left behind one group of small children sobbing uncontrollably when Ruth stopped dead in her tracks. 'Dagga!' she exclaimed, pointing to a shack incongruously surrounded by BMWs and Mercedes.

Dagga was the local slang for marijuana and we had stumbled upon the local drug dealer's house. Terrific! We squeezed sideways between two shacks, hoping that we hadn't been spotted, until we came upon another path.

The drug dealers had spooked Ruth and she insisted that I walk in front of her now. 'Don't worry,' she said, uncon-vincingly. 'You are safe.'

I didn't feel like I was. When Ruth barked out instructions of 'Left!', 'Right!' or 'Straight ahead!' there was barely controlled panic in her voice. I expected one of those hook-handled shepherd's staffs you see in cartoons to come out from between a building and drag me off with a whoosh, never to be seen again.

When we reached a small patch of scrub between some shacks that doubled as a makeshift rubbish dump Ruth barked, 'Stop!' The stench made me want to gag, but I waited silently for Ruth's next instructions. Instead, I heard the sound of a zip being unzipped and a pair of jeans being pulled down.

Such was my frazzled state of mind that I thought Ruth wanted me to have rough sex with her there on the ground.

I figured that if I didn't turn around she would get bored, pull up her jeans and continue on as if nothing had happened. But curiosity got the better of me and I turned to see what she was doing.

Ruth was squatting in the middle of the path with her jeans around her ankles. 'Just having a pee,' she said, smiling awkwardly. I felt relief for the first time that day.

We crossed a pedestrian bridge over a freeway. The bridge was caged completely to stop kids throwing rocks on passing traffic. Then Ruth announced proudly that we were in Sandy Flats.

Ruth's mother lived in a caravan with extra rooms built on the side made from cardboard and tin. She was as shocked as anyone in Cape Flats to see a white man standing on her doorstep, but accepted it as something that her wayward daughter was bound to do sooner or later. I tried to call Vicki on Ruth's mother's phone but there was still no answer. So Ruth's mother invited me to watch TV in the bedroom at the back of the van and try again later. Ruth hit me for five rand and went off to the local shebeen (bar).

Ruth's father was lying on the bed watching 'Days of Our Lives'. He made space for me and for Ruth's mother to sit down. Carrie had just broken into the hospital to change the medical records of her baby. Ruth's mother tutted sanctimoniously, enjoying a little moment of moral outrage. I asked her whether she thought it was really Randy's baby.

She started to answer but checked herself. 'The Church says we shouldn't watch these things,' she said. 'The pastor says they confuse your life.'

A pastor meant that they were Seventh Day Adventists. When I told her that I had been brought up a Seventh Day

Adventist she could barely suppress her delight. A fellow Sev and a soap opera fan – what were the odds of that? She offered to make me a cup of tea, but Carrie punched her sister (who was also the hospital registrar) and we were sucked back into watching the show. The offer of tea was lost in all the confusion.

The credits rolled and I used the ad break before 'The Bold and the Beautiful' began to try Vicki's number again. I was surprised (and a little disappointed) when she answered. She was astounded to hear that I was in Sandy Flats. It was nowhere near her house and she had to borrow a friend's car to come and get me.

Ruth was still at the shebeen when she arrived so I asked her mum to thank her for me.

'She'll be too drunk to remember you,' she said, giving me an affectionate hug goodbye.

Vicki was a large woman in a flowing kaftan and a scarf wrapped high around her head. The scarf was too high and hit the roof of the car, bending the same way Marge Simpson's hair does when she's driving the family car. Vicki told me it was traditional for married women to wear the scarf, but she didn't talk of her husband. I suspected that he had abandoned her – the practice seemed exceedingly common in South Africa – and this enterprise was her way of feeding her family, a family that not only included her four children, it turned out, but her sister and her two children as well.

It took twenty minutes to drive back to Vicki's shack. It was a modest building made from corrugated iron with two decorative swans at the door made from old tyres painted white. Inside it was surprisingly homey, with a feature wall made from interestingly shaped stones and shelves loaded with knick-knacks. Everything sat freshly dusted on doilies, and in the corner a television and a sound system had pride of place. The sound system was one of those smart all-in-one units with flashing LED lights. Not Japanese – Chinese, probably. But still, by township standards, Vicky was doing all right for herself.

There was no shower. Vicki would bring me a tub of cold water if I wanted to wash. And the toilet was a pit out the back that the whole neighbourhood used. I was given the kid's bedroom with a big soft bed that all four of them usually slept in. They didn't mind getting kicked out – it meant they would be sleeping with Mum – so I threw down my bag and lay on the bed, studying the school timetable written in pencil on the back of the door. Eventually, finally, I'd made it to my township B and B.

Dinner was served promptly at six o'clock on a small table that the whole family gathered around. We ate chicken stew and drank Coca-Cola that was poured from a 1.25 litre bottle placed on the table like a bottle of fine wine. As I ate the children reached across and tentatively stroked my hair. My flat soft hair was a revelation to them, so different from the coarse, springy hair they had. In the days of apartheid hair was used to determine your colour. A pencil was stuck in your hair and if it fell out you were white. If it didn't you were deemed coloured and sent off to a township.

Vicki shooed them away with a laugh. I asked her how she had come up with the idea for her B and B.

'One day I saw a minibus full of tourists driving through Khayelitsha,' she explained. 'They were all gawking, taking pictures but too scared to get out. I wanted to show them that we were not wild animals in a zoo.'

It took Vicki a while to bring the community around. The only white people they knew were police so when Vicki had guests her neighbours would ask if she was in trouble. Then the local children stopped playing with her children because they thought the house was full of doctors. The only time they'd had any dealings with white people was to get a painful injection. Eventually the community saw the benefits in what she was doing and some neighbours were now talking about opening up their houses to visitors.

'It's mainly tourists who stay here,' she said. 'We would really like South Africans to come and see what it's like out here, but they are still afraid.'

As well as running the B and B, Vicki organised a dance troupe of young kids. They performed traditional dances for the tourists who came to Khayelitsha on day tours. She began a support group for women starting up small enterprises and was an active member of the local community's crime initiative.

When I told her that I was exhausted just thinking about what she did she laughed. 'It is up to us to change the future,' she said.

I finished my stew and Vicki took me across the road to the local shebeen. It was called the Waterfront because it had a tap out the front. People came here from all over the neighbourhood to collect water, gossiping and discussing politics as they filled their jugs. Vicki said the owners were also having a sly dig at the upmarket bars at the Waterfront down town.

The shebeen was barely distinguishable from the other shacks, except maybe for the bare power cable illegally attached to the power line out the front to keep the beer fridge running.

Vicki introduced me to a guy called Elvis and told him to bring me home when I was 'finished'.

Elvis was drinking with his friends at a table in the back corner of the bar. They looked like members of an LA hip-hop band who'd had all their jewellery stolen. Judging by the number of bottles on the table it looked like they'd been there all day.

'In the ghetto with Elvis,' I joked as I sat down. No one else seemed to get my oblique pop culture reference – I guess the King wasn't too big in these parts – so I let it slide.

'Two years ago you would have been dead by now,' said Elvis matter-of-factly. 'We'd have thought you were from the army and beaten you up, maybe even necklaced you.'

He poured me a beer and I smiled nervously, wondering if a little Fight Club action might not still be on the agenda.

'Now look!' he said, grinning, raising a chipped glass. 'Here we are in my shebeen, drinking beer.'

It seemed that drinking was all these guys did. Elvis told me that they couldn't get jobs, they didn't have homes and the money they used to buy beer came from mothers and girlfriends or 'other ways'. Most days – and nights – were spent here, in this shebeen, at this table.

When it was my shout, I decided to shell out the extra 10 cents for a bottle of Crown to show that the dark days of apartheid were over. I plonked the bottle down on the table triumphantly, expecting murmurs of appreciation. I got hostile stares instead. Blokes who had been laughing and slapping me on the back only seconds before were now muttering among themselves, perhaps wondering where they could get a tyre and a tin of gasoline at this time of night.

Even Elvis, who I'd considered to be my new best friend, was looking at me with barely concealed contempt. 'Why did you bring us this woman's drink?' he spat. 'Are you saying we're *gay*?'

I knew some people get very tribal about the brand of beer they drink. A friend of mine refuses to drink in a pub with VB on tap. But I'd never heard of anyone's sexuality being questioned because of it.

Elvis shook his head in disgust. 'It's not beer, man,' he said, indicating for me to try it. 'It's wine!'

It was apple cider, actually. Quite tasty too. But by buying it I had cast aspersions on their sexuality and mine as well. My explanation that I thought that it was Crown Lager, my favourite beer back home, was grudgingly accepted, but only after I hurried back to the bar to buy a bottle of Castle. And it wasn't until I agreed to buy the next couple of rounds as well that my credibility was fully restored.

It was well after midnight when Elvis walked me back to Vicki's place, 'just to be safe'. He knocked on the door and didn't leave until Vicki opened it and let me in. I sunk into bed that night, my head spinning from the beer, wishing that Vicki had chosen colours a little less lurid when she was decorating the guest room.

The next morning, after a delicious breakfast of hot porridge, Vicki took me on a walk around Khayelitsha. She showed me the schools and the hospitals and introduced me to Rose, a woman who single-handedly ran a soup kitchen. Another mother, abandoned and stuck with the kids, Rose got up at four o'clock every morning to serve over 600 meals a day.

Rose could have been forgiven for being tired and grumpy, but when I met her she was beaming. 'A food company just said they'd supply me with rice,' she said. 'That will make a *big* difference!'

At the end of the day Vicki walked me to the taxi stand where I had arrived the day before with Ruth. It was only a block away from Vicki's house – a 500-metre walk at most. We stopped and chatted with women who were helping a friend move, by carrying chairs on their heads, and others who were selling bags of oranges that hung decoratively on the front wall of their shacks. I remember thinking about all the bad news stories we get out of Africa and wondering why we didn't hear more about women like Rose and Vicki. They were positive, vibrant women trying to make a difference. Maybe our attitude to the continent would be different if we heard about them instead of depressing stories about AIDS and corruption.

Vicki put me in a minivan heading into town and waved goodbye. It was full of sullen men going into town to get drunk or visit prostitutes. They didn't talk to me like the women had. They sat silently with their heads bowed, avoiding contact with me, sensing, perhaps, that I was judging them. I had met their women and seen the way they were trying to make a difference. The men sat around drinking beer, letting their children play among the bare electricity wires. Worse, they would bring AIDS into their homes, contracted, in all likelihood, on nights out like this. By the time I got back to Clive and Leanne's flat the optimism for Africa that Vicki and Rose had inspired in me had dimmed.

My mood was not improved when I discovered that I had missed the season finale of 'Isidingo'. As I had suspected there *had* been an explosion and *people were still trapped*! Clive took unseemly delight in relating the details (he had started watching 'Isidingo' too, just to see what I saw in it, he claimed) and in telling me that there had been a report on the news about plans to finally finish the freeway overpass.

There was nothing keeping me in Cape Town now. It was time to see the rest of Africa.

Chapter 2

THE GARDEN ROUTE, SOUTH AFRICA

Kila ndege huruka kwa bawa lake.
Every bird flies with its own wings.

On the Sunday morning I finally left Cape Town it was raining. I scurried down Government Lane, the leafy pathway that cuts through the botanical gardens, cursing both the inclement winter weather and my decision to pre-purchase a ticket to Oudtshoorn. I'd bought the ticket in advance hoping that the prospect of losing 100 rand would force me to leave Cape Town. And I'd chosen Oudtshoorn because I thought that its famous ostrich races might be just the motivation I needed to get up before dawn. But the rain that morning was steady and cold, and when it started trickling off my pack and down the back of my neck I seriously considered turning back to my warm bed.

I didn't, of course. And it wasn't because I couldn't afford to lose the $25 or that the lure of the ostriches was irresistible. I just knew that if I didn't leave Cape Town that morning I never would. So I pulled up my collar and pressed on, through the gardens and across the streets shiny with rain, then waved down the white Translux coach as it pulled out of the Cape Town bus terminal.

I was sad to be leaving Cape Town. I'd slept comfortably and eaten well, two things I never thought I'd do in Africa. And I'd made a lot of new friends. Now I was sitting in a modern white coach with heating that fogged the windows and velour seats that soaked up the rain from my clothes. I wiped the window with the cuff of my jacket and watched Cape Town go by in the grey light of dawn. I had a dull feeling in the pit of my stomach. The whole continent lay ahead of me and I wasn't sure what was in store. I just knew it wouldn't be as, well, comfortable.

That had been a deliberate choice. Clive and Leanne had offered me a free trip to Victoria Falls on one of their overland truck tours. I could have continued my Cape Town lifestyle, passing through Namibia and Botswana in the back of a well-appointed Mercedes truck among like-minded individuals. And I would be gazing at the majesty of Victoria Falls, admittedly through hazily hungover eyes, within ten days.

I decided instead to take a month or so to travel along the east coast of South Africa, calling into the tiny kingdoms of Lesotho and Swaziland and detouring through flood-ravaged Mozambique. It would be harder travelling – I wasn't even sure if the roads had re-opened in Mozambique yet – but that was part of the appeal. I knew that life would be as easy in Victoria Falls as it had been in Cape Town. And although

I really wanted to see the falls, I felt a little bit of delayed gratification was in order.

An hour out of Cape Town it was still raining heavily as the bus driver crunched down through the gears to tackle a steep mountain pass. It was foggy and water cascaded down the craggy peaks and onto the road. Only the week before another Translux bus had crashed here, plunging down a ravine, killing the driver and leaving 30 passengers seriously injured. The wreckage was still there – I spotted it as we rounded a sharp hairpin bend. The hostess, in a neat blue and white uniform, sensibly waited until we had successfully negotiated the pass before she brought us a cup of coffee and a biscuit.

By noon the bus had reached Swellendam, a neat white-bread town nestled at the bottom of snow-capped mountains. The God-fearing townsfolk drove home from church infuriatingly slowly in perfectly maintained cars from the sixties. A young guy with ginger hair and close-set eyes got on the bus and sat next to me. He shook my hand energetically and introduced himself as Jacques. Tall and goofy Jacques stank of sheep-dip. He was off to work on his uncle's farm just outside of Oudtshoorn.

'Did you see the rugby?' he asked when he found out I was from Australia. 'Awww, I wish we could play like that!' He surveyed the interior of the coach with child-like wonder. Reaching up, he played with the air vents above his head. Then he pulled out the elasticised pouch on the back of the seat in front, letting it flick before yelping with delight. Much to the dismay of the woman sitting behind him he also discovered the lever that made his seat recline.

On the outskirts of the town we passed paddocks with the

names of the crops painted on signs. I asked him why and he thought I was testing him. 'So the farmers remember what they've planted?' he answered expectantly.

I smiled, mainly because he was probably right, and he beamed like an excited dog that had just brought a stick back to its master.

The bus turned from the main road and headed up into the Langeberg Range, bleak and jagged mountains that create a formidable barrier between the coast and a vast area of high semi-desert known as the Karoo. It struggled to negotiate the steep passes and tight switchbacks, crawling past patches of snow where boys, rugged up against the bitter cold, herded sheep. But by late afternoon the mountains were behind us and we barrelled along a high dry plain. Soon we were approaching Oudtshoorn.

Our progress along the main road of Oudtshoorn was hindered by a group of about 50 ostriches being herded down the road like cattle. They pranced down the street, fluffing their feathers, steam hissing from the nostrils on their beaks in the cold afternoon air, as a young black boy used a stick to keep them in formation.

It was an extraordinary sight and Jacques leaned across me, excitedly pressing his nose against glass. 'Ostriches!' he guffawed. '*Cool*!'

Oudtshoorn is famous for its ostriches. Just before World War I, ostrich feathers fetched extraordinary prices in Europe and there were up to 750,000 ostriches in the area. The farmers, known as feather barons, amassed ridiculous fortunes and their prosperity is reflected in the grand public buildings that dot the town. These boom days are long gone but ostriches are still the town's lifeblood. Feathers are sold to make dusters and skins are turned into handbags and wallets. Ostrich meat is exported or salted and dried to make biltong for local consumption. And the town is full of shops selling crappy souvenirs to tourists like me who come from all over the world to gawk at the birds.

It was strange to be in a place where ostriches are considered a legitimate part of the community. There was a time not so long ago when Australian newspapers were full of ads selling shares in ostrich farms so I've always associated them with dodgy investment schemes. The ads always featured a close-up of an ostrich face – have you noticed how difficult it is to ignore a picture of an ostrich looking you square in the eye? – and invariably promised ridiculously extravagant returns. Of course, the only people who made any money out of the schemes were the guys who set them up. They'd abscond with all the money to an unnamed South American country just as reporters from current affairs programs came knocking on their doors.

Call me a bastard, but I have no sympathy for people who lose their life savings investing in ostriches. Ostrich steaks are never going to take the place of snags and chops on the barbie. An ostrich egg is just a little too big to start the day with. And anyone who watches daytime television knows that technology has created a more effective way to pick up dust than a bunch of lice-riddled feathers. It's called the Dustbuster 3000 (formerly Dustbuster 2000), and I have a cupboard full of them that I am still paying off on an easy-instalment scheme.

Jacques's uncle was waiting for him at the bus station. He was a quiet, solid Afrikaner whose unearthly stillness was magnified by Jacques's manic energy. He greeted his nephew without emotion then dealt unflinchingly with Jacques's constant question of 'When do I get to feed the ostriches?' by ignoring it. But when they drove off and Jacques started winding the windows up and down, I'm sure I saw a flicker of panic in his uncle's eyes.

I took a room at the optimistically titled Backpackers Oasis. It wasn't an oasis but it was cheap and offered guests a complimentary barbecued ostrich steak on arrival, regardless of the hour, and scrambled ostrich egg for breakfast every other day.

I spent my time in Oudtshoorn immersing myself in all things ostrich. I learned that one ostrich egg is the equivalent of 24 chicken eggs and that if you are ever attacked by an ostrich it is best to lie flat on the ground (their unique knee structure means they can only kick straight out). I hired a bike and rode to outlying farms, watching chicks hatch in incubators and older birds run in races organised especially for tourists. I fed an ostrich, fed on ostrich (I thought it tasted like beef), and if I hadn't been at the beginning of my journey I probably would have bought an ostrich egg with my name carved on it in an elegant script.

As exciting as all that was I was ready to leave Oudtshoorn by the second day. After Cape Town, sitting in a pub listening to a bunch of Afrikaners bemoaning the decline of the international feather duster market held little interest. Even winding them up by espousing the superior performance of the Dustbuster 3000 soon lost its appeal.

My plan was to go back down the mountain to George, a small seaside town that marks the beginning of the Garden Route. A picturesque stretch of coast along the south of the country, the Garden Route is dotted with resort towns and backed by untouched natural parks. From George I could catch the Outeniqua Choo-Tjoe, an old steam train that trundled along the picturesque coastline to Knysna. The train left at 9.30 am. To catch it I would have to take an early morning minivan to George.

The van was scheduled to leave at six and it was still dark when I got down to the minivan station. Because minivans are used almost exclusively by the black population, the station is in the 'black' part of Oudtshoorn. In the 'new' South Africa that's the centre of town, ironically the area that blacks weren't allowed anywhere near during apartheid. Now the whites live on the outskirts of town behind bars and razor wire, having abandoned the town centre to market stalls, PEP stores and the local Pick 'n' Pay.

I joined a group of people warming their hands around a fire in a 44-gallon drum. They murmured to each other when I first stepped up – a white person not exactly a common sight in those parts – but after they spotted my backpack they shuffled aside and made room for me. A man in a beanie asked me where I was going, and I told him George. Nothing else was said, but when the van to George arrived he pointed it out to me.

The van was a Toyota Hi-Ace from the seventies. My dad had one exactly like it when I was a kid. He was a plumber and even back then he had bought his second-hand. His apprentices would roughly toss their tools in the back and drive it like they were in a smash-up derby race. That said it was still in better condition than this one. For one thing, the side sliding door on my father's van was attached and functional. But here, when the first passenger tried to open the minivan side door, it kept sliding and then landed with a loud crash on the asphalt.

The driver and his offsider set about putting it back on. They tried to line up the runners on the top and bottom of the door with the tracks on the van, but as soon as they got the top runners in the tracks the bottom runners would pop out. They tried starting with the bottom runners and the same thing happened, except this time the top runners popped out. The driver said it was because the offsider had been dropped on his head as a baby. The offsider said it was because the driver was crap in bed. Twenty minutes later they gave up trying to get both sets of runners in and just rested the runners on the bottom of the door in the appropriate groove instead. The top part of the door was held in place by passing a piece of rope through the window and tying it to the roofrack.

As amusing and entertaining as all this was, I had a train to catch. The train left at 9.30 am and I'd been told that the 50-kilometre trip to George through the Outeniqua Range would take about an hour. By my calculations that had me in George just after seven, giving me plenty of time to buy a ticket and enjoy a steaming hot coffee as I leisurely read the morning paper.

I hadn't counted on the re-engineering of the door, of course. That had been a foolish oversight. Given the poor state of minivans in South Africa if it hadn't been the door it would have been something else – the brake lines or some other such trifle. Nor had I factored in time for the pick-ups. When the van finally left the station at half past seven, we toured the outlying townships until we all had another passenger on our laps and they had one on theirs as well. We then stopped for petrol on the edge of town before cruising by the ostrich abattoir to see if anyone else wanted to go to George.

It was well past eight when we finally reached the outskirts of Oudtshoorn and headed down the spectacular Outeniqua Pass. I asked the offsider if he thought I would make my train and he stroked his chin in a concerned manner. The driver slapped him and then turned to me to say, 'Eh! Of course!' In doing so he took his eyes off the road and let the van veer across two lanes towards a guardrail. The offsider grabbed the wheel and righted the van, saving us from a sheer but eminently picturesque drop to a rock-strewn valley below.

I considered our safe arrival in George that day as proof of a loving and kind God. His hand was evident in the number of head-on collisions He saved us from. The closest call came when the driver, arguing the merits of a goal scored by the Kaiser Chiefs in a weekend soccer match, hadn't noticed that he'd let the van stray into the path of a truck crawling up the hill with a load of bricks. A scream from a female passenger alerted him to take evasive action, but by the time he was back on the right side of the road, after passing the truck on the wrong side, he was arguing about another dodgy referee decision in the same game.

More miraculous was the fact that we arrived in George before half past nine. We actually got there at 9.14, but spent the next ten minutes casually cruising up and down the wide tree-lined streets of George, dropping off passengers within millimetres of where they wanted to go. Soon I was the only passenger left in the van. The offsider turned to ask me where I wanted to go. The train station, I said, and he slapped his forehead as if to say, 'That's right!' Then he asked me if I knew where it was.

The guys had no idea where the George train station was.

Their clientele came to town to work or buy supplies, not to catch an old steam train run exclusively for tourists. We stopped and consulted the map in my guidebook, before tearing off down Market Street, scattering shoppers and school children in our wake. It was 9.31 when we hit the carpark, the driver executing a perfect handbrake stop that showered the steps at the station entrance with gravel in a dramatic, cop show fashion.

'Here it comes!' hollered the offsider, pointing to a puff of black smoke approaching the station. Against all odds, it seemed, I had made it.

Except that the Outeniqua Choo Tjoe didn't stop at George station. It was a tourist train and the guard sweeping the platform told us that it left from the platform at the Railway Museum, about 500 metres back towards Oudtshoorn. It passed through George station, he said, but didn't stop until it reached Wilderness, a small seaside community half an hour away. That we could see it coming towards us meant it had already left.

The minivan guys weren't that easily beaten. They had promised me that I would catch my train and, by George, I was going to catch it. They jumped onto the tracks in front of the train and waved crazily at the driver until he brought the train to a shuddering, wheezing stop. I clambered on board and they scrambled back onto the platform, whooping and hollering as they waved goodbye. The train had barely started moving again before they started slapping each other, accusing the other of nearly making me miss it.

I know this sounds ungrateful but it wasn't long before I began wishing that I had missed the train. I immediately found myself surrounded by grey-haired couples with blankets and thermoses and freshly cut sandwiches who seemed to be genuinely excited that the rattling wooden carriages we were sitting in were being pulled by a class 24 locomotive built in 1846.

I'd allowed myself to be talked into the train ride by a breathless woman at the Oudtshoorn tourist office. She was a bit overweight and wore a little too much makeup, and she assured me that if I didn't catch the Outeniqua Choo-Tjoe my whole trip to South Africa would be an entire waste of time.

It wasn't the first time I'd been talked into visiting a tourist attraction only to end up being disappointed. The Torture Museum in Sighişoara in Romania springs immediately to mind. That was just a pair of shackles on a stone wall and a tape player emitting the garbled sound of clinking chains. The woman running it sensibly refused to turn the light on until I'd handed over my money and pretended she didn't under-stand me when I demanded my money back.

The Outeniqualand Preserved Railroad wasn't quite that bad. The driver did all the things expected of a steam engine driver. He wore a blue and white striped cloth cap and matching bib 'n' braces and blew the steam whistle when we emerged from tunnels. The scenery was suitably spectacular too. One minute we'd emerge from a tunnel and trundle along the edge of a cliff, the surf breaking 100 metres below. The next we'd be winding through emerald-green farmland, a frisky horse galloping beside us.

I don't know why I expected it to be any different. I was on the Garden Route and a place doesn't get a name like that because it is a long stretch of bars and strip joints. It gets called the Garden Route because it has significant tracts of indigenous plants like proteas, gladioli and agapanthus as well as tea shops and craft fairs for the folk who like that sort of thing. Unfortunately I was still a couple of decades away from the uncontrollable urge to collect teaspoons.

The train arrived at Knysna with a sigh of steam, just after noon. The final approach across the lagoon along a thin man-made embankment got my hopes up that Knysna may have offered something more, but by the time I had passed my third tea shop on the way from the station to the centre of town my hopes had been dashed and I decided instead to catch a minivan to Plettenberg Bay.

My arrival in Plettenberg Bay confirmed my worst fears about travelling through this part of South Africa in the off-season. I felt like I was arriving at a party an hour after it had finished. There were indications everywhere that a good time had been had by all and sundry. But the stereo was silent, the fridge was empty and the only sign of life was the odd person passed out in a doorway.

Lodged between Robberg Peninsula and the fantastically named Keurbooms River Lagoon, and set above a long golden beach, Plettenberg Bay would be a completely different proposition in summer. The numerous ice cream parlours suggested flustered parents and noisy kids demanding a double cone not a single one. The shuttered surf shops conjured images of guys in board shorts with surfboards tucked under their arms heading off for the main beach. The posters for whale-watching tours hinted of 'right-on' girls in cargo shorts and bikini tops strolling by on their way to coo at endangered species. But it was the middle of winter – the streets were deserted and a bitter wind made shutters clap like a horror movie.

I had fancifully thought that travelling in the off-season would see me benefit from all kinds of special deals. I imagined grateful hotel owners offering me luxurious hotel suites with Jacuzzis for a dollar or two. Or desperate restaurateurs feeding me magnificent meals for a pittance and then throwing in a complimentary jug of beer to reward me for my custom. I would have the golden beach all to myself, undisturbed by the maddening crowds of gym-junkie Afrikaners in tiny Speedos. But by the look of things I'd be spending my time in Plettenberg Bay in my room playing Solitaire on my laptop.

When I walked into the Plettenberg Bay Hostel looking for a room the manager was asleep at his desk. 'Where did you come from?' he spluttered, trying desperately to get his bearings. 'The Baz Bus has already been!'

The Baz Bus is a jump-on, jump-off bus service that runs from Cape Town along the coast and then up into Johannes-burg. Once you have bought your ticket you can get off wherever you like, and jump back on when you're done. Such is its popularity with backpackers that hostel owners operate their businesses around its timetables. When I told the manager, Patrick, that I had caught a minivan he tutted and told me they were dangerous.

As I filled in the guest book I noticed an advertisement above the reception desk for the Bloukrans River Bridge bungy jump. I'd never bungy jumped before and as I was still shaking off the lethargy induced by the Outeniqua Choo-Tjoe, I figured a quick 216-metre plunge at the end of a giant elastic band might help clear the head and kick start the heart again. I asked Patrick how far away it was.

'About 40 ks,' he said. 'I can drive you there if you like.'

I should come clean at this point and admit that it was also my birthday. If I'd still been with the GND she would have surprised me with a little gift and probably arranged for us to go somewhere nice for dinner. Instead I was feeling like a Nigel-No-Friends, alone and forgotten. I could have told the grannies on the train, of course. They probably would have sung me a croaky rendition of 'Happy Birthday' and given me one of their scones or, if I was really lucky, a souvenir teaspoon. And if I mentioned it to Patrick, I'm sure he would have bought me a beer. But informing total strangers that it's your birthday smacks of desperation to me. I decided instead to celebrate by throwing myself off a bridge.

The road east from Plettenberg Bay skirts along a lagoon and past empty caravan parks before climbing up onto a high plateau. Here it crosses a series of concrete span bridges over deep gorges, cut over the millennia by rivers running to the sea. The Bloukrans River Bridge, the site of the world's highest bungy jump, spans the largest and most spectacular gorge.

The jump was from the apex of the concrete arch that supports the bridge. I paid my money at the office beside the gorge and made my way towards the jump site along a rickety walkway suspended on the underside of the bridge. This was already more petrifying than I had imagined the jump to be. It was just a cage, really, and bounced and shook as I made my way along it. I could see through the bottom of the walkway to the river below – it looked a couple of kilometres away. I shuffled along terrified, convinced that at any moment the bolts securing the walkway would come loose and the walkway and I would go hurtling towards the rocks below.

A group of four guys waited for me on the arch. There were a couple of Kiwis, an Aussie and a South African and they all acted like they had been mainlining Pepsi Max. I don't think they'd been very impressed by the way I'd crawled rather than walked upright across the arch from the walkway.

They explained the whole process and the dangers involved with an enthusiasm that frightened me even more.

'Attaching bungy to nothing in particular,' said one.

'Check,' said another.

'Tie it around jumper's leg in exaggerated manner so he thinks we really give a shit about safety.'

'Check.'

'Roll a joint to smoke while we leave him just dangling there.'

'Check.'

They didn't really say that of course. They said lots of reassuring technical things designed to put my mind at rest. But despite their professionalism and the obvious way they crossed all the i's and dotted all the t's I was shitting myself. It just wasn't in my DNA to jump off high things. Every shuffled step towards the edge was a mighty struggle against all my natural instincts. I thought I was hiding it well though. In my mind's eye my face was passive and I was the model of cool and calm. Watching the video later, I realised I was the poster boy for wide-eyed, open-mouthed panic.

I came very close to pulling out of the jump when I got to the edge. I had been dragged there whimpering, leaning back pathetically, and I made the mistake of looking down. I didn't have a group of friends to egg me on – Patrick had stayed up at the office to flirt with the Kiwi girl working there. And the Pepsi

Max guys couldn't make me do it. I think it might be against the bungy code of practice to actually push someone over the edge.

Sensing that my resolve was wavering, the South African guy quickened the countdown, starting at three rather than the customary ten. 'Threetwoonebungy!' he shouted, and the next thing I knew I was dangling at the bottom staring at the rocks 100 metres or so below me.

I had rather fancied that when I jumped my whole life would flash before my eyes. Or at the very least, the three months I dated a Spanish girl called Inez. But all I remembered – and too late, as it turned out – was that I left the key to the padlock on my backpack in my top pocket. I dangled there, my nose running like a tap, convinced concurrently that I would drown in my own snot and that the bungy was coming loose around my ankles. Eventually one of the guys lowered himself down and winched me to the top.

It was amazing the confidence the dose of adrenalin gave me. I stood on the concrete arch laughing and joking with the guys like I was in a pub, not on a concrete arch where the slightest puff of wind would blow me off to a certain and grisly death. I farewelled them with a flurry of high fives and strode over the rickety bridge confidently and without looking down. I felt so good that I shelled out the equivalent of a month's budget to buy the video of my jump.

As we drove back to Plettenberg Bay Patrick asked if I'd do it again.

'Once is enough,' I said. The adrenalin had worn off already.

Not even the need to find a locksmith to pick the padlock on my backpack could keep me on the Garden Route any longer. I decided that if worst came to worst I would use the patently inadequate metal saw on my Swiss Army knife to hack through it.

I spent the next two days travelling to Bloemfontein, the last South African town of any size near the mountain kingdom of Lesotho.

Chapter 3

LESOTHO

Shoka lisilo mpini halichanji kuni.
An axe without a handle does not split firewood.

J R R Tolkien was born in Bloemfontein. You wouldn't know it though. The house he grew up in has been turned into a cut-price furniture store and there isn't a single statue or plaque in the town acknowledging that this was where the creator of *The Lord of the Rings* took his first breath. There's a guy who runs a Tolkien-themed guesthouse with rooms named after hobbits and a menu heavy on ale and berries, but that's it. I think the good folk of Bloemfontein are a little miffed that Tolkien left when he was four and never came back.

I mention J R R not because like him I was in a hurry to leave Bloemfontein (which I was) but because my next stop, the tiny mountain kingdom of Lesotho, struck me as a very Tolkien kind of place. It is perched in high jagged mountains that rise from the dusty plains of Free State like the mountains of Mordor. How much of an influence this intimidating landscape had on the young J R R Tolkien is difficult to gauge. He barely mentioned the place in interviews. But I challenge anyone to look at those mountains from Bloemfontein and not think they are full of orcs and goblins.

Of course, Lesotho is not full of orcs and goblins. The Basotho people are friendly and gregarious and without any of the bitterness that lingers in South Africa because of apartheid. During those troubled times Lesotho was an independent kingdom, having been granted self-government by the British in the 1960s. Although poor and overpopulated, Chief Jonathon, the ruler back then, portrayed his country as a small, embattled nation fighting its racist neighbour, and the aid dollars came flooding in. The money was wasted, of course, and nothing was done to alleviate the long-term problems of poverty and dependence. Lesotho is once again reliant on wages sent back from migrant workers and the money the South Africans pay for water from the Lesotho Highlands Water Scheme.

For the trivia buffs out there, Lesotho is completely sur-rounded by South Africa, one of only three countries in the world completely encircled by another single country (the Vatican and the Republic of San Marino are the others). It also has the highest low point of any country in the world at over 1300 metres above sea level.

Maseru is the capital of Lesotho and in the afternoon sun it reminded me an awful lot of Kathmandu. It is in a valley surrounded by a ridge and while it has a few modern buildings, once you get out of the small city centre it is positively rural. Here people live in modest mud brick huts with smoke from cooking fires seeping from the roof. Each home has a couple of goats and some chickens and small gardens that they tend expertly. Even the parliament building is unassuming for a structure of national importance and looks more like the sort of place a poultry farmer on the outskirts of Sydney might build after he subdivided his property and came into a bit of money.

The most striking thing about Lesotho is that everyone wears a blanket. They sling it across their shoulders in a jaunty fashion that suggests wearing bedding is the most natural thing in the world to do. And who is to say they are wrong? With a bit of practice one could get out of bed without having to bother getting dressed. Even the children wear them, albeit of a smaller, more practical size.

The Basotho started wearing blankets shortly after their first contact with Europeans in the 19th century. The missionaries who first ventured into the mountain kingdom were disturbed by how little the local folk wore and they encouraged them to cover up. Canny traders introduced the Basotho to blankets and they quickly replaced traditional but skimpy animal skins as the attire of choice. Part of the reason for the rapid uptake of blanket wearing was that they were perfectly suited to the climatic extremes of the country. In fact, the Basotho believe that if you carry a blanket and a pocketknife you can always sleep and you can always eat.

The Basotho have a wardrobe of blankets of varying quality and featuring different designs. Which ones they wear depends on the circumstance. Simple blankets are used for utilitarian purposes. The ones with more complex designs are dusted off for important occasions. (British designs like the Sandringham, named after the royal palace at Sandringham, and the Victoria England Crest, associated with Queen Victoria, are held in particular high regard.) It is a commonly held belief that a correctly chosen blanket adds gravity, elegance and a certain symbolism to an event.

I was shown to my room at the back of the St James church by a guy wearing a plain grey blanket. Obviously my arrival had not been expected.

The next morning I wandered up the Kingsway into the centre of Maseru. The Kingsway is the grandest road in the kingdom and had been asphalted especially for a visit by Queen Elizabeth. For a long time it was the only sealed road in Lesotho and even now it is where you find most of the important government buildings and shops. Or what is left of them. Most of the buildings were razed during the riots of 1998, when people took to the streets to protest against another dodgy election result (it is not unusual for the king to declare results invalid). South Africa sent in troops, 100 people died, and lots of businesses didn't bother starting up again because they hadn't been insured.

Funnily enough, the sight of concrete steps leading to nowhere seemed perfectly natural in this strange town. The charred sandstone entrance to the old post office looked like a memorial of some sort. And the single surviving wall of the High Point Cinema – featuring a crude hand-painted advertisement for *American Pie*, the last movie to be shown there – had the feel of an art installation. Cell phone shops and shoe stores operated out of shipping containers while other businesses flourished on blankets laid out on the ground. That morning it felt like Maseru should always be this way.

The long queues outside the banks looked like a natural feature of the town too. They snaked their way past hawkers selling fruit, some queuers sitting in the gutter or on a low wall to take the weight off their feet. For a moment I considered joining a queue to change some money. Perhaps there had been a run on the Lesotho maloti. But then I remembered that the South African rand was interchangeable with the maloti and I still had a pocketful of the stuff from Bloemfontein.

So instead I made my way to the government-run internet cafe in the new post office building. It was empty except for the manager, who sat behind one of the terminals in a neat suit and tie. He was downloading songs from Napster.

I smiled when I noticed what he was doing. 'Napster, eh?' I said, in that sarcastic tone teachers are so fond of using.

He looked up startled. 'Are you a Napster user too?' he whispered, unsure of my answer.

I told him that I had been known to dabble, and he greeted me as if we were both part of a secret society. 'It is an excellent service,' he said, opening a drawer to show me a pile of CDs he had burned. 'I can download songs that we would never get here in Lesotho.'

He loaded one of the discs into his computer and clicked on a folder then showed me his collection of MP3 files. His tastes ran to hardcore American gangsta rap – Biggy Smalls, Tupac Shakur, Snoop Doggy Dogg, that sort of thing – which should have struck me as odd music for a government employee in a suit in a tiny mountain kingdom in southern Africa. But it didn't. He asked if I'd like him to burn me a CD, but I declined. I didn't have anything to play it on.

Mr Napster turned on another computer for me to use to

check my e-mail and as I waited for Windows to load I asked him about the queues. He told me it was payday for government employees. Once a month offices are closed to allow workers to get their pay. Even classes are stopped while the teacher goes down to the bank. I asked him why he wasn't down at the bank.

'I am just waiting for this song to download,' he said. If the amount of time it took me to open Hotmail was any indication of the speed and quality of internet connection in Lesotho I suspected he would be going hungry this month.

Once I had checked my e-mail there was nothing to keep me in Maseru, so I grabbed my pack and headed down to the minibus station. It was just behind the cathedral and was little more than a line of vans with their destination roughly painted on signs placed on the dash. I was heading to Malealea, to Malealea Lodge to be exact, where you can go pony trekking and stay in traditional villages. Malealea is in the far south of the country, but Lesotho being the tiny country it is that was only 84 kilometres away.

Within minutes of departing we had left Maseru on the Main South Road, passed the airport and were hurtling into the wide-open spaces of southern Lesotho.

Lesotho is known as 'The Kingdom Without Fences', but perhaps a more accurate description would be 'The Kingdom Where Cattle Are Allowed To Wander Freely Into The Path Of Oncoming Vehicles'. Over the 84 kilometres to Malealea we nearly hit half a dozen cows. The driver seemed quite adept at avoiding them and did it with a nonchalance that suggested he had been doing it for years. Still, I was disturbed when a long-neck bottle of Castle Lager was cracked open and passed around for everyone to take a swig, including me and, alarmingly, the driver.

, At Mafeteng we turned off the main road and passed through the Gates of Paradise Pass. There was a plaque at the pass that read 'Wayfarer – Pause and look upon a gateway of Paradise'. Paradise, as it turned out was a vast valley of terraced fields dissected by a gorge. In the distance the tin roof of Malealea Lodge caught the afternoon sun, blinking like a flashlight. The driver seemed to regard it as some sort of signal because he floored the van and covered the remaining 5 kilometres in no time at all.

Malealea the village is really just Malealea the lodge. It is a working property with a trading centre attached and was bought by its current owners, Mick and Di Jones, in December 1986. They opened a small lodge for travellers soon after and started the pony trekking operation in 1991. It has been one of the most popular places in Lesotho for visitors ever since.

A small community has evolved around the lodge and the focal point is the trading centre. It had a country general store vibe about it, with sacks of grains and bales of hay against the walls and bridles, reins and other accoutrements of horse-manship hanging from the roof. It stocked the kind of items that are sadly missing from the shelves of supermarkets back home – like molasses.

The most popular items in stock are the blankets. People come from all the outlying villages to buy them, trying them on first and asking their wives or their mates how they look in them.

My room was at the back of the shop, in a section that had been converted into a backpackers' lodge. There was nowhere to eat in the village, so I had to cook my own dinner over a gas

fire in the kitchen. I'd picked up a pack of dehydrated Knorrox
Tasty Soya Mince at the general store. I had been taken in by the
photo of a suitably beefy cow on the packet and by the claim
that Knorrox Farm, from where I assumed this fine product
had come, was known as 'the place where the meat never ends'.
You can't get much beefier than that, I thought.

Well, apparently you could. As I waited for the water to boil I
scanned through the list of ingredients on the side of the packet
and was surprised to learn that there wasn't actually any meat in
my fine Knorrox Farm product. It had plenty of textured
vegetable protein, monosodium glutamate and hydrolysed
vegetable protein, as well as a host of enhancers and acidifiers,
but no actual bovine flesh. It filled a hole and sat heavily in my
stomach that night, but I felt I had been cheated somehow.

I got up early the next morning to start my pony trek.
Readers of *The Full Montezuma* will be surprised to learn that I
was even contemplating getting onto the back of a horse again
after my experiences in Nicaragua. Unfortunately the memory
of the battering my testicles took had faded and my head was
again full of romantic lonesome cowboy notions. I imagined
myself sauntering along a ridge, a solitary figure at one with the
landscape. Or stopping to light a cigarette, bowing my head and
using the rim of my hat to stop the wind blowing out the
match. I hadn't completely forgotten the pain, though, and had
the good sense to restrict myself to a two-day, one-night trek.

A group of local village men had gathered outside the barn,
hoping to be picked as my guide. They were dressed in blankets
and shifted from one foot to another, rubbing their hands
together to keep warm. Ponies were waiting in a corral, steam
coming from their nostrils.

There was a notice on the door of the barn where the saddles were kept. 'Important Notice,' it read. 'For tall people we have tall horses. For short people we have short horses. For fat people we have fat horses. For skinny people we have skinny horses. And for people who haven't ridden before we have horses that have never been ridden before.' Ha bloody ha.

All jokes aside, Basotho ponies are renowned for being sure-footed and strong. They tackle the treacherous mountain passes of Lesotho with a dexterity and bravery uncommon in most horses. What appealed to me most about them, however, was that they are also regarded as one of the more docile horse breeds.

I was given a horse called Lapile, the Sesotho word for hungry, which I took as a good sign, figuring that a horse with food on its mind just had to be slothful. And my guide was Clements, a quiet, unassuming guy whose main distinguishing feature was that he laughed like Eddie Murphy.

We set off across the valley at a gentle pace. The air was still crisp and farmers in thick blankets were heading off into the fields with crudely made hoes over their shoulders. They nodded as we passed but didn't greet us verbally. I fancied it was because any sound would have been startling in the stillness of the morning.

An hour later we reached the gorge and followed a path that snaked its way down towards the river at the bottom. It was like a scene from an old western, but there were no injuns or rogue cowboys hiding behind boulders to take potshots at us. Our wellbeing was instead threatened by a huge slab of slippery rock the size of an ice rink that stretched across the path.

The rock was shiny and smooth, without any visible footholds. I wanted to get off my pony and walk across.

A stumble or trip would have seen me tumbling into the gorge with 400 kilos of pony right behind me. But Clements assured me our ponies would take it in their stride, and they did, clip-clopping across the stone as nonchalantly as reviewers treat my books.

At the bottom of the gorge we forded a river with a pebbly bottom and then rode up an equally steep path on the other side. This side of the gorge hadn't yet seen the sun so there was still ice on the path. At the top we came upon a village of round mud huts with thatched roofs and wooden holding pens for livestock. A group of men were sitting in a circle under a tree. Judging by the blankets they were wearing, something important was happening. 'They are discussing what crops to plant,' said Clements.

It must have been a highly confidential discussion because they stopped talking as we rode by, waiting until we were out of earshot before continuing.

The day passed to the gentle rhythm of our horses' gait. We rode over ridges and through valleys and for a while followed a river lined with willows and ploughed fields. By late afternoon we reached a village sitting on a ridge, just past a waterfall surrounded by snow. This was where I'd be staying for the night, in a small hut on a dirt floor. The soundtrack was the river below, the tinkling of cowbells, chickens clucking and the clank of pots as women prepared the evening meal. I had barely settled into my hut before a woman brought me dinner – it was part of my trek. It was Knorrox Tasty Soya Mince.

'You are lucky!' said Clements, genuinely pleased for me. He'd been given papa, the Lesotho version of mealie-meal.

My butt was too sore to sit down so I ate my dinner

standing. I looked out over the valley towards the mountains. The sun had sunk behind them and it was getting cold. Thin plumes of smoke rose from the huts dotted around the valley. Young boys wielding sticks were herding cattle, goats and pigs home to roughly made corrals. They waved and laughed as they passed me. This was the Africa I had been expecting.

I asked Clements if there was anything happening in the village that night and he laughed. 'After they have eaten they will go to their huts and sleep,' he said. 'This is the traditional Lesotho lifestyle. Rise at dawn and sleep at sunset.'

It was so quiet that night as I lay on the floor of my hut that I heard ringing in my ears. The more I tried to ignore it, the louder it became and I was soon convinced that it was the start of tinnitus, the result of playing my Walkman too loud. In retrospect, I think it was just my body adjusting to the alien environment. Like the microphone on a cheap cassette recorder, the levels had been turned down low to filter out the excessive clamour and din of city life. Now they were being whacked up high, searching for a sound to register. Unfortunately that sound was a cock crowing at dawn and at the levels my body was now operating on it sounded like the bird had sneaked into my hut and crowed straight into my ear.

Clements had already saddled the horses and stood outside my hut waiting for me to stir. The rest of the village was busy too, getting ready for another day of herding, threshing and grinding. We rode back to Malealea along a different route, across rolling hills planted with crops and ridges dotted with jojoba plants. We crossed the river at the same point we had the day before and a group of small boys waited with a clutch of fish they had caught. They had threaded them on a reed, passing the reed through their gills to form a neat carry handle. I bought some to cook for dinner. They would make a pleasant change from Knorrox Tasty Soya Mince and besides, it only cost me 2 maloti (50 cents) for half a dozen.

When Lapile, my horse, reached the top of the gorge he realised he was nearly home. He knew that there was a sack of feed waiting for him back at the lodge and he broke into a canter. There was nothing I could do to stop him. When I tried pulling on the reins the previously docile beast turned and tried to bite me. So I gave up and jiggled around in a most undignified manner, my testicles taking their customary battering.

Back at the lodge that night the Malealea Band performed on the lawn, the trees and the mountains behind them forming a natural amphitheatre. They played guitars fashioned from cooking oil tins and drums made from metal cans with inner tube rubber pulled over them. People from the nearby village, drawn by the sound of music and the warmth of the fire, wandered across from their huts and soon joined in. At first they simply clapped their hands or murmured appreciatively at a well-struck chord. But soon they were dancing energetically and calling for me to join in. It was the first authentic African music I had heard on my trip and it was wonderful. Before that it had all been sappy Western pop like Craig David, or bad American rap music. I wondered how long it would be before Peter Gabriel found out about these guys and signed them to his Real World label.

With my pony trek completed, my plan was to cut across the middle of Lesotho through the Central Mountains to Thaba-Tseka, a remote town right in the centre of the kingdom. From there I would go to Molumong – a friend had recommended staying at another farm lodge there – and then on to Sani Top. I could then cross back into South Africa through the spectacular Drakensberg Range. The plan entailed going back to Maseru – most journeys in Lesotho do. But I was in luck. Mick, the owner of Malealea Lodge, was picking up guests from the airport and he said he would give me a lift.

Mick was white, but he had been born in Lesotho. He wore large glasses that made him look bookish, and like most people I'd taken lifts from was appalled that I had been catching local minivans. Like the ones in South Africa, the minivans in Lesotho were badly maintained death traps driven by drunk, unwashed deviants, Mick claimed.

About halfway to Maseru he made a point of showing me a spot where he had seen a minivan accident. 'There were bodies everywhere,' he said. Then he pointed to a spot on the rise ahead. 'I nearly ran over an arm just there.'

I decided to catch a bus to Thaba-Tseka. So, it seemed, did everyone else in Maseru. The bus station was seething with wannabe passengers and hawkers trying to sell them provisions. Some hawkers sold fruit juice, others chicken and papa. One guy sat on a stool in the middle of the maelstrom, whittling patterns into walking sticks. In Lesotho a walking stick is as essential a fashion item as a blanket and individuality in the carvings is much sought after. This guy must have been good because he had a long line of customers waiting.

The bus to Thaba-Tseka was old and worn, with broken windows and battered panels that suggested a number of close encounters with rocky ledges. I had hoped the run to Thaba-Tseka would be serviced by one of the more modern buses that featured murals of Lesotho village life done in the style of 1970s panel-van art. The images were representations of the country-side I had ridden through down at Malealea – mud huts, fields of green, herds of goats and pigs – with a few embellishments, notably a chief in full traditional battle regalia and bare-breasted maidens in grass skirts. Unfortunately those buses were only used on the prestigious international routes back into South Africa.

The only seat available on the bus to Thaba-Tseka was a window seat next to a guy carrying a large pane of glass. He sat in the middle of the three-person seat, resting the pane of glass across my lap and the lap of the guy sitting closest to the aisle. He fretted as other passengers came on board, especially those with bags or daypacks that could catch on the corners. 'Please, be careful!' he pleaded. '*Please!*'

On noticing that I was watching the whole charade with interest, he felt the need to explain why he was going to so much trouble over a pane of glass. 'Glass is much cheaper in Maseru,' he said. 'This glass cost me 28 rand here. In Thaba-Tseka it would cost 100!'

He also had a penchant for school choir tapes and got me to negotiate with a hawker who has standing outside the bus selling them. This is always a potential pitfall of sitting in the window seat on a bus in the developing world. You unwittingly become the middle-man in passenger–hawker transactions for food, clothing and, in this case, music cassettes. It's a thankless task, especially if the bus drives off before you get the person's change. Buying this tape was a particularly complicated process. The hawker would reach up to the window and pass me a tape. The guy would examine it – perusing it like a connoisseur – before tutting at the obvious crapness of it and making me hand it back. It took ten tapes before he found one to his liking. 'This one is from St Paul's!' he said, his eyes lighting up. 'It is one of our finest schools.'

He insisted that I listen to it on my Walkman. It sounded as you would imagine a school choir from Lesotho to sound.

The journey to Thaba-Tseka is a dramatic 110-kilometre journey through the heart of Lesotho. The gravel negotiates the suitably named God Help Me Pass and crosses the mighty Makhaleng River. Unfortunately all I remember about it is a series of police checks. Our bus couldn't go 5 kilometres without a member of Lesotho's finest pulling it over, ordering off every passenger on board and giving us a thorough frisking. It wasn't made any easier by glass man insisting he take the glass with him.

'These people cannot be trusted with precious things,' he said after I humphed a little too loudly the third time he carried it off.

For a moment I ungraciously wished that it would break, but after all the trouble he had gone to I realised that glass man would have been devastated. Instead I crankily asked him what the hell the police were looking for anyway.

'They are looking for guns,' he said. 'There has been a spate of arms smuggling.'

By Mantsonyane the police checks became less frequent and over the last 25 kilometres there were only three. The last and the most thorough was just outside Thaba-Tseka. The policeman at this checkpoint wore a fur hat and had waxed the tips of his moustache so that they stuck out like cat's whiskers. He looked through my passport at length, particularly the visas, turning it on its side to admire some of the more unconventionally stamped visas, and then asked me where I was staying.

My guidebook had suggested the Farmer Training Centre. It was used to promote fine farming practices among the country's agricultural personnel, but they also rented out rooms to travellers. I imagined sitting around in the common room talking crop rotation with the eager trainee farmers. But the policeman said it was closed and insisted that I stay at his house. I wasn't sure if it was an offer or a demand, so I went along with it.

The policeman's name was Joel and he said I could ride into town in the back of the police pick-up. Thaba-Tseka is a new town on the western edge of the Central Ranges, built to service the villages in the mountain ranges around it. It is set in a dry, barren valley and is blighted by the ugly grey concrete block buildings that seem to scar every new town in Africa. The town centre featured a PEP supermarket and a caravan that operated as a photo development centre called Come Shine Photo Gallery. The police station was next to the bus station, out on the edge of town on the road to Sehonghong. It was another grey concrete block building with a compound full of cars stolen from South Africa.

Joel was from Maseru and had been posted to Thaba-Tseka in line with the Lesotho Police Force's policy of stationing officers as far away from their home town as possible. He said it was to cut down on corruption – if he worked in Maseru he might be tempted to turn a blind eye when friends or family broke the law. But it left him in an unenviable position. If he made new friends in Thaba-Tseka his integrity would come into question and he would have to be moved again. 'It makes it very hard to find a wife,' he said. It also explained why he befriended scruffy backpackers he'd just frisked moments before.

Joel's quarters were modest. There was a lounge room, a kitchen, a bathroom and a bedroom, but that was all. He heated some stew his superintendent's wife had left him on an old gas stove and served it on beat-up metal plates. I asked him what sort of cases he handled.

'The biggest problem was stock theft,' he said. 'I used to help the police from South Africa trace sheep and cattle rustled into Lesotho. But now I am seeing more guns.'

South African drug lords were starting to grow marijuana among the maize in the isolated mountains of Lesotho. And in doing so they were bringing new problems to the sleepy mountain kingdom.

'Now *I* have to carry a gun,' said Joel. 'You never know when a situation might arise.' He stared wistfully at his bowl, remembering a time when life in Thaba-Tseka was a lot simpler.

❖　　❖　　❖

The next morning Joel had to investigate an attempted robbery in a village nearby and he gave me a lift to the turnoff for Mokhotlong. It was a couple of kilometres from Thaba-Tseka, but Joel assured me that this was the best place to find a ride to Molumong Lodge. There was no public transport as such in this part of Lesotho. People simply gathered in groups according to their destination and waved down trucks heading in the same direction. I found the bunch of people heading in the direction I wanted to go and stood among them smiling weakly. They let two trucks pass before rushing the third and clambering aboard as it crawled by. A guy in a suit was one of the first to get on board and he beckoned for me to follow. He dragged on my pack and then me.

The back of the truck was dusty and uncomfortable but I was ecstatically happy to be on it. It was the first rough travelling I'd done on my African adventure and it felt good. South Africa had been too easy. I simply turned up at a minivan station and there was a death trap waiting for me. Now I was on a painfully slow truck that shuddered and groaned in a manner that suggested that it wasn't long for this world.

I felt like I was part of a tiny community. A woman leaned against the cabin, breastfeeding her child. Two old men played cards. A small boy huddled, listening to the radio. (The top news story that day was that a TV set had been donated to a Lesotho prison providing 'much needed recreation for prisoners'.) Food was passed around and shared by everyone. I imagined this was what it was like for the boxcar hobos in the States.

The scenery was breathtaking too. One moment we were crawling through a grey barren moonscape, the next crossing a river that rushed across rocks in a white foaming frenzy. Then we were in the high country and the truck was trundling along a road that cut through wild heath. I'm sure I spent most of the journey with a beatific smile on my face.

The guy in the suit who had helped me on board crawled across to where I was sitting and started chatting to me. He was going to a meeting in Mokhotlong. I asked him what time it was starting and he said nine. It was already past eleven.

'Yes,' he nodded solemnly. 'I think I will be late.'

I asked him what the meeting was about, trying to ascertain if he was missing out on something important.

'I don't know,' he said. 'They did not tell us the agenda.'

He asked me if there were black people in Australia and

when I said that there were he told me that our goats were famous. There isn't much scope to develop a conversation after such a startling revelation, so we both went silent, holding onto the rail and staring at the dusty road ahead. By late afternoon we had reached Molumong.

The driver stopped at the point of the road just above the lodge and waited for me to clamber down.

The suit man reluctantly lowered my bag to me. 'Are you sure you want to get off here?' he asked. 'Tomorrow is Sunday. You could get stranded here.'

I shook my head. The lodge looked stunning, an old whitewashed farmhouse looking out over a gorgeous valley. Even if I did get stranded there for a day or two, I was sure I would cope. He shrugged his shoulders and waved half-heartedly as the truck drove off.

The lodge was deserted. I knocked on the back door of the farmhouse and it creaked open from the force of the knock. I entered cautiously, calling out 'Hello?' but there was only silence. The place was empty. I had the whole lodge to myself. Cool.

It was the first time I'd had a place entirely to myself in Africa. I tried each bed and decided on the most comfortable one, before having a hot shower to wash away the dust and grime from the truck ride. I wandered through the house naked, towelling my hair, and into the lounge room. The walls were lined with bookshelves, and there were large comfortable chairs and bay windows with views out over the valley. It also had an old stone fireplace and I noticed with alarm that someone had lit a fire and brought in a pile of logs to keep it going.

I checked every room in the house again but no one was

there. I got dressed and looked around outside but I couldn't find a soul there either. I went back to my room and checked my bag, concerned that stuff had been stolen while I showered, but everything was there. I went back to the lounge room and looked at the fire again, spooked. Who the fuck had lit it and where were they now?

I noticed a guest book lying open on a table and flicked through it, looking for a clue. Maybe other guests had commented on the mystery. 'Don't worry about the fire,' I hoped an entry would read. 'It's just Pedro the farm boy playing tricks. He'll be around again at eight with the complimentary roast lamb dinner.'

Instead it was full of the usual guff in guest books – 'lovely place . . . peaceful . . . so restful' – that sort of thing. Except for an entry by two Dutch girls: 'It is scary to stay in the middle of nowhere just two girls.' I turned the page looking for the rest of the message but the entry stopped abruptly. I picked up the guest book to look at it more closely and noticed that a page had been ripped out.

I began to wonder why. Did the page have a message warning guests to get out while they still could? I began to imagine the Dutch girls looking up mid-sentence to see a mad woodchopper standing above them. They would scream. He would chop. Then he would tear the bloodied page from the book. Such was my spooked frame of mind that this seemed the most rational explanation for the missing page.

The mystery of the miraculously lit fire and missing page began to play heavily on my mind. I should have enjoyed having a beautiful old farmhouse all to myself, but I couldn't. When the shadows danced across the valley in a beguiling manner in the late afternoon, I saw something more sinister. When the fireplace crackled with warmth and vitality that night, I jumped at every loud pop. It was the kind of peaceful solitude that stressed-out executives pay good money for and I used it to torture myself with tales of murderous axemen.

After a long restless night I was up at dawn and waiting at the roadside with my pack. It was a Sunday, the worst day to travel on, but I had to get out of Molumong. The solitude was freaking me out.

Chapter 4

ZULULAND

Mficha uchi hazai.

One who hides his private parts will never have a child.

I got a lift from Molumong in a battered Toyota Landcruiser with a creased roof and a smear of blood across the bonnet. The blood had come from the previous owner when he crawled through the broken window after plunging down a ravine. The Landcruiser had been extricated from its rocky resting place by an enterprising young man called Vincent. He was driving it north to sell it for parts and it veered along the road at an angle like a drunk crab. Vincent simply turned the wheel in the opposite direction to get it to go where he wanted it to.

I only rode with Vincent for 15 kilometres. He had a prospective buyer waiting in Mokhotlong and I wanted to go east to Sani Top and the border with South Africa.

He dropped me off at Matsoaing, the village where the road

to Sani Top starts, and wished me luck. 'I don't think you will get a lift,' he said cheerfully. 'It is a Sunday, and no one goes anywhere on a Sunday.'

He was right. I stood beside the road at Matsoaing for two hours and not a single car passed. The landscape was dry and barren with an emptiness that seemed to swallow me up. It made me feel small and isolated so I decided to start walking. It was only about 40 kilometres to Sani Top and walking would be a way of taking a little bit of control. And if a minivan or a car passed by I would wave it down.

The first kilometre was exhilarating. The sky was clear, the air was crisp and my pack didn't seem that heavy. The low brown hills stretched off into the distance and the sky seemed to go on forever. By the time I reached the next village, however, I was tiring and foolishly waved to a bunch of kids playing with rocks by the side of the road.

A white man with a pack on his back was obviously not a common site in this part of Lesotho because the kids quickly abandoned the rocks and started to follow me. It was an indication of just how little there is for kids to do in this part of Lesotho that they followed me for 5 kilometres.

I know it was 5 kilometres because I was counting off my progress against the stone road markers on the side of the road. At first the kids were a welcome distraction. They asked me my name and where I was from and helped me forget that this walking caper was bloody hard work. But then a smart one pulled on my pack, hoping that I would react, and it all went pear-shaped from there.

I smiled, hoping that if I didn't react the kids would lose interest and go away. But that only made them more determined and it soon become a competition to see who could get a reaction from me first. They took turns to tug on my pack, each one getting more aggressive than the one before. Finally, when one of them jumped onto my back and clung to my pack, I snapped.

I thought I was being quite scary – I waved my arms about and growled – but they thought I was hilarious. They all jumped on my back, the smaller ones taking a longer run up to get the required velocity. I'd lost any authority I may have had. I was just a plaything for them now. I simply trudged along, metres at a time with a young Basotho child on my back. Eventually they tired of the game, and realising that they were now quite a long way from home, turned back. Previously I had been impressed by Lesotho's untouched isolation. Now I was wishing that these kids had been inside glued to a Sony Playstation when I passed.

Even without a small kid clinging to my pack, it still took me most of the morning to walk to Nokeng. It was the last village before a sparsely inhabited wilderness that stretched the rest of the way to Sani Top and I arrived as the villagers were heading off to church.

Two well-dressed girls giggled when they saw me and called me over to ask me where I was going. I told them Sani Top. 'Eh!' said the pretty, most confident one. 'That is 30 kilometres away!'

The other one told me that there wasn't any public transport to Sani Top on Sundays, and probably no private vehicles either. I could walk, she said, but it was getting a little late for that.

'Perhaps you can stay with the shepherd boys who live up there,' said the pretty one, laughing at her own joke. 'Maybe they can make room for you in their caves.'

They also told me to be careful of robbers. Why robbers would lie in ambush in an isolated wilderness was beyond me, but these girls seemed to think it was a distinct possibility.

'We will pray for you,' said the pretty one. They both laughed.

At the edge of the village I realised the foolishness of what I was doing. The huts of the village stopped abruptly and the road started climbing at a steep angle up into a rugged sandstone escarpment.

I took my pack off and sat by the side of the road, my head in my hands. I'd left Molumong six hours earlier and the only vehicle I'd seen was the damaged Toyota and that had only taken me as far as the turnoff. Now I was in front of the last house for 30 kilometres beside a road that was about to become more of a steep mountain pass than a major byway.

Intrigued as to why a white man was wailing in front of his house, a man came and spoke to me. His name was Steven and he didn't like my chances of getting a ride either. 'Maybe a private car will come today,' he said, picking at his hair with a perm comb. 'But I think you will have to wait until tomorrow. You can stay at my house if you'd like.'

I thanked him, but stayed beside the road. I still hoped to get to Sani Top that night, but it was nice to know that I had somewhere to sleep if I didn't.

I sat beside the road for an hour, straining so hard to hear a car or van coming that it hurt. Eventually a small blue ute passed and headed up into the mountains, but when I tried to wave it down the driver simply gave me a resigned shrug. Over the next hour the same ute shuttled up and down the mountain at least half a dozen times, and each time the driver gave me the same resigned shrug. I must have looked terribly despondent because on the seventh time he passed, the driver stopped to explain that he was collecting water from a river a couple of kilometres into the wilderness reserve. After that he made a point of waving and smiling when he went past.

The owner of the house I was sitting in front of must have said something to his wife because she brought me a meal of fried fish and papa and a warm bottle of Castle beer. I was touched by the generous offer but a little reluctant to take it. I was convinced that a car would come along before I could finish it, or worse, drive right by me because my hands and mouth were too full to wave it down. I needn't have worried. I was able to finish the meal, pick my teeth and start on a second bottle of Castle before another car came along.

It was the water guy again, but this time he stopped and waved me over. 'I have found you a ride!' he said, excitedly. 'Get in!'

He drove me to the place up in the mountains where he was getting water. Up there it was beautiful, a sea of greens, reds, yellows and greys, dominated by an immense sandstone escarpment and flecked by fleshy green succulents and delicate alpine flowers. The river was crystal clear and cut through the escarpment about 20 metres below the road. There was a white dual cab Nissan parked on the road and a white couple watched a group of guys clamber down to the river with plastic drums and then drag them back up full. The couple had come up Sani Pass from South Africa to do a bit of bird watching and were heading back to the lodge at the top of the pass to stay the night.

'We're not going straight away,' said the man, who introduced himself as Garth. 'We still have a few birds to spot yet.'

He pointed towards a thick book resting on the bonnet. They had marked the birds they had seen but, disturbingly, there were still at least ten they hadn't yet spotted.

Garth drove slowly while his wife, Laura, scoured the escarpment through binoculars. If Laura spotted anything interesting, Garth pulled over so they could get a better view.

'Look, there's an orange-breasted rockjumper,' said Laura excitedly, pointing to a spot halfway up the escarpment.

'And there's a Layard's titbabbler,' said Garth. 'I thought it was time they started coming out!'

Soon I was scouring the escarpment for birds too. I figured the sooner we spotted the birds the sooner we'd head back to the lodge at Sani Top. But then I found that I was starting to enjoy looking for titbabblers. Immensely. Convinced he had a convert to the world of bird watching, Garth handed me a pair of binoculars and gave me a list of birds to look out for.

'Look!' I cried, handing Garth the binoculars and pointing to a ledge about halfway up. 'A black-shouldered kite!'

Garth nodded, impressed.

By late afternoon we reached the top of the escarpment, a vast moor of heath and gorse, and Garth pointed to a peat marsh in one of the valleys. 'It is supposed to be spongy, collecting water,' he explained. 'But since they've started grazing cattle here the ground has gone hard. The grass stops growing and the cattle move on to destroy another part of the reserve.'

It would have an impact on all the other wildlife in the reserve as well. If the ground became too hard for insects the birds that fed on them would disappear too. Chances were that if I came back in two years' time I wouldn't be able to spot a titbabbler for love nor money. It was a sobering thought.

◆   ◆   ◆

The lodge at Sani Top was a classic sixties-style ski lodge that looked like something out of an old Peter Stuyvesant ad. There were wooden skis hanging on a stone wall at the entrance and out the back there was a dark, smoky bar with a sign declaring that it was the highest bar in Africa. In one corner there was a full-length window overlooking the pass, in the other, a stone fireplace with a crackling fire. The only thing missing were the people in jumpers with knitted snowflake patterns sipping liqueur from huge brandy balloons. Even my bunk bed was from a different era, hewn from solid slabs of wood that made the Ikea-style ones I'd slept on elsewhere look positively flimsy.

At sunset I put on every piece of clothing I had with me and walked out to the edge of the ridge. Here the mountains dropped away suddenly and dramatically and if I looked to my left or right I could see their sheer face. It was like Lesotho was a multi-layered sponge cake and South Africa was the plate it was sitting on.

I walked right to the edge and sat down to watch the sun sink, my legs dangling over the edge of Lesotho. The next day I would be back in South Africa and it struck me that close to three weeks after leaving Cape Town I still hadn't left the southernmost country of my journey. All the things I had been looking forward to on this journey – Victoria Falls, Mount Kilimanjaro, Zanzibar, Ethiopia, the pyramids in Egypt – all seemed as far away as they had done from the couch in Clive and Leanne's flat.

A young guy with a tattered blanket slung over his shoulder came up and sat next to me, scaring away the sentinel rock thrush that had been pecking at a rock nearby. 'I am hungry,' he said, sticking out his hand.

I shrugged my shoulders and told him that I had no food to give him.

'I have no mother or father!' he replied.

He obviously thought that the orphan line was a winner so I asked him how old he was.

'Twenty-seven.'

I chuckled at his audacity and told him that he was old enough to look after himself. Still, his plight was a reminder that for all its friendliness Lesotho was a country struggling to support itself, having to import over 90 per cent of its food. If I'd had something to give him I would have.

❖   ❖   ❖

All the other guests staying at the lodge that evening were white South Africans. They were all heading further into Lesotho to go fishing or hiking or to broker some kind of dodgy deal with corrupt government officials. I got the impression they felt more comfortable in Lesotho. Not because they were still treated like masters – because they weren't – but rather because there wasn't the downright hostility towards them that there was back in their home country. Of course, I could have been reading way too much into it. They might have simply been impressed, as I had been, that you could dine on a giant grilled trout and sip brandy in such convivial surroundings for only a couple of dollars.

I got a lift back into South Africa the next morning with

a diesel mechanic called Wayne. I found him at the border, boiling a billy of water, and he said he could take me all the way to Durban. He drove a V8 Landcruiser, which was handy because the temperature had dropped to minus seven overnight and there was talk that the road had iced over. The pass was treacherous enough at the best of times. Covered with ice it would be doubly so.

The road wound its way down the escarpment like a brown snake, dropping 2850 metres over 8 kilometres. On one bend a small stream that cascaded down the mountain and across the road had turned to solid ice. It looked like a limestone formation in a cave and three guys from the Lesotho border post were throwing salt onto it. Wayne crunched down through the gears and came to a stop. The ice was cracking and groaning like a dying beast.

'We'll wait for it to break up a bit,' said Wayne. 'If we lose our grip we'll just slide over the edge.' He pointed to the crumpled wreck of a truck lying on its side between the esses. 'That's what happened to that oke,' he said. 'You might want to get out and walk through.'

The passengers from a minivan were doing just that, and were shuffling cautiously along the icy road. One woman lost her grip and skated down the road, flapping her arms wildly. Everyone laughed when she landed rather ungraciously on her butt but took extra care in case they ended up in an undignified position themselves. I got through okay, skating in the same spot as the woman had but managing to stay upright.

We all waited in the sun, warming ourselves as our vehicles attempted the corner. The minivan tried first. The driver was obviously of the 'get it over and done with' school. He drove into the corner at what I regarded as a reckless speed, fishtailing his way across the ice and through the corner. Astonishingly, the van didn't career over the edge.

It was the kind of driving you'd see on 'World's Worst Drivers 7' and reminded me of a childhood trip to the Snowy Mountains in Australia. My father had never driven in the snow before and when a blizzard hit decided that the best thing to do would be to put his foot to the floor and get us back to the lodge as soon as possible. He lost control of our Valiant stationwagon on the first corner and we spun in slow motion through a blurry white world for what seemed an eternity. My sister Lesley-Ann screamed hysterically, even after we came to a stop, the front bumper of the Valiant resting against an embankment made by a snow plough that morning. We drove home the next day and my father has not been back to the snow since.

Unlike the driver of the van and my father, Wayne was a model of restraint and skill and piloted his Landcruiser carefully through the curve in low gear. I jumped in and we edged our way around the van as its passengers clambered back on board.

Wayne was furious. 'Maniacs!' he spat. 'And they'd expect *me* to pull them out!' I wondered what he would make of my father's driving.

Twenty minutes later we were 3000 metres lower and it was 20 degrees warmer. I was back in South Africa and the barren highlands of Lesotho had been replaced by the lush farmland of Natal.

The driving was easy and Wayne started to chat. 'My mate went to Australia,' he said. 'He's a diesel mechanic like me. He lined me up a job there too.'

Wayne had decided to stay in South Africa. I told him he

was mad. I mean, South Africa was okay, but from what I could see there wasn't much of a future for a white diesel mechanic in his mid-forties. The government's affirmative action policies meant that most jobs were offered to the black or coloured populations first.

'You're right,' he said. 'But in five years' time things'll be different.'

Wayne pulled over to the side of the road and grabbed a pen and a piece of paper from the glove box. He was eager to explain his theory and drew an L-shaped graph with a line starting high on the vertical axis, but finishing low along the horizontal one. 'At the moment, the black population is up here and they're getting all the jobs,' he said pointing to high point. 'But in five years they'll be decimated by AIDS.'

I looked at him incredulously.

He took it as incomprehension. 'There'll only be this many left!' he said, pointing at the low spot of the line. 'Black and white populations will be about equal and my skills will be needed again.'

I was flabbergasted. Wayne was basing his career decisions on the AIDS epidemic. What's more, he didn't seem the least bit uncomfortable about planning his future on the misfortunes of others.

'It'll be boom times,' he said, putting the Landcruiser back into gear and pulling back out onto the road. 'I'm just a bit worried about the safety of my daughters. Rape is real bad here.'

I nodded, not really sure what to say. We passed the rest of the way to Durban in silence.

❖   ❖   ❖

Durban was 25 degrees and humid. I stayed up in the hills in a
big old house that had been converted into a hostel. It was nice
up there. There were lots of trees and all the houses were smart
and well maintained. The hostel had a bar on the top floor, in a
room that looked out over the city and bay and caught a sweet
afternoon breeze laden with the perfume of frangipani. The bar
was run by a German girl with hair dyed neon red. She was
from a small village outside of Stuttgart and had been a bar girl
back home too. Her name was Nina.

'Like Nina who sang "99 Luftballons",' I said.

She looked at me quizzically. I think she may have even
thought I was mad.

'You know,' I said. 'Na, na, na, na Captain Kirk. Na, na, na,
na fireverks.'

'Oh, yes,' she said. 'I think my mother used to like it when
she was pregnant with me.'

Ouch.

Like all good barmaids Nina was a sympathetic listener and
I found myself telling her all about my break up – the
accusations, the bitter recriminations, even the incident with
the sister-in-law. She listened attentively, getting me another
beer just as I finished the previous one. It felt good to get it all
off my chest and I stumbled into bed that night convinced that
Nina really cared.

I didn't stay long in Durban. I had imagined it would be an
exotic place, pungent with the aromas of the east courtesy of its
large Indian population. Instead it was dirty and decaying, with
a grubby beach that had grey sand instead of white and pigeons
instead of seagulls. Worse, the block along the beach was lined
with seedy bars, strip joints, adult shops and mini casinos. I had

expected lassies and saris, but got fruit machines and prostitutes instead.

The 13th International Conference on AIDS had just been held in Durban. The South African President, Thabo Mbeki, had caused a ruckus by refusing to recognise a link between HIV and AIDS, claiming that the problem was one of poverty. It was an exercise in semantics and unfortunately it took the focus away from the real problem at hand – 4.2 million people in South Africa are infected.

The rest of the figures quoted at the conference were equally horrific and sadly backed Wayne's theory for career advancement. One in five adults in South Africa are HIV positive. More than 1600 people become infected each day. Sixteen thousand die every year. The rate of infection among prostitutes is over 90 per cent, yet astoundingly, Durban's working girls claimed that they had never been busier than during the conference.

The affluent suburbs of Durban were no less perplexing. I went out to the Pavilion, a huge shopping mall modelled on a 19th-century English pleasure dome, and found Durban Guns'n'Ammo trading between a women's fashion store and an electronics shop and opposite the Game supermarket. When I got back to the hostel my confusion was compounded when I found another guy pouring his heart out to a sympathetic Nina. I decided then that it was time to go to Zululand.

I dug out my copy of *Coast-to-Coast*, a little booklet-sized magazine that lists all the backpacker hostels in South Africa. Put out every couple of months by a South African couple, it gives a quirky but honest description of each place and is more up-to-date than the other guidebooks. When I was in Cape

Town a girl called Barbara went through my copy and marked all the places she liked. She was lovely and I had to madly concentrate on not doing anything rash like telling her I loved her since she had an equally nice boyfriend called Barry. Even so, I remember her absolutely raving about a hostel called Inyezane in Gingindlovu, Zululand.

Coast-to-Coast described Inyezane as 'the most off-the-wall backpackers in South Africa'. It is part of a 150-hectare sugar estate, the hostel set in the middle of the fields. Guests sleep in the old workers' huts, each one converted into a unique art installation. My hut was the aeroplane one and had a 'jet' motif throughout. There were crude wooden models hanging from the ceiling and the walls were covered with thousands of stamps with a small bi-plane on them.

It was an extraordinarily relaxing place. I spent each day doing nothing and each night I took an open-air bath in a tub surrounded by low, broken walls dotted with candles. The staff boiled the water and added special Zulu oils. All I had to do was lie back and look at the stars. Then I'd return to my hut, drifting off to sleep to the sound of distant fires burning off cane debris. Spring was coming and here, in the north of the country, the weather was already warmer. Five days later I was still there.

Inyezane was run by Brad, a South African, and his French wife, Katie. They had to go to Durban for a few days and sensing that I wasn't going anywhere asked me if I could look after the place while they were away. In return I could stay for free and use their car to visit the Zululand battlefields. Trying to figure out how to get to the battlefields was the reason I'd given for still being at Inyezane, you see.

I've got to say I rather enjoyed being a hostel manager. I had been worried that under my management the place would degenerate into a Zululand version of Fawlty Towers. But it didn't. I greeted people and showed them to their huts. I registered them in an officious-looking ledger and took their money. I answered any queries about things to see and do in the area quickly and accurately. And the cleaning staff continued to perform their duties punctually and professionally. I'd like to think that the guests who stayed at Inyezane under my auspices didn't realise just how unqualified I was to serve them.

My favourite job was working in the bar, giving generous servings of Amarula to the girls who were staying there. Amarula is a creamy liqueur made from the intoxicating plum-like fruit of the marula tree and is not unlike Baileys.

Elisabetta, an Italian fashion photographer staying in the African wildlife-themed hut, was particularly fond of it. She couldn't speak much English, but she propped up the bar most nights, keeping me company. 'Much beauty, si?' she'd say, motioning towards the fields as I gave her a slug of Amarula. 'Is it like this in your country?'

It was actually. This part of Zululand reminded me an awful lot of northern New South Wales – the low, rolling hills, the endless fields of sugar cane. When I walked into town, it was through the fields, past the cane cutters and tractors loaded high with cane, just like the fields near Murwillumbah.

The only downside to being a hostel manager was dealing with the Baz Bus. It was always late or overbooked and it was always left to me to sort it out with the guests. Most took a cancellation in their stride. Another day or two at Inyezane was not entirely burdensome, especially if they were drinking Amarula. But for some the Baz Bus was like an umbilical cord that they didn't want to let go of. It picked them up at one hostel and dropped them off at the next and they had planned their whole Southern Africa trip around its timetable.

Soon it was the night before Brad and Katie were due back. As I closed the bar, I mawkishly thought, 'This is the last time I will be closing the bar.' Then when I locked up the office I thought, 'This is the last time I will be locking up the office.' I wandered through the grounds, lingering a little after I flicked off each light, soaking up the poignancy of the moment. It was like a TV show where the retiring teacher turns the light off in the classroom in which he has just spent 40 years teaching. I'd been manager for three days.

When I went to lock up the TV room Elisabetta was still there, reading with the TV on in the background. I asked her if she could switch it off before she went to bed.

'I am going bed now,' she said, closing her book.

I remember thinking how sexy that simple statement sounded in her Italian accent. And how if I were to say the same thing in Italian with an Australian accent it would have the totally opposite effect.

As we walked out of the room Elisabetta turned and grabbed my arm. 'Peter, show me the Southern Cross,' she said. 'I must see it before I go!'

It was a strange request but, officially, I was still hostel manager, so I felt compelled to meet it. We wandered out into the cane fields and I scanned the sky for the distinctive marker star. As I looked, Elisabetta stood in front, leaning back into me and looking up at the sky.

'Well, that's the moon,' I said, pointing towards the slither of a crescent moon, trying to buy a bit of time. 'And that's the Milky Way, I think.'

To be honest, I was a little distracted by Elisabetta's closeness. I hadn't been this close to a woman for a while. Sure, I had been squeezed between my share of African mammas on minivans, but this was more intimate. It made me more desperate to impress her and, perversely, less able to find the Southern Cross.

After a fruitless half hour, Elisabetta broke free. 'No matter,' she said. 'Time for bed.'

I nodded, still searching the night sky. I was determined to find it.

'Night night,' Elisabetta called from the door of her hut, lingering a little.

'Yeah, okay,' I said.

About ten minutes later I found the Southern Cross, low on the horizon. It had only just risen. 'I found it!' I said. I turned triumphantly to point it out to Elisabetta but she was gone and her hut was dark.

The next day she got on the Baz Bus and I never saw her again.

Chapter 5

JOHANNESBURG, SOUTH AFRICA

Asiyefunzwa na mamaye, hufunzwa na ulimwengu.

He who was not taught by his mother will be taught
by the world.

I arrived in Johannesburg on the day it was declared the murder capital of the world. The story was front-page news and the newspapers had obviously struggled to get the tone right. It was terrible news of course. In the past year there had been 57 homicides per 100,000 of the population. The next city in the list, Moscow, didn't even come close. It could only manage 21 per 100,000, and that was with the help of a Mafia fond of old-school concrete boots-style intimidation. I couldn't help but feel that the South African papers wanted to trumpet the figures as a world-beating achievement. Murder was something, at last, that the country led the world in.

Instead, the papers quoted the Minister for Safety and Security, Steve Tshwete. He found it deplorable that there were over 20,000 murders a year in South Africa, a good deal of them in Johannesburg. I suspect that a good percentage of those murders were committed in and around Johannesburg's long-distance minivan station. It is in the centre of town, beside the main railway station, and it's a ghetto of makeshift stalls, greasy food and broken muddy streets. Hundreds of vans leave from there to every part of the country, either from a huge parking lot or from the corners of the streets around it, creating a maelstrom of confusion that pickpockets and petty thieves use to their advantage.

It's a dangerous part of town. Illegal immigrants from the Congo Republic live in the crumbling tenements (locals call it 'Little Kinshasa'), attempting to make a living as best they can. Some try selling crappy plastic things, but most have opted for a more lucrative career in drugs, prostitution or crime. The most ambitious have tried all three and only the dullest would have failed to see my potential as a victim that afternoon. I wandered among the street stalls, looking for a telephone and feeling like I had a sign on my back saying 'Rob me!'.

I finally found a phone that worked and waited patiently for the guy using it to conclude a drug deal. I was calling Craig, a friend I'd met when I was living in London. He was another antipodean, with an even funnier accent, earning pounds and pissing it away on lager. He had said that if I ever got to South Africa I should call him.

I did, and when I told him where I was he was horrified. 'Go stand near one of the security guards at the KFC,' he said. 'I'll get there as fast as I can.'

I put on my best 'don't fuck with me' face and waited for him to arrive.

I had passed through Swaziland to get to Johannesburg and the contrast between the two places couldn't have been more pronounced. Swaziland is the smallest country in the southern hemisphere, a tiny rural kingdom whose population could be squeezed into a couple of Johannesburg suburbs. It is so diminutive, and the degrees of separation are so slight, nearly every person living there is related to the royal family. I met a princess in a pie shop (she served me) and a prince propping up the bar at the Salt & Pepper Club. Even the backpacker hostel where I stayed had a royal connection. His majesty King Mswati III had just signed an edict to have it demolished.

Traditional culture is still strong in Swaziland too. It is not unusual to see girls wearing an Umcwacho, a 'purity' tassel, even on the streets of the capital, Mbabane. The tassel indicates that the girl is still a virgin and if any man violates her purity, even by touching her, he is required by law to pay the fine of one cow. And unlike the rest of the continent the big events each year in Swaziland aren't sporting ones. They're cultural festivals like the Incwala, where the king gives his people permission to eat the first crops of the year, and the Umhlanga, or Reed Dance, that my guidebook described as a 'week-long debutante ball for marriageable young Swazi women'.

I had hoped to be in Swaziland for the Reed Dance. As many as 20,000 girls come from all over the country to collect reeds and do a bit of DIY on the queen's house. Then they jump into a traditional outfit and dance bare-breasted in front of the king. He checks them out and if he likes what he sees he'll choose one to be his bride that year. It's the kind of cultural event Sir Les

Patterson might commission if he were ever put in charge of the Festival of Sydney.

I missed the Umhlanga at the Royal Kraal at Lombaba by one day. You know all those TV travel shows where the presenters just happen to be in a village when a colourful gypsy wedding is taking place or an ancient sporting event is being revived for the first time in centuries? Well, my own journeys are the antithesis of that. I had a vague idea when the festival was on, but figured fate would deliver me there on time. Instead fate decided that I wasn't ready for the sight of 20,000 semi-naked women. The bunting was still up and the royal viewing platform hadn't been dismantled. But the field was empty, the grass tantalisingly flattened by thousands of feet. The girls were already back in their villages, grinding the maize and reminiscing about the time they danced bare-breasted before their cousin, the king.

❖   ❖   ❖

In Johannesburg Craig lived with his wife and young daughter in River Club, a pretty suburb in the north of the city. Unlike the ugly city centre or the outer suburbs scarred by gold mining slag heaps, River Club was leafy and green and could have been an affluent suburb anywhere else in the world. The only indication that it wasn't were the mechanics who sat among the shrubs along the roadside. They had little ramps, spare parts and oxy bottles and were ready to do running repairs on any car that pulled over.

'You'd be surprised the kind of okes that use them,' said Craig. 'In fact they fixed the muffler on this – only cost me 100 rand.'

There was a boom gate across the road leading into River Club, manned by a black guy in a uniform. He recognised Craig's car as it approached and raised the boom gate with a smile and a wave. We drove past cul-de-sacs of neat houses with clipped lawns and telegraph poles with signs saying 'Let me teach your maid to cook'. When we pulled into Craig's townhouse, his wife, Sarah, came out to greet us, holding their baby daughter, Emma, in her arms. It was the perfect suburban scenario, the sort of thing you saw in 1950s American movies. Except here there were bars on every door and window.

'This all used to be a treeless mining veld,' said Sarah, keen to distract me from the bars. 'Now it's the largest man-made forest in the world.'

It really was beautiful. Low hills covered in trees stretched as far as I could see. Birds tweeted. Cicadas hummed. And a lawnmower buzzed in the distance. It was almost as if I had imagined the horrors of central Johannesburg. In the north, where most of the city's white population lived, it was quite easy to convince yourself that 'Little Kinshasa' didn't exist.

'I guess I should show you how everything works,' said Craig.

Dealing with the little idiosyncrasies of another person's house is the price you pay for their hospitality. Usually it's a dodgy shower or a toilet with a temperamental flush. At Craig's house it was the security system.

'Make sure the alarm is on all the time, not just when you go out,' he said. 'And if there is an intrusion, just press one of the panic buttons and the rapid response guys will be here within minutes.'

There was a panic button in the kitchen, another in the bathroom and toilet and one above my bed.

Noticing that I was a little freaked out, Craig tried to reassure me. 'We only have them to keep insurance costs down,' he said. 'This suburb actually has the lowest crime rate in Jo'burg. Only 2 per cent of crimes are committed here.'

I wondered what he meant exactly by only 2 per cent of crime. Did he mean 2 per cent of *all* crime committed in Johannesburg, which I would regard as still being pretty high? Or 2 per cent of the *range* of crimes – a little petty burglary and mugging, but not the other 98 per cent of crimes like murder, perhaps. I decided it was best not to know.

That night Craig took me to the Baron and Jester, a mock Tudor English-style pub in a posh area a couple of suburbs away. Australia was playing the Springboks in the Tri-Nations decider and the pub was packed with South African rugby fans drinking copious amounts of Castle Lager, eating thick rump steaks from the bistro and cheering their boys as they walloped the Wallabies on a large-screen television. It was a white South African's idea of a perfect night out until Australia snatched an unlikely victory and the Tri-Nations Cup with a Stirling Mortlock penalty goal right on full-time.

I sensibly kept my exclamation of delight down to a gulped yelp but when I went to the bar to buy the next round, my accent was noticed. A rather large Afrikaner told me I was in the wrong place, rising from his stool so I could appreciate just what a big motherfucker he was. Then he poked me in the chest and said that Australia didn't deserve to win.

I smiled weakly and agreed. Australia probably didn't deserve to win, but the South Africans wouldn't have won the Tri-Nations Cup anyway. New Zealand would have and surely nobody wanted that to happen. It's so much fun when the

All Blacks lose and the New Zealand nation goes into collective therapy.

Jonty the giant didn't agree. 'I'd rather see anyone win it than you bunch of sheep-shagging convicts!' he barked.

I very nearly pointed out to him that, *again*, it is the New Zealanders who are sheep shaggers, but as it was his navel that I would be trying to convince I thought better of it. I paid for my beers and got the hell out of there.

The incident was just another example of the anti-Australian sentiment I had noticed among white South Africans. Frankly it surprised me. They were all lining up to migrate to Australia – Perth was particularly popular – but seemed to take great delight in portraying us as unsophisticated slobs. That month's issue of the South African version of *FHM*, for example, had just run a feature on Aussie 'babes', claiming they were crying out for intelligent men with manners.

'Sheilas don't exactly have it easy,' it read. 'Apart from felons in the family tree, their romantic prospects, by and large, are limited to Australian men. Honestly, how steamed up can a girl get over a bunch of fly-blown, beer-swilling, sheep-shagging, no ball-bowling World Cup thieves?' To illustrate the point, they ran a photo of former Aussie cricketer Merv Hughes, not a good-looking man at the best of times, making cross eyes.

'Fortunately,' it continued, 'the antipodean ladies have been swamped by a new breed of male – the South African refugee. These down-to-earth imports are the silver lining to the Aussie ladies' cloud, treating them to perfect manners and intelligent conversation.'

I mentioned what happened at the bar to Craig and he shrugged his shoulders.

'Just friendly rivalry,' he said. 'You guys must say the same things about us.'

Well, no. To be honest, South Africans rarely cross an Australian's mind. We enjoy beating them in cricket and rugby, but only because they seem to get so upset about it. But as a day-to-day rival, South Africa rates as highly with Australia as Australia does with the rest of the world – barely a blip. I didn't say that to Craig of course. I just nodded my head, said something innocuous like 'Good point!' and drank my beer. Jonty the giant was still glaring at me from the bar. If I had to fight my way out of the pub I'd need Craig's help.

❖   ❖   ❖

The next day I visited Soweto, the black township in the south-west of Johannesburg. My trip out to Khayelitsha had been the highlight of my time in South Africa so far and I hoped that Soweto, being the most famous of the South African townships, would prove just as educational and inspirational.

My guide was a black guy called Steven and when he picked me up in his car he apologised that I would be the only one taking the tour. 'Things are slow,' he said. 'The crime figures are keeping people away.'

It took us an hour to reach Soweto from the northern suburbs, along freeways that looped and shot off in all directions and past Gold Reef City, a mock recreation of the gold fields with its own authentic slagheap.

Steven passed the time by torturing me with feeble tour guide banter. 'See the GP on the number plates?' he said, pointing to the car in front of us. (All number plates in South Africa feature the two letters that represent the province they were registered in. Johannesburg is in Guateng Province.) 'It stands for Gangsta's Paradise.'

The turnoff into Soweto was marked by a billboard saying 'Welcome to Omoville'. It struck me as strange to associate a township with a washing powder, especially one that promised 'whiter whites, more colourful colours', but I quickly discovered that nothing in Soweto was as I imagined it would be.

It was more established than I had expected. Soweto has grown beyond the slums and hostels that black labourers lived in when they first came to Johannesburg. Now there are pockets that are unashamedly suburban. One brick veneer home in Diepkloof even had a Mexican-sleeping-beside-a-cactus house number on the wall. The only indication that you were in South Africa's largest township was a hostel for day workers on a ridge and the constant buzz of helicopters tracking BMWs carjacked in other parts of Johannesburg and taken back to Soweto to be stripped.

As we drove past some of the more impressive houses I noticed that most of them had bars on the windows and signs warning they were protected by a private security company. I asked Steven if there was much crime in Soweto.

'There is no crime whatsoever,' he said. 'The community watches out for things. If someone tries to steal something they shout "Bambani!" – catch him.'

I pointed out the bars and he shrugged his shoulders. 'They are purely for decoration,' he said without skipping a beat. 'They see white people have them on their houses and copy them.'

Before I could say anything more, Steven started explaining the taxi system within the township. 'There are 38 suburbs in

Soweto,' he said. 'And each of them has its own hand signal if you want to wave down a taxi as it goes past you. You make an "o" for Orlando, an "o" with a finger down for Orlando West, and crossed fingers for Crossroads. If you want to go to Orange, you pretend to pick an orange.'

We soon reached one of Soweto's squatter camps, a suburb of dusty lanes and dilapidated shacks. It was more like the Soweto I had imagined, except for the line of taxis and minibuses full of tourists and the enterprising locals who had set up handicraft stalls that you were forced to walk past.

A guy with dreads and wearing a beanie came up to the car and gave Steven a complicated handshake. 'This is Max,' said Steven. 'He will take you into the squatter camp.' Steven was obviously subletting this part of the tour because I noticed him slip Max a 20 rand note.

The squatter camp tour consisted of going 100 metres down a dusty lane and visiting a 'typical' house owned by a woman who got gnarly when I wouldn't buy her township jewellery. Max trotted out inane patter like 'Come back in peace, not in pieces', and ten minutes later we were back at the car and the handicraft stalls.

I was beginning to suspect that coming to Soweto had been a mistake. My visit to Khayelitsha had given me a real insight into life in a township. And meeting women like Vicki and Rose had filled me with hope for the new rainbow nation. Soweto, on the other hand, seemed cynical and mercenary. I was dreading going to Nelson Mandela's old house in Vilakazi Street in Orlando West. It was bound to be a tourist trap.

'This is the only street in the world where two Nobel Prize winners lived,' said Steven, as we approached it. 'Of course,

Nelson Mandela has moved, but Desmond Tutu is still here.'

Mandela's house was an unassuming little hut, set among similarly unassuming huts below a low ridge. Mandela had lived there with Winnie before going to jail. And it was where she lived while he was incarcerated. Surprisingly, there wasn't a large neon sign screaming Casa Mdiba, and even the juice shop Winnie had built opposite to cash in on the tourists had a suitably township look about it.

Driving through Soweto that day it was easy to forget just what a vital role Soweto had played in overcoming apartheid. On 16 June 1976, on the same streets I was driving along, South African police fired on students protesting against a plan to make Afrikaans compulsory in all black schools. It sparked a national uprising that saw 600 people killed. Then in 1984 Soweto exploded again when the National Party changed the constitution to give Indians and coloureds limited rights, but not the African majority.

The unrest continued throughout the eighties and a state of emergency was declared. The South African Defence Force began patrolling the streets and the ANC, still illegal at this stage, organised a series of strikes and stayaways that crippled the economy, already suffering from international sanctions. Finally the National Party conceded defeat and negotiations began in 1992 over the transition to an elected government based on universal suffrage. As I got out of the car it struck me that the surprising thing about two Nobel-prize winning residents living here was that there hadn't been more.

I was shown around the house by Ngugi, a dashing guy with a thin moustache and long hair kept in ringlets. He wore a white T-shirt under a cream suit jacket, looking very 'Miami

Vice', and was married to one of Winnie's daughters from a previous marriage. 'So I am not quite royalty,' he joked.

I liked Ngugi. He was quietly spoken and respectful and he clearly admired both Nelson and Winnie deeply. 'Winnie was harassed every day she lived here,' he said. 'The army raided the house every day and snipers would take pot shots from that ridge. Those wattles out the front were planted to protect her from the gunfire.'

He pointed to a wall that dissected the front room in two. Winnie had had it built to stop the bullets. 'It was years before the police who "visited" her realised its purpose,' said Ngugi. 'Then they started shooting from the back of the house.'

The walls of the room were lined with old black and white photos. At a glimpse they looked like family photos, but on closer inspection they were snapshots of history. Nelson with Oliver Tambo and Walter Sisulu. His wedding day with Winnie. A photo that looked like a group of mates with their arms around each other, was a shot taken in the headquarters of the Umkhonto We Sizwe (Spear of the Nation, the ANC's underground military wing).

Even the clothes in the house were a part of history. A coat made from jackal pelts laid out on the bed in the bedroom was the one that Mandela famously wore to his trial for treason back in 1956. 'There was an uproar when he wore this,' said Ngugi. 'It was like he was an emperor.'

To be honest, I had been a little cynical about the whole Nelson Mandela deification thing. Don't get me wrong, Mandela is a great man. (We share the same birthday!) But like the Dalai Lama, he seems to attract the devotion of people with scary smiles and a very tenuous grip on reality.

So I was surprised how inspired and uplifted I was by Ngugi's stories. And how emotional I became witnessing a great man being honoured by someone who really respected him.

At the end of the tour I thanked Ngugi, shaking his hand a little too vigorously. He waved goodbye and then called after a white female guide who had brought a minivan full of tourists. 'Bring more South Africans,' he yelled.

I got the feeling that if she did, and Ngugi was their guide, things in South Africa would improve out of hand.

❖   ❖   ❖

Steven didn't say anything to me until we got back to River Club. I think he was a little freaked out by my reverential silence. 'Perhaps you would like to do our city tour tomorrow,' he said as I got out. 'An armed guard is included.'

When I told Sarah about my visit to Mandela's house and how it had affected me she went to her bedroom and got out a scrapbook. She had been at university when apartheid ended in 1994 and had been very involved in the first free election. The scrapbook was her record of that time. 'Craig says I was a bit of a lefty,' she said. 'But it was such an exciting time.'

She flipped open the scrapbook and smiled. There was a wristband stuck on the first page. 'I was a scrutineer,' she said. 'We all had to wear one of these.'

The scrapbook was full of newspaper articles and advertisements from the time. It gave a real sense that history was being made, that they were witnessing the birth of an exciting and exhilarating new nation. The groundswell of goodwill was almost palpable.

'I kept these to show my children,' Sarah said, flicking

through the pages. 'I wanted to show them how it was, how we had to fight for their rights.'

Seven years on, however, the rainbow nation was looking a little tarnished. Even Sarah's optimism was dimming. 'I was hoping that by the time Emma went to university she would be taking it all for granted,' she said, stopping at a page with a picture of Mandela's inauguration. 'But now I'm not so sure.'

Nothing I had seen in my travels in South Africa had suggested things were getting better. Blacks are allowed back into the city centres, but the whites have retreated to outer suburbs. Affirmative Action is having some success, but there are still millions struggling to put a meal on the table. New houses are being built. But the black population are certainly not enjoying the same economic status as whites.

My impression from reading the papers was that the country was following the same path towards greed and corruption that other African nations have followed. Headmasters were using school funds to buy themselves BMWs. Government ministers were using their power and influence to make money.

For the moment, the mood on the streets was good. There was still a general feeling of optimism and people seemed happy enough to be free. But I wondered how long it would last once bellies began grumbling.

That night we had dinner in Melville, a funky suburb of cafes, restaurants and bars close to the centre of town, and once again I was surprised by how 'un-Johannesburg' it was. Over a plate of particularly good nachos, I asked Craig and Sarah if they ever thought about going back to England.

'We're in a bit of a dilemma, actually,' said Craig. 'I have a good job with Standard Bank here but there's nothing to say it will continue.'

Sarah picked at her food silently. It was obviously a discussion they'd had before.

'We have UK patronage, so it wouldn't be a problem working there,' said Craig. 'I'd earn pounds. It'd be safer. I just have to talk Sarah into it.'

Sarah was torn between her idealism and her instincts as a mother.

'I *am* worried about Emma growing up here,' she said, more to Craig than me. 'But if we go back to London it would be like I am abandoning everything I believed in. Sure, it's difficult now. But maybe it is Emma's generation that will make it work.'

We drove back to River Club in silence, cruising through red lights to minimise the chance of carjacking and past homeless people warming their hands over fires in 44-gallon drums. The security guard on duty at the boom gate looked in the back window to check I wasn't a hijacker before raising it. And as we pulled into the driveway a car belonging to one of the private security companies cruised by, just making sure that everything was all right. It was meant to be reassuring, but somehow it had the opposite effect.

If I were Craig and Sarah, I thought, I'd be on the first plane to the UK.

Chapter 6

MAPUTO, MOZAMBIQUE

Akili nyingi huondoa maarifa.
Great wit drives away wisdom.

Heading north of Johannesburg I spent three days in Kruger National Park, one of the biggest and most famous wildlife parks in the world. I took a tour led by a South African guy called Paul who had a pathological dislike of a) the Australian cricket team and b) Steve Irwin, the Crocodile Hunter.

I could understand his aversion to the Australian cricket team. No one likes a team that wins all the time. And while I admire what the team has achieved, I'm the first to admit that they're not really a likeable bunch of blokes. Glenn McGrath could do with being a little less surly. Steve Waugh should walk more often instead of waiting for the umpire to give him out. And Shane Warne, well, he could pretty much work on all areas of his life. But diss the Crocodile Hunter? Crikey, the guy's a legend!

I put Paul's dislike of the Crocodile Hunter down to plain old jealousy. Paul was stocky like Steve Irwin and wore the same uniform of khaki shorts and shirt a couple of sizes too small. His hair was the same sandy blond but had a more cinematic wave to it. And I suspect that in his own mind Paul felt he was more the real thing. But while the Crocodile Hunter had an internationally successful TV series, Paul was still driving tourists around a national park in a country fewer and fewer people were visiting. That's got to hurt.

Paul's dislike of Steve Irwin had become even more intense after the Crocodile Hunter came to his turf and filmed a documentary on African snakes. It wasn't so much the Steve Irwin antics that upset him – he was expecting him to climb trees, grab poisonous snakes by the tail and generally piss them off. It was the fact that the Crocodile Hunter turned up with an entire support crew that grated. 'People think he's some kind of action man,' Paul grumbled. 'But in Kruger he had a car follow him with anti-venom!'

Personally, I didn't have a problem with that. In fact, it raised my opinion of Steve Irwin immeasurably. He might be crazy, it seemed, but he wasn't stupid. As far as Paul was concerned, though, the Crocodile Hunter just wasn't sufficiently dangerous or out there.

Funnily enough, that was the exact problem I had with Kruger National Park. It might be as big as Wales and have 147 species of mammals, 507 species of birds, 114 varieties of reptiles and 34 different types of amphibians. But it was a politically correct game park. You had to keep to the roads and try to spot wildlife from your car, letting the animals come to you rather than going off cross-country harassing them.

And don't get me started about the campsites. They were brand new and spanking clean, securely fenced to keep the animals out and boasting the kind of amenities that would shame many upmarket hotels.

To give Paul his due, he might not have had the charisma of the Crocodile Hunter, but he was very good at his job. By the end of the second day he had managed to get us within a car length of all of the big five (elephant, lion, leopard, buffalo and rhino) as well as a fair number of the other less sought-after species like zebras and giraffes. But his constant carping about Steve Waugh and Steve Irwin got on my nerves.

On my last morning in Kruger I decide to have a little bit of fun. 'Look,' I said. 'There's a Jaguar.'

Paul instinctively slammed on the brakes. When he was driving he'd rely on passengers to spot something he'd missed.

'Where?' asked Paul, still not thinking straight.

'Just there on the road,' I said, pointing to a fine example of Coventry engineering. 'It's an old XJS, I think.'

I thought it was funny, and it got a laugh from a few of the other passengers. But Paul was furious. I'd made him look like an idiot – there aren't any jaguars in Africa, they're endemic to the jungles of South America – and at the end of the tour he didn't actually stop to drop me off at Nelspruit. I got more of a slow-down-a-little-open-the-door-and-kick-the-Aussie-out kind of farewell.

Nelspruit lies on the Crocodile River among dome granite hills. It was another South African town caught in a sixties time warp, with box-shaped buildings and arcades instead of malls, and I stayed only long enough to organise a ride in a long-distance minivan heading to Maputo, the capital of Mozambique.

I was really looking forward to going to Mozambique. It's a country with a name that is laden with promise for adventure and excitement. Crossed by two legendary rivers, the Limpopo and the Zambezi, and the setting for many a Wilbur Smith novel, it's the kind of country you could mention you've been to at a dinner party and before you know it you're standing in the lounge room with one foot on the coffee table, cradling a brandy balloon and thrilling a captive audience with tales of your derring-do. Well, that's the effect it has on me, anyway.

To be honest, I was also getting a little tired of the underlying tension in South Africa. It manifested itself in all kinds of little ways, but most annoyingly in the way no one really trusted anyone else. For example, in Johannesburg a check-out girl gave me the wrong change (she thought I'd given her a 20 rand note instead of a 50). Back home, they'd apologise and give you the correct change. But that day the manager was called over and the girl had to close the till and go to a back room to count the money. Half an hour later she came back and gave me the proper change. I had been right, but I didn't even get an apology.

In Nelspruit I had a beer while I waited for my minivan to leave and I was given a scratch card as part of an Amstel Draught promotion. The prizes were free beers and T-shirts, nothing to get excited about, but get this: you only won the prize if you scratched the card in front of the waitress. In fact the instructions stated that you had to 'scratch quickly in front of Waitress'. It didn't say *where* you had to scratch but I figured that in a conservative town like Nelspruit rearranging the wedding tackle would not be appreciated.

Psychologically it was time to get a move on too. Nearly six weeks had passed and I was still in South Africa, a country that, quite frankly, reminded me of home. The landscape, the vegetation, the weather, the big skies were all terribly familiar so for most of my time there I had the uneasy feeling that I wasn't so much in another country as in a parallel universe of Australia where the people talked even funnier and all the kangaroos had been turned into springboks.

The other passengers in the minivan to Maputo were mainly Mozambique folk going home to visit their families. They had been working as gardeners or maids in South Africa, sending money home whenever they could, and were now crammed in a minivan surrounded by striped bags full of stuff their families couldn't buy in Mozambique. The prized front seats, however, were taken by two self-confessed businessmen: Leonard, a tall Indian guy, and Claude, a half-Portuguese half-Mozambican chap who was round and short. They were going to Maputo to check out a business opportunity.

'Now that the civil war is over there are many opportunities in Mozambique,' said Leonard. 'You would be wise to invest.'

I don't know where people like Leonard get the idea that I have a lazy couple of grand lying around to invest in third-world business opportunities. I certainly don't look like I've got money. When they give me these sure-fire investment tips I'm invariably unshaven and wearing dirty crumpled clothes. And surely the fact that I'm in a minivan rather than a private taxi or even a luxury coach must suggest that things are a bit tight. Maybe I just look like a sucker.

The South Africans obviously think there is money to be made in Mozambique – the road from Nelspruit to the border is a brand new dual-lane freeway. The border post at Komatipoort, however, must be regarded as a poorer investment opportunity because it was a complete shambles.

Such was the state of the border post that people wandered from one building to another looking for the appropriate immigration/customs/bank department to process them. More often than not they wandered into the stinky toilet by mistake, coming out again almost immediately with a look on their face that suggested they had seen something they rather wished they hadn't. Meanwhile other people with boxes and bags wandered through constantly, only some of them being stopped by officials. There may have been some sort of system at work but it wasn't immediately apparent.

The driver of the van indicated for us to abandon his vehicle and go through the formalities on foot. He would wait for us on the other side. I had got my Mozambique visa back in Johannesburg so I went through quickly and waited on the Mozambique side of the border beside a sign that read 'Welcome to Mozambique. Beautiful people, beautiful country'.

The sign also featured the Mozambique coat of arms, a hoe crossed by an AK-47. The AK-47 was a reminder of how much this country's history had been decided at the point of a gun. The Portuguese had taken the country by force, of course, and in 1964 Frelimo, the outlawed Mozambique Liberation Front, launched the war for independence with guerrilla attacks on targets in northern Mozambique. After independence was won in 1975, Rhodesian Intelligence Services created Renamo, the Mozambican National Resistance, to destabilise the young Marxist state using the same guerrilla tactics. That civil war has ended, and now the two sides fight it out at the ballot box. But the coat of arms suggests that it wouldn't take much for the warring parties to take up an AK-47 again.

I was disturbed from my thoughts by Leonard, the tall, thin businessman. 'Do you notice the difference?' he asked, sweeping his hand across the Mozambique side. 'The difference is money.'

The change from the South African side of the border was quite startling. On the Mozambique side everything was ramshackle, dusty and broken, especially the people. Boys sold crappy cassettes from grubby grape boxes as goats wandered among them. I've long held that you can judge a country's economic plight by the number of goats it has. The more goats there are, the more desperate the situation in that particular village, town or country. Judging by the number of goats nibbling at scrubby bushes and rooting through piles of garbage, Mozambique was in a heap of trouble.

After half an hour most of the passengers had passed to the other side, but we were still missing two. Their bags were in the van but they were nowhere to be seen.

'They didn't have visas,' explained Claude. 'They were going to sneak across but they must have been caught.'

No one seemed particularly disturbed by this, even an hour later when there was still no sign of the two errant passengers. The driver had obviously factored such an occurrence into the trip. I asked Claude what would happen if they didn't turn up.

'Oh, they will get through,' he said confidently. 'And if they don't they have given the driver an address in Maputo. He will drop their bags there.'

By 4 pm the sun was getting low in the sky and Leonard and Claude decided that it was time to take matters into their own hands. 'It is very dangerous to drive at night in Mozambique,' Leonard said. 'Many of the vehicles do not have lights. Only last week a taxi ran into the back of a tractor that was driving without lights. Everyone was killed. If you are lucky we will be able to see the wreck.'

Leonard and Claude strode back purposefully towards the border post and I soon lost them in the crowd of people making the crossing. There was nothing to do but wait, so I leaned against the van, in the shady side, batting off boys who were convinced I needed a poorly pirated copy of a tape of a 1950s Portuguese pop star. After 40 minutes there was still no sign of Claude and Leonard. Even the driver, who had spent most of the afternoon comatose, his head using the steering wheel as a pillow, was starting to get antsy.

Just as he was about to start the engine, I spotted Leonard and Claude, silhouetted against the afternoon sun, bathed in golden light diffused and softened by the dust. It was like a scene from a western. They sauntered over the rise, the two missing passengers beside them. When they reached the van everyone shook their hands and slapped them on the back. It was like they'd just returned from a successful mission behind enemy lines.

'The guard wanted 140 rand to let them through,' Leonard told anyone who would listen. 'We simply distracted him by showing him our passports and they slipped through. It was easy, really.'

The rest of the journey to Maputo passed quickly. The van hurtled along an impressive toll road, recently opened and unaffected by the flooding that had devastated other parts of the country not long before. It was a black ribbon through scrubby savanna. The sun was setting as we passed the twisted remains of the tractor and taxi.

Unlike the border post, the toll stations on the Mozambique side were gleaming and modern, probably to justify the heinously expensive toll. I had noted the toll at each of the booths we had passed since Nelspruit, and by my calculations the trip to Maputo would cost a motorist $76. This section of the freeway had replaced the old road completely and was the only way from the border to Maputo. I asked Leonard how people could afford the toll and he said that they took the road through Swaziland.

It was dark when we hit the outskirts of Maputo. The roads were badly potholed, the street lamps were broken and gizzards were being grilled on roadside barbecues. I immediately decided I liked the place. As we got closer to the town centre Claude asked me where I was staying and I told him Fatima's. Other travellers had told me that it was a dank, dour place where they crammed as many people as possible into tiny humid rooms with broken fans, but it was the only budget option in town.

Appalled, Claude insisted that I stay with him and Leonard at his sister's place. 'She is not expecting us,' he said. 'So three guests instead of two will not make much difference.'

Although I wasn't sure about Claude's reasoning, I happily accepted his offer. I was going with the flow again, taking chances and being dragged into people's lives. As an added bonus, Claude talked the driver of the minivan into dropping us off right at the door, saving us an uncomfortable bus ride from the city centre.

As it was there were four extra guests at Claude's sister's

house. Claude's mother had returned unexpectedly that day after spending two years in Portugal. It was quite the family reunion with all the attendant hugs, tears and pinching of cheeks. Leonard and I hung back – we were the only ones not related – but Claude's mother spotted us and hugged us warmly, dragging us into the family too.

The whole family sat in the lounge room while Claude's sister prepared a feast. It was a huge, delicious meal eaten at a crowded table where everyone laughed and sang, passing plates of steaming hot vegetables and lightly spiced meats. I couldn't understand a word, of course – everyone spoke in Portuguese. But I didn't need to. The warmth of the family and the cheap red wine poured from glass carafes gave me understanding enough. The celebrations continued into the early hours of the morning when we retired to the lounge room to play old vinyl records – Portuguese – on a sixties-style record player. I ended the night sharing a bed with Leonard. When he stripped down to a singlet and Y-fronts I insisted we sleep head to toe.

Leonard snored like a jet fighter so I was awake and out of bed at dawn. Claude's mother was already up and was preparing a big breakfast for the family, so I sat in the lounge room reading. She came and spoke to me in Portuguese, expecting a reply. I couldn't understand so I shrugged my shoulders and smiled. Claude came in, rubbing his eyes, and hugged his mother. She asked him to translate.

'She wants to know if you slept okay,' he said.

'No problems,' I answered. 'Leonard stayed on his side of the bed.' He translated my answer and his mother reached across and pinched my cheek, laughing. I knew who'd be getting extra helpings at breakfast that morning.

Later I headed into the city centre with Leonard and Claude. They were checking out sites for a spare parts business. Their plan was to import parts from South Africa and sell them cheaply in Maputo. It was a sure-fire thing they said, and they spent the entire morning trying to convince me that my fortune was there waiting to be made.

I liked Maputo. It was crumbling and decaying like all Portuguese colonial cities, with wide streets and tree-lined boulevards. Women hung washing from cramped balconies, calling out to friends who passed below. Portuguese pop warbled from beat-up transistors in shops. Old men sat on benches under trees smoking hand-rolled cigarettes while children played football on the broken pavements with balls they had made from twine. Life seemed slower and somehow more enjoyable there.

I'm not sure how long it will stay that way. The skyline was dotted by a forest of construction cranes carrying out the work of South African investors. They were throwing up office blocks, warehouses and port facilities at a frenetic pace. Despite backing the wrong side in the civil war, the South Africans were determined to transform Maputo into a major port, to suit their purposes, regardless.

'The South Africans have already invested many millions in infrastructure,' said Leonard as we drove through the city. 'Maputo will be their most important cargo port.'

Whether this would benefit your average Mozambican is debatable. Ever since the Portuguese, outside forces have been taking from the country and not putting much back in return. On the strength of its resources, Mozambique should be southern Africa's most important energy producer and exporter. But past military unrest and, now, the need to get rid of a crippling foreign debt, has seen the country pawn its most valuable assets just to get by. For the South Africans, Maputo is a quality deep-water port close to their industrial heartland of Johannesburg and Guateng Province. I couldn't help wondering what lengths they'd go to protect their 'investment'.

At lunchtime we visited Claude's father. He was an old, balding Portuguese guy who had once been a bigwig in the fishing department and had separated from Claude's mother not long after Claude was born. He was semi-retired now and ran a bar-cum-restaurant in a ramshackle part of town. He greeted Claude like a prodigal son, although they had only seen each other a few months before.

As I watched them hug – Claude black, his father white it struck me that its Portuguese heritage seemed to make Mozambique a more emotional and passionate place than South Africa. Unlike the Afrikaners the Portuguese inter-married, got involved, started families, integrated. I know they weren't angels – the Portuguese were as savage and greedy as other colonial powers – but that afternoon, seeing Claude and his father hug, made me think there wasn't the chasm there between the colonisers and the colonised.

Claude's father's restaurant could be described, graciously, as modest, just a bare concrete area with tables and more than its fair share of Maputo's put-upon nursing beers and staring at a spot on the table in front of them. But within fifteen minutes we had a feast laid before us that was one of the best seafood meals I have ever eaten. (I come from a city with some of the best seafood restaurants in the world, so I know what I'm talking about.) We tucked into crab, lobster and prawns, leaving a pile of shells a foot high. When we had finished eating

Claude's father went to rustle up some more beers. He shuffled, bent over as most 70-year-old men are.

Claude watched him and smiled. 'When I was 16 I got into a lot of trouble with the police,' said Claude. 'I hit one with a rock from my slingshot. My father got me out of jail and sent me to South Africa. His contacts there looked after me. It was better for me, even with apartheid.'

By mid-afternoon we couldn't eat or drink any more so we made our excuses and left. Claude's father stood at the door and gave each of us a big bear hug as we left. It was my second day in Mozambique and I already had an extended family.

The guys dropped me off at the town centre while they went and looked at more shop fronts. I visited the market, checked my e-mail at an internet cafe with a loyalty scheme (you were given a card that was stamped each visit and got your tenth visit free) and dropped into the Museum of Art. The work there didn't reflect the new Mozambique that I had been embraced by. They were bleak and angry pieces that captured the spirit of darker times when the country was wracked by civil war. The paintings were gloomy, populated by wide-eyed people looking suspicious and unsure, whispering to each other and accusing.

I told the guys about it when they picked me up and Claude nodded his head solemnly. 'It was a terrible time,' he said. 'People didn't trust anybody – even their own families. That's why my mother went to Portugal. That's why my father sent me to South Africa. Even with apartheid, he felt I would be safer there.'

When we feasted again that night, with everyone laughing and joking, I found it hard to believe that it could have ever been like that, the country, families, friends, divided down political lines – Renamo or Frelimo. The really sad thing was that Mozambicans were being manipulated by outside sources the whole time. Frelimo was backed by Tanzania, keen to thwart South African ambitions in Southern and East Africa. Renamo was set up by the whites in Rhodesia, who were worried that the Africans in their country would want Mozambique-style independence there. The 25 years of misery inflicted upon Mozambique is a sobering example of why other countries should just butt out of another's affairs.

Claude borrowed his sister's car and dropped me off at the long-distance bus station at four o'clock the next morning. Every long-distance bus left at 4.30. I didn't bother asking why – it was just the way they did things in Mozambique.

I was heading north to Inhambane, a town just over 250 kilometres away, partly because it was close to long, untouched beaches but mainly because it was as far as any bus would get that day. The road north was in terrible condition. I'd like to believe it was in such a bad way because of the recent floods, but I think it had always been bad. The South Africans had no interest in the rest of Mozambique. They just wanted access to the port at Maputo. There was no reason to sink a north–south road that they would never use.

By 10 am the bus had reached Chisano, the point where the sealed road degenerated into a dirt track. Since the floods the road had only ever been open in one direction, for a few hours in each direction at a time. When we arrived it was open to vehicles heading south. The vehicles heading north, including our bus and every other one that had been at the main terminal in Maputo that morning, stopped. Their passengers were milling around or lying under trees.

It was grey and overcast and the passengers used the break as an opportunity to tuck into beer and cheap wine that they bought from roadside stalls. I was alarmed by the way they looked like they were settling in for a long wait. One guy, clutching a half-drunk bottle of Ballantines Whisky and already a little worse for wear, came up and gleefully informed me that the buses wouldn't be going until 1 pm, a three-hour wait. I asked him why the buses didn't take the three-hour wait into account and leave Maputo later.

'But they are express buses!' he exclaimed.

At twelve, a convoy of arrogant Afrikaners with big bellies and big moustaches in big fuck-off four-wheel-drives pulling sparkling new boats arrived. They spoke with the only seemingly authority, a soldier sitting under a tree in battle fatigues and a red beret, an AK-47 lazily on his lap. Their reaction suggested he had told them to wait. They gesticulated, yabbered, and when that didn't seem to have any effect, jumped in their vehicles and drove right past him and the long line of waiting vehicles.

There was a hushed silence as everyone in the crowd watched to see what the soldier would do. He simply stood up and let them pass. When he sat back down again it triggered a tsunami of activity. Drivers sprinted for their vehicles, motioning wide-eyed for passengers to follow. People gathered up their food, beer and wine in a mad scramble and skipped among the puddles back to their buses. Engines roared to life, horns honked and then came the sound of a hundred over-revved vehicles dropping the clutch and spinning their wheels on the loose gravel. The soldier stood up again, even raised his gun this time, but figured that it was too late and sat down.

It reminded me of the 'Wacky Races', a cartoon series I used to love as a kid. There was a different race every week, with the same teams, using all kinds of tactics, legal and illegal, to win. But instead of the Ant Hill Mob or Penelope Pitstop, that afternoon in Mozambique it was a motley collection of buses, vans and pick-up trucks that jockeyed for position, tearing up the thin, bumpy road, three or four abreast at a time. It must have been a shocking sight for the last of the southbound vehicles. Most sensibly pulled to the side of the road and let the northbound swarm pass. One, a heavily overloaded truck that couldn't pull over, simply stopped in the middle of the road as the traffic passed him like a torrent around a rock.

At Chiboto it became apparent why the traffic only ever operated in one direction at a time. Here the road had been washed away, leaving gaping potholes the size of houses. The traffic was diverted around the village, alongside a school with 'Viva Marxism' painted on the side, past a guy selling bows and arrows with nasty looking tips and across a rickety temp bridge barely wide enough for the buses. An hour later we passed the South Africans, broken down by the side of the road. (I joined the bus passengers in jeering them!) By late afternoon we were in Inhambane, a crumbling, colonial cashew town perched picturesquely on an inlet of the Mozambique Channel. And so began my meanderings up the coast of Mozambique.

I blame my father for the high expectations I had of the Mozambique coastline. When I was a teenager he bought *Desire* by Bob Dylan and played it to death. His favourite song was 'Hurricane', the song about the wrongful imprisonment of Rubin Carter. My favourite was 'Mozambique'.

Dylan purists will argue that it's not one of Bob's best tunes. In fact, I'm sure that many will argue that it is probably his worst. But to a teenage boy the line about there being lots of pretty girls in Mozambique with plenty of time for romance had a certain allure. If I remember rightly the sky was also aqua blue and all the couples danced cheek-to-cheek. If I'd been getting a bit more pocket money, I would have been on the first plane to Maputo.

My first stop, Bamboozi's at Tofu Beach, looked the goods. It was nestled in the sand dunes behind a long stretch of white beach and had a restaurant-bar where you could lie in a hammock and watch the ocean. There were no rooms. You either camped under the palm trees or slept on a camp bed in the big open tent up the back. It was like being shipwrecked but with the knowledge that a packet of dry biscuits or the next van out of there was only a 20-minute walk down the beach away.

Unfortunately, I didn't get to lie beside a girl on the beach or say hello with just a glance, two things promised in the Bob Dylan song. Instead I spent a Saturday night at the local 'nightclub', a reed hut in the middle of nowhere, where young men shuffled about getting pissed on palm wine and the dance floor reeked of BO.

From Tofu Beach I made my way north to Vilankulo, a crumbling seaside town opposite the Bazaruto Archipelago. My guidebook promised sandy beaches and azure waters. Instead I got a malicious tide that went out during the day, leaving wooden fishing boats stranded and leaning on their side and giving the whole place the demeanour of mud flats. Sure, it came back in at night, but what good is that when you want to work on your tan?

I was staying in a place on the outskirts of town called the Last Resort. It was appropriately named. My bed was a foam mattress on the floor of a hut and the shower was a bucket and a drum filled with rain water. Each evening I'd buy fresh seafood from kids on the beach and cook it on the charcoal fire in the rudimentary kitchen. After a few days I realised that Vilankulo was nothing like the Bob Dylan song either and decided to leave.

There was a problem though. The bus north to the Zimbabwean border at Machipanda left at 4 am and my bag was locked in the storage hut. John, the English owner, had the keys but he had gone out on a bender. Worse, no one knew where.

There were a dozen or so drinking establishments in Vilankulo. Some, like Smugglers, were bright salubrious places with chatty bar staff and freshly polished glasses. Most were dingy, dark places where patrons didn't care what they drank as long as it helped them forget who they were. I visited them all that night, some of them twice. John wasn't at any of them.

At eleven o'clock I gave up and walked back towards the Last Resort along a sandy road illuminated by moonlight filtering through the palm trees. A guy with a teddy bear haircut riding a bike stopped and offered me a lift. I sat on the rack, my legs dangling to one side. He had an old transistor radio strapped to the front. He couldn't speak English. I couldn't speak Portuguese. So we rode in silence, the only sound the squeak of the bike and Sade singing 'Smooth Operator', the bongos synchronising perfectly with the rhythm of the ride. Then the DJ played Louis Armstrong's 'It's a

Wonderful World'. I thought, 'Yeah, it is!' I decided then that I didn't care if I missed my bus.

Which was kind of lucky because I found John passed out drunk in the dorm and the word was he had lost his keys.

Chapter 7

HARARE, ZIMBABWE

Mpanda ovyo, hula ovya.
He who sows in a disorderly fashion will eat likewise.

You know the feeling when you see someone famous in real life and they look nothing like you expected? Somehow they're not as glamorous or dashing as they appear on the big screen or in their photo and for a second your whole world gets a little skewed: 'God, they look a bit rough/fat/short!' Well, that's how I felt coming into Mutare, the first Zimbabwean town I came to across the border.

Mutare had once been a pretty place with wide streets lined by jacarandas and flame trees. But the buildings had fallen into disrepair and all the papaya and mango trees that grew in the gardens were stripped bare. The streetlights were smashed. The traffic lights didn't work (I found out later that they had been stolen and sold to discos). And the prices in the shops had all been crossed out and new, higher ones marked in.

There were very few cars on the roads. The petrol stations were closed because of fuel shortages. The only sign of life were the groups of people gathered around ATMs, waiting for the machines to momentarily flicker on so they could withdraw their money. When I walked down the street beggars stopped me with plaintive pleas of 'I'm hungry, man', and I believed them.

I was the only guest staying at a hostel close to town that my guidebook had described as 'always buzzing'. Milo, the owner, was a white Zimbabwean of advancing years, and when I asked him if he was expecting any more people, he laughed like a drain. 'It's your first day here, isn't it?' he said.

I nodded and he gave me the kind of pitying look that suggested it wouldn't be long before it all became a lot clearer.

At Milo's all your meals were provided and you spent the evenings watching television with the proprietor. It wasn't exactly how I thought I'd be spending my time in Zimbabwe but there wasn't anything else in Mutare competing for my entertainment dollar. Most of the restaurants and pubs were closed because of power and fuel shortages and the alluringly lurid 'Miss High School 2000' had been cancelled because of a teachers' strike.

The viewing that night was a specially edited interview with the Zimbabwean president, Robert Mugabe. It wasn't an address to the nation, just an informal chat about the importance of seizing land from white farmers, but it was on every channel.

When the president appeared, with that unfortunate little Hitler moustache he insists on wearing, Milo hissed at the television. 'That bastard has ruined a beautiful, beautiful country,' he spat. 'I hope he rots in hell.'

The president used the interview to defend the rights of so-called 'war veterans' to use force to reclaim land.

When Mugabe had finished, the station ran a news report about the Minister of Agriculture accepting a donation of ploughs and cattle from World Vision. 'You must be grateful for these gifts,' he told a group of dishevelled folk who looked like they'd been rounded up from the local bar. 'They show why land is so important.'

Land was important to the government because they could use it to buy support from rural voters. They'd already lost support in the cities to the opposition Movement for Democratic Change (MDC) party. The city folk were tired of the chronic food and fuel shortages and the effects of rampant inflation. But in the countryside the lure of a block of land, and hence the means to support your family, was irresistible.

'You are visiting at a very interesting point in this country's history,' said Milo. I got the feeling he was using 'interesting' in the same manner people describe the way I dance. That is, in its derogative form.

I suspected that Milo was not normally a political person. But tourists – his livelihood – were being frightened away from Zimbabwe by the reports of violence and intimidation that they saw each night on their televisions and he was livid. Milo cut out political cartoons from newspapers and stuck them around the hostel as a kind of protest. One featured Mugabe walking through a hostile crowd with Ian Smith, the white president who ruled Zimbabwe when it was still Rhodesia. 'It seems I have more black friends than you,' he says in the cartoon. Another featured a taxi driver being told by a petrol pump attendant that prices have gone up 10 per cent. The driver turns around immediately and tells the passengers in his van that the fares have just gone up 10 per cent.

Zimbabwe, it seems, was always destined to end up like this. When Mugabe led the country to independence in 1980 his previously pragmatic approach was progressively replaced by more nationalistic and Marxist policies that weren't going to get the country on top of the international investors' 'must sink wads of cash here' list. More recently, he has been amassing a vast personal fortune, at the expense of his country, which has only made things worse. Add to that the destruction of the few agricultural enterprises bringing in foreign currency by dividing them up into tiny allotments and giving them away to buy votes and you have a country going down the gurgler big time.

On my second evening a group of Milo's friends came over for dinner and I was spared another television interview with Mugabe. Milo's friends were all white and they were all being affected by the president's antics. One distinguished-looking chap had recently 'retired' as a lecturer on farm management at the local university. Another fellow had been forced to shut down his import–export business when his suppliers started insisting on payment in US dollars. They all relied on the BBC and the South African press for truth about what was going on in their country.

'Take that oke who defended his farm against 300 attackers,' said the former lecturer. 'It didn't even make the news here.' The farmer had spotted a mob approaching and had put a loaded rifle in each room. When they attacked he ran from room to room, firing through the windows, killing 17 of his attackers before they finally got him. The former lecturer had heard the story on the BBC. 'Mugabe and his henchmen don't want us to hear about it,' said the former import–exporter. 'They don't want the blacks to hear either. The blacks love a hero and that's what that guy was – a hero.'

The talk turned to a mutual friend who owned a tobacco farm nearby. The former lecturer said that the farm had been earmarked for 'seizure'. I asked him how he knew.

'He tried to get some diesel delivered the other day and they wouldn't give it to him,' he said. 'Closed his account. Sure enough, when he got home there was a letter from the government telling him to surrender his farm.'

The cities were suffering as well. The *Sunday Mail* that weekend ran a story about students turning to prostitution to pay for increased food fees at the University of Zimbabwe. In another seemingly related story, most of the backpacker lodges in Harare were being turned into brothels. Even the advertisements told a sorry tale. A furniture store offered free delivery within a 25-kilometre radius – subject to the availability of fuel.

The driver of the bus I caught to Harare certainly wasn't taking any chances. He kept a couple of 44-gallon drums full of fuel at the back of the bus, positioned strategically to explode on impact.

The four-hour drive to Harare was unremarkable except for the rock formations beside the road (they looked like a pile of giant marbles stacked on top of each other) and the most bizarre drink driving campaign I think I have ever seen. The police had set up a roadblock and after a sufficient number of people had stopped, they walked along the line of vehicles holding up a sign that said 'Drinking and driving don't mix'. When the drivers acknowledged that they had read the sign – a simple nod of the head would suffice – they were allowed to drive off.

The long-distance bus station servicing Harare is situated in the Mbare township about 5 kilometres from town. It is as noisy, muddy and chaotic as any in Africa, but the harsh economic climate meant that the touts were the most intense I had come across on my journey so far. From the moment I stepped off the bus and into what I hoped was dog shit, I was besieged by men desperate to get a commission out of me, no matter how tiny. 'Where are you *going*?' they pleaded. 'You must take taxi! I have a meter – only 300 dollars! *Pleeeaasse*!!!'

I told the assembled crowd of would-be helpers that I didn't have enough for a taxi and asked where the minivans for town left from. The older hands refused to tell me, but a teenage boy wearing only tattered shorts without a shirt pointed to the road running along the edge of the bus station and told me the ride should only cost $Z20 (about 80 cents). I thanked him and made my way towards the exit.

The other touts were not so easily defeated. They bounded ahead of me and blocked my way, demanding money to let me pass. 'Give us $200!' they demanded angrily.

I refused.

A van heading to the city came along and they dropped their demand to $Z100. When I didn't budge they blocked the van door and demanded $Z50. Just as the van was about to drive off I pushed my way past them and fell face first into the lap of a lady so large that she had taken up most of the bench seat herself. My pack was still on my back so it took quite a while for me to extricate myself from her cushiony thighs. When I did, the touts waved their fists at me as we drove off.

'It is desperate times,' said the conductor, shaking his head.

I decided to stay at Possum Lodge, a 20-minute walk from the city centre and one of the few hostels that had not been turned into a brothel. It was a large house with a huge wooden staircase, a pool and enough beds for 50 backpackers. The manager told me that they needed 18 people a night to break even. Over the three days I stayed there were never any more than six.

One of the other guests at the lodge was a young Zimbabwean farmer called Bryce who had just been kicked off a property that his family had farmed for generations. He was on his way to Zambia to manage a rose farm. 'They took our farm only three months ago,' he said. 'But already it is in ruins.'

It wasn't just Bryce's family that was affected. The farm had employed over 200 locals who lived in workers' huts with their families on the land. The war veterans had chased them off the land as well, even though the workers could have shown them how to run the farm.

According to Bryce, it wasn't easy running a farm in Zimbabwe, especially with inflation out of control. 'You have to get finance for millions of dollars at interest rates of 78 per cent,' he said. 'It can be five years before you see a return. Are these war veterans going to be able handle that?'

Bryce said most farmers were just abandoning their farms. The Commercial Farmers Union had said they'd get market price for the land, with extra for improvements, but the reality was that they got nothing. 'The bastards just come and take it,' he said. 'Most farmers sabotage everything before they go now. Throw rocks down bores, put sand in the petrol tank of tractors, that sort of thing.'

I asked Bryce what the farmers did for money once they had lost their major asset – and their livelihood. He said the smart ones had been spiriting money away for years. 'I have a secret bank account in the Channel Islands,' he said. 'So I'm lucky.'

As one of only a handful of tourists in Harare, I was surprised to see that the souvenir stalls in African Unity Square were still operating. Each morning the stall owners carefully laid out the soapstone animals, the wooden masks and the African jewellery and each evening they packed them all up again without making a single sale. I wondered why they even bothered but I figured that they had nothing else to do and nowhere else to go.

I made the mistake of wandering through the stalls on my second day in Harare and immediately regretted it. I had no intention of buying anything – I just wanted to see what kind of stuff they were selling. But it was like walking into a medieval dungeon and having all the prisoners lunge at you through the bars, demanding that you help them get out.

'If you do not buy this you are killing me!' said a soapstone carver, thrusting a soapstone elephant at me that was bordering on life size.

I had barely shaken the soapstone guy off when a jewellery hawker rushed up and tried to put a bright, beaded necklace around my neck. 'There are no jobs, no food,' he pleaded. 'I am relying on you to survive!'

I wanted to tell him that he should speak to his president, but I was completely surrounded by souvenir sellers clambering for my custom. I broke free and scurried towards the park exit, a wood carver still clinging to my shirt. 'Help promote me!' he cried as I brushed him off. 'Do not kill me!'

I found Harare depressing. Like Mutare, it had once been a blushing belle, probably in the seventies, judging by the architecture. But now the roads were potholed and the pavements broken, and the entrances of even the grandest buildings were home to entire families with nowhere else to live.

I wandered through the scruffy Harare Gardens, stepping over drunks passed out on the patchy lawn, and visited the National Gallery. My guidebook described it as the 'last word on art and culture from around the continent' but it looked like it was full of the same things I had just seen down at the markets. It crossed my mind that perhaps it was. The curator may have flogged the real stuff to feed his family.

I realised that it was time for me to leave the Zimbabwean capital when I seriously considered going to the cricket match between Zimbabwe and New Zealand at the Harare Sports Club. So instead, I got on a bus, thinking it would take me all the way to Bulawayo, Zimbabwe's second biggest city, but it ran out of petrol just outside of Shangani and I had to hitch the rest of the way.

I got a ride in a small pick-up from a black guy who made granite bench tops for a living. I couldn't imagine that there'd be much of a market for his product in Zimbabwe and asked him if he exported.

'My life would be wonderful!' he replied, with a wistful look on his face. Then he turned and asked me if I believed in Jesus. I mumbled an indistinct answer and he told me that Jesus was coming soon. 'The signs are everywhere!' he cried, with an evangelical fire in his eyes. 'War . . . plague . . . famine. We hear a lot about these things in Africa.'

It struck me at that moment that the horror stories in the Bible that seem almost unbelievable to us in the West have a particular resonance in Africa. Day-to-day life in Zimbabwe was like a chapter from Revelations. Disease, hunger and cruelty are all part of the daily Zimbabwean experience.

The conversation turned to Jesus miracles and Satan miracles and, in particular, how to tell them apart. Jesus miracles, it transpired, are always free. And Satan miracles always involve snake or bull's blood.

Once I had demonstrated that I could distinguish between the two, the bench top man offered me a banana. 'Let us eat,' he said reverentially.

I felt as though I should bow my head.

As we approached the outskirts of Bulawayo we passed three buses abandoned by the side of the road. 'The buses ran out of fuel last week,' said the bench top man. 'The passengers walked the rest of the way or got a lift.' The buses would stay there until the company that owned them could afford the fuel needed to retrieve them.

Bulawayo is Zimbabwe's principal industrial centre so it was even more depressed than Harare and Mutare. The textile factories that had once brought it prosperity were closed and trade with nearby South Africa had slowed to a trickle because Zimbabwe had nothing to sell. In Ndebele, one of the languages spoken in Zimbabwe, Bulawayo means 'Place of Slaughter'. When I was there it felt more suicidal.

The rain didn't help. It gave the town a dull grey aura that only served to emphasise how hopeless things were. I went down to the dilapidated railway station (disturbingly also the national headquarters of Zimbabwe Railways) and bought a ticket on the overnight train to Victoria Falls.

It was still raining heavily when I returned to catch the train that night. Porters were plying their trade with stolen shopping trolleys, waiting under a sign that read, 'Passengers are earnestly requested to abstain from the dangerous and objectionable habit of expectorating'.

I was delighted to discover that the train was as old as the sign. My compartment for the journey was lined with timber veneer and had a silver metal wash basin and little hidey holes for my toiletries and my shoes.

The man who had sold me the ticket had warned me that the train's departure was dependent on the availability of diesel so I was surprised when it left Bulawayo right on time at 7 pm, just as thunder rumbled and then clapped, right above the train.

The man sharing my compartment, a middle-aged man in a crumpled suit, looked out of the window, concerned. 'Very bad,' he said. 'Very, very bad. The thunder will affect the signals.'

He introduced himself as George and told me that he worked for the railways. He was from Dete, a small town about three-quarters of the way to Victoria Falls, and had travelled to Bulawayo to visit his 13-year-old daughter in hospital. 'She had a stroke,' he said, shaking his head. 'She just fell down on her way from school and never woke up.'

He was obviously upset and looked out the window, the rain dribbling down it, so I wouldn't see his tears. He turned to me and pointed to his wet jacket. 'I was going to say, "Look, it rained on me!" ' he said with a sad smile. 'But she was still unconscious.'

The train struggled slowly through the night. Occasionally the countryside was lit by lightning and I was alarmed to see people standing beside the track getting wet, staring blankly at the train.

'They have nowhere to go,' said George. 'The crops have failed. Prices have risen. We are all hungry.'

The conductor came along to prepare our beds for the evening. His uniform was bright and clean, but there were telltale patches where it had been repaired. 'Good evening Mr Moore,' he said. 'May I see your ticket?'

I gave him my ticket and he marked it off his list. 'And who is this?' he asked, motioning towards George.

'It's George,' I answered.

'George who?'

'Ncube,' answered George.

The conductor flicked through his list before finding George's name. 'You're in compartment B,' he said. 'Please go there so I know where you are when I need to wake you up at Dete Crossroads.'

I waited out in the corridor while the bed was made and watched George shuffle off to his compartment, his shoulders stooped under the weight of his own, and his country's, problems. It certainly put my personal problems into perspective. I'd just come out of a relationship that hadn't worked – nothing more, nothing less. I had my health. And the fact that I was able to travel proved that the Australian dollar wasn't as bad as we all made out. I still had hope. George was being sapped of his.

❖　　　❖　　　❖

I woke the next morning to a different Zimbabwe. It was green and lush and the railway station was neat and tidy with freshly clipped lawns. The rain had cleared and the sky was blue, but a strange light mist fell on my face. It freaked me out a little until I realised what it was.

It was spray from Victoria Falls.

Chapter 8

VICTORIA FALLS, ZIMBABWE

Si kila mwenye makucha huwa simba.

Not all that have claws are lions.

I'd heard from other travellers that Victoria Falls hadn't been as badly affected as the rest of Zimbabwe. It was in the far north-west of the country, a long way from the troubles in Harare and Bulawayo, and it had its own international airport that the well-heeled international tourist could fly directly into. I'd been told you couldn't go 5 metres without a tout muttering a mantra of 'Change money . . . drugs . . . rafting . . . booze cruise . . . taxi'. But that morning I walked from the railway station and up into town unnoticed and unmolested.

That didn't lessen the buzz I got from just being there. Finally, I'd reached the greatest falls in Africa, one of the natural wonders of the world. The first big sight of my trip. One of the boxes I wanted to tick on my way north to Cairo.

Victoria Falls is a tourist town, there was no hiding that. It is a collection of pastel-coloured malls selling clothes with safari motifs and tour companies promising *Out of Africa* vistas or the adrenalin rush of white water rafting or bungy jumping. There's a photo development lab for every five visitors and a bar for every three. But it's a tourist town that was having a hard time of it.

The guy who ran Shoestrings was as surprised as anyone to see me. He relied solely on business from overland trucks now. They crossed directly into Victoria Falls from Botswana and Namibia in the south or Zambia in the north, avoiding the rest of Zimbabwe, and the trouble, altogether. They were proving to be the lifeblood of the town.

'Never used to take overland trucks,' he said as he checked me in. 'Too much grief, and frankly, too much trouble. Now they are my best customers.'

I found my room and tossed my bag on the bed. Then with that night-before-Christmas feeling in the pit of my stomach I hurried out and down the hill towards the Victoria Falls National Park.

The only indication that I was near the greatest waterfall in Africa was a pall of mist that hung over the trees like smoke and a gentle roar in the distance sounding like a jet passing 35,000 feet overhead. I ran the gauntlet of souvenir salesmen and umbrella hirers, and happily coughed up the outrageous $US20 entrance fee for the park. I stopped briefly to read a plaque that read, 'Victoria Falls, peerless jewel of Africa. Soul stirring power. Breathtaking power. Life elevating majesty!' and, I'm sad to say, became even more excited.

It was a clear and sunny day but I was soaked to the skin before I was anywhere near the falls. It was like walking through a heavy rainstorm, but a rainstorm of weird, gravity-defying rain that went up into the air first and got you again on the way down. I walked through it, laughing like a mad man.

By the time I reached the rim of the gorge I was drenched and I had to wipe the water away from my eyes to truly appreciate what was before me. Five million cubic metres of water plunging into a gorge and onto rocks 107 metres below. Every minute.

Can I just say that it was one of the most impressive things I've ever seen? The lip of the falls stretches for 1.7 kilometres, and although it was on the other side of the gorge, it looked close enough to touch. The roar was deafening now, like the sound of a jet engine as you approach a plane across the tarmac. The water looked like a giant version of a Sydney flash flood, a murky brown liquid littered with debris rushing down a gutter too pitiful to contain it. The smell was a pungent, organic mix of vegetation and mud churned together. My guidebook said there's a rainbow but in fact there were several. Previously I had thought that David Livingstone's famous quote that angels would be compelled to stop and look at Victoria Falls was a little over the top. That day I felt he had undersold them a little.

Perhaps the most astounding thing about the falls is that there are no guardrails along the rim to stop visitors from falling in. Back home they stick up signs screaming 'Danger!' even if it's a 1-metre drop onto a bed of spongy moss. Here you can get as close to a 107-metre drop as you want. If you wanted to stick your face over the edge to be caressed by the mist there was nothing to stop you.

I made my way out to Danger Point, the furthermost point west on the Zimbabwe side, and discovered that it is aptly named. As I crept towards the edge to peer at the river 100 metres below I lost my footing and slipped on the wet rocks. As soon as I felt myself slip I dropped to the ground immediately – it was the only thing that stopped me from tumbling over the edge and falling to a terrifying death. Looking up, my heart pounding, I saw an old Japanese couple taking my photo.

I spent the rest of the morning wandering down paths looking for new vistas of the falls to mesmerise me. When I had exhausted all the options in the national park I made my way to the Zambezi Bridge. Built in 1905 it is an old steel-arched bridge that seems as natural a part of the falls as the walls of the gorge it stretches across. It also offers a postcard perfect view of the falls, framed either side by the rugged walls of the gorge. It is possible to bungy jump from the bridge, although no one was, but having already done the world's highest jump I wasn't compelled to do the most picturesque.

The border between Zimbabwe and Zambia is a line across the middle of the bridge, and although I would be crossing it when I went into Zambia to continue my journey north, I felt compelled to see it. A policeman stood beside the line, ostensibly to check on people crossing into Zambia, but no one was crossing so he stood leaning against the rail. He'd chat occasionally with the bungy jump folk who were similarly underemployed, but most of the time he just looked at the falls.

He asked me where I was from and when I told him Sydney his eyes lit up. 'I saw your city in the Olympics,' he said. 'It is so beautiful!'

I motioned towards the falls and told him that he didn't have a bad view himself.

He shrugged his shoulders. 'A beautiful view does not fill your stomach,' he said.

An overland truck from Nairobi had arrived at Shoestrings while I was down at the falls and its occupants, mainly Aussies and Kiwis, were sprawled in the lounges around the outdoor bar and overlooking the pool when I got back. They had already been down to the craft markets and had bought ridiculously large wooden carvings. Now they sat around drinking Zambezi Lager, admiring the things they had bought and comparing prices.

'I got these three elephants for $Z500,' said one guy, pointing to three intricately carved wooden statues on the table. Each one had cost him less than $7 but the craftsmanship was amazing.

'Mine cost $Z700,' said another girl, pushing forward an even more finely carved elephant. 'But it's made from teak.'

'Polished,' said the first guy, picking up the piece and looking at it more closely. '*Nice!*'

There were certainly bargains to be had in Victoria Falls. The curio sellers were as badly hit by the lack of visitors as everyone else. I made the mistake of wandering through the craft market and was besieged by a woman offering me two lovely hessian figures for $Z100, then $80, $60, $40 and finally $20. (You couldn't even buy a loaf of bread down at the local SPAR for that price.) When I said that I didn't want them she started wailing. I ran away and never went back to the craft markets again. I didn't know how the overlanders could handle it.

By their second day in Victoria Falls the truck folk were

tired of shopping and had decided to design a T-shirt to commemorate the trip instead. While they had bargained with curio sellers until they made them cry, the overlanders seemed happy enough to shell out $US20 each for a shirt and sat around devising a design that would incorporate a Womble and their overland truck nicknames like Chalky, Blue Balls and Big Tits. They decided to throw in the names of two mystery passengers called Di Rea and Murray J Wana as well. Hilarious.

As they sketched a Womble for the T-shirt, the girls debated which raft guide they wanted to sleep with. Raft guides were highly sought after by women on overland trucks, apparently. It was the unfortunately monikered 'Mr Herpes' who had taken the fancy of these girls.

'Best piece of eye-candy I've seen in a long time,' said one, a rough Aussie girl with freckles called Kylie. I'd already tagged her as the most likely to flash her boobs.

'But he's got herpes,' said her mate.

'That's just his nickname,' reasoned Kylie. 'I reckon he'd be a top root!'

Another girl, a Kiwi, interrupted and told a story about a girl who came over to Vic Falls for eight months and slept with 26 of the raft guides. Then she had to send them all a letter telling them that she had AIDS. Everyone 'oohed' appropriately, except for Kylie. 'AIDS isn't so bad,' she said. 'You're HIV positive for ten years before it really starts to affect you. Some people get cancer and are told they only have five weeks to live!'

'Yeah, but it's a social disease,' said the Kiwi, unconvinced.

'Just don't tell anyone you've got it!' Kylie said triumphantly.

I was pleased to see that the Australian government's massive education program was having such an impact!

There is a ritual to a night out in Victoria Falls and it remains the same when business is slow. The early part of the evening is spent watching rafting videos – if it's your first day in Vic Falls it'll be the video of the rafting trip you did earlier that day; if it's not it'll be someone else's. Then at 10 pm you go to the Explorers Travellers Club.

There's no reason the Explorers should be more popular than anywhere else in town. The beers are the same price. The decor is merely functional. And there's nothing special about its location above a crappy arcade overlooking a carpark. But every night it gets packed with raft guides, overlanders and independent stragglers like myself.

The guy in charge of the music there certainly knew his audience. He played the sort of stuff you hear at parties back in Australia – 'American Pie' by Don Maclean, '500 Miles' by the Proclaimers, that sort of thing. And if a night got a bit slow he'd whack on 'Down Under' by Men at Work, knowing that the Aussie truck girls would be up on the bar dancing within seconds.

Now, call me shallow, but if I walk into a pub and there are girls dancing on the bar, I tend to stick around. Unfortunately, on my third night in Victoria Falls I stuck around too long at the Explorers and got horribly drunk. I woke up the next morning to what sounded like baboons jumping on the tin roof at Shoestrings and promptly discovered that there were baboons jumping on the tin roof. Luckily Victoria Falls is the kind of place where you can get the big greasy breakfast a hangover demands.

A huge billboard had been erected overnight outside the SPAR supermarket informing the good people of Victoria Falls

that President Mugabe was coming to their town the next day
to celebrate his birthday. The celebration included a public rally
at the stadium with free beer and steaks for everyone. Apparently he chose a different town each year.

The party was being held in a stadium in Chinotimba, the
black part of town. Here people sleep in shacks, not hotels, and
buy their food from scruffy market stalls instead of restaurants.
It is where the touts, the maids, the waiters and the cleaners that
serve the tourists live and I was interested to see how they
would react to Mugabe. After all, his policies were affecting
their livelihood just as much as that of the tour companies and
tourist hotels.

I told the guy running Shoestrings that I wanted to go and
he said I was crazy. 'Mr Mugabe isn't too fond of white people,'
he said. 'I'm not sure that you would be welcome.'

The presidential visit transformed Victoria Falls. On the day
of the birthday party there was a group of policemen on every
corner. Busloads of school kids in crisp, neat uniforms were
trucked in from all over the country. They waited in lines at the
Municipal Camping Ground, practising their singing and
clapping while their teachers marked a roll.

Well-dressed dignitaries and party faithful wandered the
streets, sweating in the heat and killing time before the show
began. The men wore suits; the women wore bright sarongs, or
kangas, as they are known in East Africa, featuring the
president's face. Everyone wore a laminated pass.

I followed a line of school children, still singing and clapping,
as they filed across an empty block towards the stadium. The
stadium was completely walled, but I could see the tops of white
marquees being put up especially for the occasion. It was only

10 am but there were already thousands of people lining up to get in. I decided to have a Pepsi before I joined the queue.

A tout I had befriended during my stay spotted me and came over to say hello. His name was David and he asked me what I was doing up in Chinotimba. When I told him that I was going to the president's birthday party, he didn't seem surprised. Nor did he tell me that I wouldn't be welcome. I had noticed that with black Africans. Unlike the whites, it didn't even cross their minds that I shouldn't be in a particular part of town, or in a minivan or at the birthday celebrations of an African president.

They weren't letting anyone into the stadium until lunchtime so David invited me back to his place to drink some chibuku.

Chibuku is native beer, a white effervescent liquid made from sorghum, maize and yeast that is cheap and potent. It comes in two sizes: one-litre cardboard cartons (like milk), or the more affordable two-litre 'scuds' (brown plastic bottles with a blue screw top). The scuds have the advantage of being returnable and David kept a stash of empties that he had found abandoned, using the return fee to help purchase the next one.

David lived in a shack at the side of an established house. The owner had divided the house into lots of rooms and filled all the space in the yard with shacks to maximise the earning potential of the property. David lived in one of the bare-floored shacks. It was tiny, with only room for a bed, so we sat on the steps, under the shade of a frangipani tree, passing the scud of chibuku between us. It was awful, a fibrous liquid with a tangy aftertaste that left me feeling ill. I took little sips and when it was finished I gave David some money to buy some more.

David showed me a certificate he had received from the Salesman Institute of Harare. He was doing a correspondence course in marketing through them. He sent them $Z600 a month and in return they sent him books and course material. It sounded a bit dodgy to me, but he was very happy with the course.

Sensing I wasn't convinced, he demonstrated some of the techniques he had learned. 'Sometimes a customer thinks he knows everything,' he said. 'You must agree, but bring him around. Others are scared and say, "No! No! No!" But they really want your product, so you must allay their fears.'

Other tactics were needed when dealing with people that David described as 'big shots'. The example he gave was Michael Jackson, and while I had a hard time imagining just what a raft trip tout from Zimbabwe would be flogging Mr Plastic Surgery, I let him continue.

'He will say I have no time,' explained David. 'So you say, "I would really like to tell you about my product. When can I come and see you. Let's make an appointment." He agrees and that's when you know you have him!'

I nodded my head. I hadn't realised it was that easy.

When we returned to the stadium, the queues were longer but at least they were moving. David dragged me towards the entrance, using my whiteness as an excuse to get to the front of the queue. No one complained. They smiled, happy to see me as a guest.

Inside it was like a normal sportsground. There was a podium on the far side of the ground, backed by a poster of Mugabe like the one that had mysteriously appeared in town. (I figured this was where Bob would make a passionate speech about the importance of kicking white farmers off their land.) For the moment though, everyone's attention was focused on the two marquees that had been erected on the soccer pitch. One served beer – litre cartons of chibuku tossed from plastic milk crates to outstretched hands. The other dished up barbecued kebabs of gristly meat. I grabbed a spot on a grassy hill and David went off for the beer and meat. He successfully used his queue-jumping techniques and was back within 15 minutes. I gave the chibuku a miss and after chewing the kebab for 20 minutes gave up on that too.

'I am really looking forward to the marching band,' said David, wiping grease from his chin. 'It is always a highlight.'

Just after two the president's limousine entered the stadium through a side gate. I stood up with the rest of the crowd and strained to catch a glimpse of the man. Just as a lackey in a uniform went to the back of the car to open the door for the president I felt a tap on my shoulder. It was a big black guy in a tight-fitting suit. Judging by the earpiece he was a member of the CIO, the Zimbabwean secret police. 'What are you doing here?' he snapped.

I said that I was celebrating the president's birthday and a dark look came over his face as though he thought I was taking the piss. He clearly didn't like me and, judging by the way the vein on his temple was throbbing, he was only just controlling an urge to thump me. Just when I thought his eyes couldn't look any crazier he spat on the ground beside me. 'Get lost!' he shouted. Just in case I didn't understand what he was saying he opened his jacket to reveal a revolver in its holster.

David gave me the kind of look that suggested I should do as the man said, and while I was at it, not mention that I was there with him. As it was, the guy grabbed me by the arm and forcefully took me to the entrance anyway, tossing me onto the street just as the marching band struck their first note.

I dusted myself off and walked back into town. Just outside the Kingdom Hotel a policeman yelled out 'Hey Aussie!' and motioned me over. I thought the word was out that I was some international troublemaker to be arrested on sight, but it was the policeman I had chatted to on the Zambezi Bridge. He shook my hand vigorously and I asked him what he was doing in town.

'Just waiting for the old man,' he said, referring to the president. 'He'll go back to his hotel room and then out to the airport. He's not hanging around, never does.'

A wail of sirens announced the arrival of the presidential cavalcade, and soon a convoy of limousines, police cars and army jeeps full of soldiers swept by us and into the drive in front of the hotel. The drive was circular, and not designed to accommodate so many vehicles so it quickly became grid-locked. The soldiers jumped out of the jeeps and tried directing the cars, but their efforts at clearing the traffic jam were thwarted by a milk truck that had arrived to make a delivery and was blocking the only entrance.

It was a farcical scene captured for 'Funniest Home Video' shows around the world by well-heeled tourists with digital video cameras. Eventually Mugabe was hustled into the hotel surrounded by bodyguards. My friend the policeman just shook his head.

❖   ❖   ❖

I had heard there was a flagpole in the gardens of the Victoria

Falls Hotel with a plaque noting the distances to both Cape Town and Cairo. I decided to visit it that afternoon.

In my mind Victoria Falls had always represented the end of the first leg of the journey and I was still feeling a minor sense of achievement. But soon I would be heading north towards the Equator and to Malawi, Zanzibar and Mount Kilimanjaro.

I walked to the hotel and took a stroll through the gardens. The flagpole was in the middle of manicured lawn. Behind I could just make out the Zambezi Bridge and the falls. And there was the plaque, cast in bronze and set into the base of the pole. I was pleased to note that Cape Town was 1647 miles behind me but alarmed to see that after three months of travelling there were still another 5165 miles to Cairo.

I found myself thinking I had better get a move on.

Chapter 9

LUSAKA, ZAMBIA

Yote yang'aayo usidhani ni dhahabu.
All that glitters, do not think it is gold.

The dearth of independent travellers in Victoria Falls meant that I could arrange a ride to Livingstone, the town on the Zambian side of the falls, for only $US10. The price included my Zambian visa, entrance to the falls on the Zambian side and a night's accommodation at Jolly Boys Backpackers. Just to make sure they got my business they chucked in a free beer and my first evening meal as well. If my mother had been with me she would have scolded me for taking advantage of other people's misfortunes.

I was picked up from Shoestrings by Dan, an Englishman with a big white beard. He drove an old Land Rover that had been converted for game watching and after introducing himself he told me that his daughter had gone to school with

Craig David. 'He used to be a chubby little tyke,' he said, shaking his head. 'But now look at him.' That would be buff, multi-million selling, R'n'B sex god with chocolate-block hair.

I liked Zambia. It was humid and dank, with crumbling roads lined with enormous banyan trees. Women dressed in brightly coloured kangas balanced bowls on their heads as they dodged puddles full of orange-brown water. There were hand-painted road signs rather than mass-produced ones and the cars that drove on the roads looked like they had been stolen from a wrecking yard. It was laidback, almost to the point of being comatose, without the angst Zimbabwe suffered because it had once been something better. In Zambia I got the feeling that nothing had changed since the British left.

Livingstone was briefly the capital of Zambia back in 1911 when Cecil Rhodes's British South Africa Company (BSAC) combined its two administration zones, North-East and North-West Rhodesia, into the more manageable Northern Rhodesia. The BSAC had been granted a charter by the British government to grab as much land north of Southern Rhodesia (now Zimbabwe) to thwart the designs of other European powers. In return the company got a prime source of labour for its gold and coal mines as well as some of the richest copper deposits in the world. The local population, it seems, got not very much at all in return.

Jolly Boys was a house that may have been grand once but was now falling into disrepair. The bedrooms had been converted into dorms and the one existing bathroom had to service all the guests. The bar was a hut with a fridge down by the pool (that was an unexpected bonus!) and I made my way there immediately to collect my complimentary beer.

I chose a Rhino – mainly because it had a rhino on the label – and chatted with two local Indian shopkeepers who were already sitting on stools beside the bar drinking. One was a tall, thin man with a mullet haircut and full of energy. The other was a short round chap with a brow-beaten demeanour.

I wondered why it is that duos always seem to fit the tall and thin and short and round stereotype. Leonard and Claude, the business partners I had met on the trip to Mozambique, had fitted the stereotype too. Perhaps it is something in our DNA that draws us to our complete opposites. After my second Rhino I decided to file this particular phenomenon with others I have difficulty fathoming – like where all my money goes and why stunningly attractive women always take a plain girlfriend with them to nightclubs.

When the short, round Indian discovered I was from Australia he congratulated me personally on our decision not to become a republic. He remembered the Queen visiting Zambia when he was a child and claimed it was the happiest day of his life. It was his belief that the British should never have left. 'The Queen has said, "Give me my people back," ' he moaned. 'Why can't they? *Really*, why can't they?'

The tall, thin guy told him it would never happen and that he should get over it. The British would never come back, and if the truth be known, his precious queen probably never gave Zambia a second thought.

One of the girls staying at the hostel came down to the bar and the tall Indian became distracted. Whenever it was his turn to throw in an anecdote about the British or bemoan how bad business had become, he simply stared, open-mouthed, at the girl. 'You know you have beautiful eyes,' he said to her finally.

She gave him a dismissive smirk and took her beer back to the main house. The tall Indian never really recovered.

Her name was Zoe, a sharp-featured, cynical English girl, and yes, she did have beautiful eyes. She was 'in-between' trucks – she'd just finished a Cape Town to Vic Falls tour and was waiting for a Vic Falls to Nairobi tour to start the following week.

Over the few days I was in Livingstone we hung out together. There seemed to be chemistry between us – I have always had a bit of a thing for sarky English girls – but I was so out of touch I couldn't be sure.

For example: each night we'd go to a nearby bar for drinks. When it was my shout, Zoe wanted a Bacardi Breezer at 8000 kwacha (about $5) a pop. When it was her shout she drank Diet Coke. She could have been pacing herself but I suspected I was being used. I needed a mate to tell me whether Zoe was just taking me for a ride. In the end I decided that I'd rather miss an opportunity than take up one only to be humiliated.

On my third day in Livingstone there was a cholera out-break in the town. All the public schools were closed and the restaurants were taking greater care washing their dishes. Over her nightly Bacardi Breezer (at my expense, of course) Zoe told me that she thought that she might have a slight dose. In 90 per cent of cases that's all you got – a sudden onset of the shits – and it was difficult to differentiate it from any other diarrhoeal illness. Perhaps it was an attempt at intimacy, but I decided to get out before they sealed off the town and the men in space suits arrived. Besides, keeping Zoe supplied in Bacardi Breezers was sending me broke.

My journey from Bulawayo to Victoria Falls had re-acquainted me with the joys of travelling on trains in old British colonies, so I had hoped to catch a train out of Livingstone to Lusaka. But there had been a derailment about an hour up the track so I was forced to take a bus. And the only bus with seats available at short notice was the Super Luxury Bus.

From what I could gather, all I got for the extra 10,000 kwacha that the Super Luxury Bus to Lusaka cost me was a driver in a uniform and a video from Nigeria as onboard entertainment. The bus itself was as battered as any of the other buses I had seen in Zambia and the air-conditioning, naturally enough, did not work. The radio did though and as we pulled out of Livingstone the DJ made an important public announcement urging people to wash their hands after going to the toilet to avoid spreading cholera. 'When you shake hands and they ask how are you,' he intoned, 'you can say fine thank you!'

Lusaka is the capital of Zambia and it lies roughly in the geographic centre of the country. From what I could see that is the only reason it has been built where it is. It doesn't sit on the picturesque bend of a river. And there isn't a lake or a mountain of note nearby. It just sits on a scruffy plain, its colourless buildings crumbling into disrepair, another African city with a few half-arsed high-rise buildings that no one would miss if some day, somehow, it was wiped off the face of the planet.

Having said that, it does have its pleasant corners, especially around the diplomatic triangle, where huge shady trees have been allowed to grow instead of being cut down for firewood. And the people, on the whole, are laidback and friendly. If they had stopped calling me 'Big Man', 'Bwana' and 'Masser' it wouldn't be too bad a place to visit at all.

I was staying at Chachacha Backpackers, a place that charged

$US6 for a dorm bed. It was probably only worth about a third of that but it was the cheapest place in town and anyone travelling in Zambia, admittedly a small and select group, passed through here. On my first night at Chachacha I met a South African guy called Hugo, who had driven overland from London in a Land Rover. My plan was to travel along the same route, but in the opposite direction and going only as far as Cairo. I asked him about getting a visa for Sudan – it was essential to my plan to travel from Cape Town to Cairo overland.

The news was not good. Hugo had spent two months trying to get a Sudanese visa in Egypt. He couldn't get one and had to ship his car to Djibouti and pick it up from there.

'The embassy in Cairo is a mad house,' he said. 'There are people screaming and shaking the gates. They take your application, all right, but fob you off by saying they have to contact Khartoum and to call back in four weeks. It's just their way of saying no.'

Apparently demanding your 'rights' didn't help either. Hugo told me the story of an Aussie bloke who visited the Sudanese embassy in Cairo every day for six weeks. He finally lost it and insisted the consul give him the visa he had promised him. The consul just opened a drawer and handed his passport back to him.

I must have looked devastated because the South African guy offered me one small ray of hope. 'If I have any advice, it is to apply as far away from Sudan as possible,' he said. 'We met another Dutch guy who applied for his visa in Jordan and he got it within twenty-four hours.'

I decided to visit the Sudanese embassy in Lusaka the next morning.

The embassy was in a large house in the diplomatic triangle, a little further out than the rest of the embassies. Apart from a few Moorish flourishes that gave it a slightly Arabic feel, it could have been a suburban house in Sydney, except that the lawn needed mowing and it didn't have a Hill's Hoist out the back. I knocked on the metal gates and a guard opened a little eye flap to see who it was. When I told him that I had come to apply for a visa, he unlocked the gate, swung it open and pointed me towards a small office attached to the back of the house. So far, so good, I thought.

In the office I was greeted by Rose, a local Zambian girl with a lovely smile. She told me I needed two passport photos, a letter from my employer and $US50. When I told her I was self-employed (in the IT industry – being a writer tends to set off alarm bells in Africa) she told me that I'd have to write a letter for myself, laughing as she pushed a blank piece of paper towards me. I filled in a form, wrote myself a glowing letter of recommendation and gave Rose my photos and the kwacha equivalent of $US50.

'Call me on this number at three o'clock this afternoon,' she said, slipping me a piece of paper with the embassy's phone number on it. I was surprised by how easy it had all been.

Finding something constructive to do to pass the time until 3 pm proved more difficult. There's not an awful lot going on in Lusaka. The main drag, Cairo Road, is lined by banks and telecommunication offices, with a few dusty corners where people urinate. Walking the streets wasn't really an option – Lusakans walk along the railway tracks because it is easier than trying to negotiate the cracked pavements. Nor was going to the movies. The city's only cinema had been closed down long ago, despite the peeling posters offering Lusakans all the classics from the Jean-Claude Van Damme oeuvre.

I once met an English guy in Turkey whose goal was to watch a Jean-Claude Van Damme movie in every country he travelled to. He had travelled overland from Egypt to Istanbul and had already seen *Kickboxer* in Cairo, *Double Impact* in Amman and *Universal Soldier* in Damascus. That afternoon in Istanbul he had been off to see *Nowhere to Run*. It was a slow, hot afternoon so I went along with him, and after seeing Jean-Claude simultaneously jump onto a motorbike and kick start it I was ready to make the same J-CVD vow myself. Then in Bodrum I saw *Double Team*, co-starring Dennis Rodman, and got over it.

There are no public phones in Lusaka, so when 3 pm came I had to call the embassy from one of the private telecommunication centres on Cairo Road. Local calls costed a ridiculous 1000 kwacha (75 cents) a minute – it was actually cheaper to call overseas – but I rang Rose anyway, hoping that the news she gave me would make any costs incurred worthwhile.

I took heart from the fact that she seemed genuinely happy to hear from me. 'How are you!' she said. 'Tell me, what have you been doing today?'

I filled her in on my movements, trying to keep the call as brief as possible. She asked me if I was enjoying Zambia and I said I was, and then she asked me about my favourite parts. I nervously looked at the meter and noticed with alarm that it was ticking over faster than the foreign debt counter in New York. I desperately tried to think how I could turn the conversation to my visa.

Then Rose did it for me. 'Come and pick up your passport tomorrow,' she said, chirpily.

If I didn't think the bloke behind the counter would have taken it the wrong way I would have hugged him.

That evening at Chachacha I told everyone who would listen that I had got my Sudanese visa. Hugo, to his credit, congratulated me, even though he had missed out on getting one himself. Paul, a fifty-year-old Canadian real estate agent on a grand African adventure, bought me a beer to celebrate. I didn't sleep very well that night. I was too excited.

❖   ❖   ❖

Rose was not in a good mood when I arrived at the embassy the next morning. She was on the phone talking to the consul, and by the sounds of the loud tinny voice she was getting a right bollocking. 'Excuse me, I must go!' she said a little brusquely after hanging up. '*He* wants to see me!'

She came back into the room a few minutes later and told me that *he* wanted to see *me* now. This was an unfortunate turn of events. The day before I'd worn a neat collared shirt, but that day, thinking I was simply picking up my visa, I had worn a scruffy T-shirt and jeans. It was not exactly the outfit to wear when meeting diplomats.

The consul sat behind his desk in flowing robes and a little skullcap. He was very black, with a thin moustache, and I remember thinking that he looked very regal and that I didn't. I greeted him with 'Salām 'alēkum', a polite Arabic greeting, hoping it would score me some sorely needed brownie points.

He gave me a withering look that suggested that it hadn't worked. 'Are you living in Zambia?' he asked. I said that I wasn't and explained that I was in transit, in the hope of speeding up the process. It was another mistake.

'Then you can apply in Dar es Salaam,' he said, pushing my application towards me. I said I probably could, but there was a chance I wouldn't get to Dar. (This was a lie.)

He thought about that for a moment before saying the words I had been dreading. 'I will have to send your details to Khartoum for approval,' he said. 'It's an Islamic holiday on Monday, but I should hear from them by Thursday next week.'

I wondered if this was just a polite way of saying no. I mean, that's how these guys operate. But the consul assured me I had a 90 per cent chance of being approved, although he tellingly gave me back my passport as well as the money I had handed over for the visa. 'Call Rose next Thursday,' he said. 'Maybe she will have good news for you.'

I wouldn't be counting on it.

I returned to the hostel in low spirits. Of course everyone asked to see the visa – I think I'd made some drunken claim that they were the most beautiful in the world – and I had to tell them the whole sorry tale. The South African offered his commiserations, but I swear I saw the traces of a smug smile on his face. Paul offered to buy me another beer. I suspected, however, that he just wanted an excuse to drink beer at 10.30 in the morning.

'I was so close,' I said to him as I slouched over my Rhino. 'What if I get this treatment all the way through East Africa?' Like all good consolers, Paul just nodded his head sympathetically and kept buying the beers.

I decided to leave for Malawi the next morning. It didn't make sense to hang around on the off-chance that I might get a Sudanese visa. I had a bad feeling that the consul was just tagging me along. I would call from Malawi and if, by chance, approval had come through I would double back to Lusaka to pick up my visa. That was the plan, and after three or four beers it had seemed a very good one. Even Paul had agreed.

Somehow I got to the Lusaka bus station the next morning by 4.30. I was still tipsy from spending the previous day and most of the previous evening drinking with Paul. It was raining and the other passengers huddled under the eaves of the main building, trying not to get wet. Most had slept there for the night, swathed in blankets, their meagre belongings pulled close. They were wrapped completely, like woollen mummies, and lay lined up like cocoons in what little dry space there was. I grabbed a spot, pleased and surprised to have found it, only to suffer a drip falling constantly on my left shoulder. Great!

At 5 am the passengers stirred from their sleep and collected their belongings. They wandered like zombies in the pre-dawn drizzle until they found their bus, and after waking the driver who slept on the floor inside, they clambered aboard. I found my luxury bus in the far corner of the compound. It wasn't that luxurious. It had velour seats, but no air-conditioning, and the TV hung at a disconcerting angle from the roof, as if the slightest bump would dislodge it. When dawn came, grey and wet, the bus pulled out of the compound and onto the empty streets of Lusaka. Its destination was Chipata, the last town in Zambia before the border with Malawi. Exhausted from getting up early and my whole Sudanese visa ordeal, I promptly fell asleep.

I woke up an hour or so later with a start. We were in low green hills now, among drab olive-coloured trees under an escarpment, and the bus driver had lost control of the bus going into a corner. Something in my body's equilibrium, even as I slept, had warned me of the danger and within seconds I was alert and gripping the back of the seat in front of me. Inches from the edge of the road and a considerable drop, the driver wrested control of the bus and righted it. He smiled, feeling like a hero and expecting the passengers to congratulate him for saving them. Instead they abused him, angry that his reckless driving had put them in the situation in the first place. I was tempted to shake my fist at him as well.

Soon we reached the Luangwa Bridge, a giant suspension bridge close to the Mozambique border and about halfway between Lusaka and Chipata. I was disappointed to learn that we had already passed Rufunsa. I had read in the *Times of Zambia* that the local magistrates court there was hearing a case about a local woman allegedly caught making love to a goat. Under the compelling caption 'Bestiality case pulls crowd' the story reported that judicial workers and prosecutors were surprised to find so many people waiting outside the court, keen to sit in on the case. I had hoped to catch sight of the crowds, or maybe even the woman herself, being ushered into the court.

The level of the Luangwa River was high, and judging by the way the passengers were all straining to look at it, this was unusual. Once we crossed it, however, Zambia became drier and flatter. I had read that this was the poorest part of the country and noted with some satisfaction that my goat-poverty index proved as accurate here as it did in Mozambique. The buggers were everywhere, stripping what little vegetation there was. They'd had the heavy rains here too, but the soil was so hard the water simply formed waist-deep puddles that naked children played in.

In Chipata I resisted a generous offer to charter a car into Malawi for more than the car would have cost its owner in the first place, and instead squeezed into a taxi with a dozen Zambians on their way to Malawi on business. With so many people in such a small car I wasn't sure where I would fit my backpack. But surprisingly I was the only passenger with luggage so my pack had the entire boot to itself. I'm not sure what kind of business these guys were on but it obviously didn't involve a fresh change of clothes and toiletries.

The exit formalities on the Zambian side of the border went quickly and smoothly. The immigration officer in charge that day correctly assumed that I had already spent more time in his country than I had wanted to and stamped my passport and sent me on my way within minutes.

On the Malawi side the immigration official wore a crisp uniform and cap and was of a similar disposition to his Zambian counterpart. There was a sticker on the glass door that read, 'Warning! You are entering a corruption-free zone! Resist, reject and report corruption to the Anti-Corruption Bureau.' We were stamped into Malawi swiftly and with a smile.

But while the Zambians were allowed to leave without further ado, I was ushered over to the health division – a desk with a sign that said 'Health Officer' on it. A man in a similar crisp uniform but without the hat asked to see proof of my yellow fever vaccination.

I pulled out my yellow international vaccination booklet and showed him the stamp. I was happy to actually. It made me feel like all the pain and suffering I had gone through at the hands of Dr Chu had been for something. Of course, the vaccinations had probably saved me from any number of horrible, disfiguring diseases already but I didn't know that. The Malawian health officer asking to see a stamp, however, made me feel like it had all been worthwhile.

Then the health officer asked to see the stamp for polio. I showed him. Then typhoid. Then meningitis. Each time he appeared to become more disappointed that I was able to show him the stamp. Then, when he had just about exhausted every disease listed in my *Rough Guide to Travel Health*, he asked to see the stamp for cholera, the only vaccination I hadn't had.

Dr Chu had assured me that I didn't need a cholera shot. I was up for it – after all, what difference would getting another needle make – but he told me that the current vaccine had proved unreliable, giving only 50 per cent protection for just three to six months. Not only was it ineffective, it wasn't a prerequisite for entry into *any country*. He wasn't even sure if it was available any more because a new oral vaccine was being developed. This wondrous news obviously hadn't reached the Zambia–Malawi border near Chipata. The health officer told me that he'd have to send me back to Zambia.

It was obvious to me that he was angling for a bribe so I didn't react in the way that he hoped I would. I didn't wail or gnash my teeth or beg him to reconsider. I just shrugged my shoulders and sat there.

Thinking that I hadn't heard him correctly, he repeated his threat. 'You don't have a cholera stamp so I am going to have to send you back.'

Of course, he expected me to panic and give him anything rather than endure the bus trip back to Lusaka. Any normal person would have. But I just sat there, employing the same eye-acting techniques that I had just seen Clint Eastwood use in

The Good, the Bad, and the Ugly, the video provided as onboard entertainment on the bus. You know – hooded stares, arched eyebrows, slight eye twitches, that sort of thing.

It took a good ten minutes before I noticed a bead of sweat trickling down the health officer's forehead and knew that I had him. 'You're only in transit, right?' he asked, wiping his brow.

I nodded. As much fun as pretending to be Clint was, I wasn't going to be silly and not tell him what he wanted to hear. He stamped me into Malawi for two weeks, without the cholera stamp. I'd like to think he'd been impressed by my resolve, and I sauntered out the door whistling the haunting signature tune from the movie.

The Zambians were waiting patiently in the taxi for me and asked me what had happened. I told them the story and they laughed. 'He wanted money!' one said. 'I am impressed you did not give it to him.'

I don't think the taxi driver was. I caught sight of him in the rear-vision mirror and he looked a little disappointed. I think he'd been planning to try it on himself when we got to the bus station in the first town in Malawi.

Chapter 10

NKHATA BAY, MALAWI

Maji ya kifuu ni bahari ya chungu.
The water in a coconut shell is like an ocean to an ant.

There was a time not so long ago when you couldn't get into Malawi unless you could slide a Coke bottle between your leg and your jeans. You had to stick the bottle in at the waistband and under the watchful gaze of the Malawi police move it between the denim and your pelvis and down your inside leg until it popped out through the leghole near your foot. The government claimed that it was to protect the country from the moral decline caused by tight jeans. But I put it to you that if anyone had ever filmed one of these jeans tests, there is not a television station in the world that would air it before 8.30 pm.

The Coke bottle test was the brainchild of the first Malawi president after independence in 1964, Hastings Zazuma Banda. He had visited London for a Commonwealth Heads of

Government Meeting during the swinging sixties and had been shocked by what he had seen. Guys with long hair. Girls in trousers. Gerry and the Pacemakers on top of the charts. He returned to Malawi determined that his country would not travel down the same degenerate path. That's why Gerry and the Pacemakers have never toured Malawi. And why I didn't go there on my first visit to Africa ten years before.

I'd been all set to go. Indeed, I was rather looking forward to it. Everybody I met who had been to Malawi raved about the place and said that it was their favourite place in Africa. The people were friendly, the lake that ran along the length of the country was stunning and the dope, known affectionately as Malawi gold, was cheap and plentiful. But I had long hair and when I came across a group of passengers from an overland truck in Tanzania with crew cuts I started having serious second thoughts.

'Just come from Malawi, man,' said one of the guys in a thick south-London accent. 'Can't 'ave long 'air.'

He pulled out his driver's licence and showed me the picture. He looked like Neil from 'The Young Ones' in the photo on his licence. Now he looked like a thug. 'It was even longer by the time I got to the border,' he said. 'But bzzz, bzzz, bzzzz – it all had to go.'

I can admit now that I was a little bit vain about my hair in those days (I think I must have had a subconscious inkling that it wouldn't always be with me). I wore it long and blond like Fabio, only pulling it back into a ponytail when a strong breeze threatened to knot it. It had taken me two years to get it to that length, including a particularly difficult three-month period when it looked like a mullet, so I was reluctant to have it cut off.

Sadly, I decided that having long hair was more important than visiting Africa's friendliest country. It's not something I'm proud of.

Ten years later Banda was dead and the rules had changed. You didn't need to perform kinky acts with Coke bottles in front of Malawi immigration officials. Nor did you need a haircut, although my genes had made sure that wasn't as much of a problem as it once had been. Still, I thought it was appropriate that one of the first places I spotted from the minivan on my way into Lilongwe was the Tycoon Barber Shop.

Barber shops are easy to spot in Africa. They're the places with colourful hand-painted signs of heads out the front. The signs usually feature 20 heads at a time, all with slight variations on the classic short back and sides. One might be shaved a little closer on one side. Another might have a zig-zag pattern cut into it. When your customer's hair is like Velcro there aren't really many coiffurially artistic options available.

Customers get more of a choice inside the barber shop, though. This is where the African barber keeps his prize possession – a poster featuring pictures of African-American movie stars and musicians. Tupac Shakur and Will Smith, mainly, modelling the various hairstyles over the years.

'I'll have a Will Smith *Independence Day*,' a customer might say. 'No, make that a *Bagger Vance*.'

At the border I told the driver of the minivan that I wanted to get off near St Peter's church. It was close to the centre of town and offered accommodation that my guidebook said was 'quiet and clean'. According to the map it was only a couple of hundred metres from the banks and post office and a short walk from the bus station, so I was surprised when he dropped me off on a corner with unmown verges and unkempt hedges. I thought he had made a mistake, and it was only after he pointed to a sign on a gate saying 'St Peter's Guesthouse' that I let him drive off. I was moments from the centre of a nation's capital and birds were chirping and cicadas humming like I was in an outer suburb of Sydney.

That's Lilongwe for you. Words like compact, sleepy, green and pleasant spring immediately to mind. The church was surrounded by an abundance of flowering trees, frangipanis in particular, and the short walk to town passed by the golf course and a number of manicured gardens. The city centre itself, an area of only a block or two, was drab and scruffy with dull concrete buildings, but it soon gave way to vacant lots used as impromptu maize fields.

There is also a new part of town. It's a couple of kilometres away and consists of a few office buildings that the South Africans threw up by way of thanks for President Banda's support when the rest of Africa was against them. There is an incongruously grandiose parliament building too that had once been Banda's palace. But these few dashes of modernity only seem to emphasise how laidback the capital is.

I decided I liked Lilongwe. A lot. The people were friendly too. They smiled and waved as I walked past, or shook my hand vigorously like I was a long lost friend. Even the handicraft salesmen in the carpark in front of the post office seemed more intent on making a friend than making a sale. They showed me how they made cheap wood look like teak by polishing it with a brand of boot polish called Lude. Or how they aged 'antique' items by lighting fires in garbage cans and holding the carvings in the flames. None of them seemed particularly disturbed that

I didn't buy anything. Most of their sales came from tourists on passing overlander trucks. They were just happy to have someone new to chat to.

As beguiling as Lilongwe was, there was no real reason for me to stay. The banks did not give cash on credit cards and internet access was expensive and flaky. I still had close to a week before I had to ring the Sudanese embassy back in Lusaka to see if they had given me a visa so I decided to head for the lake.

Lake Malawi is the southernmost and third largest of the Rift Valley lakes. It is 584 kilometres long and between 16 and 80 kilometres wide. Its western shore forms much of the country's borders with Tanzania and Mozambique, while its eastern shore is backed by the spectacular Livingstone Mountains. I wanted to go to the lake, and in particular to Cape Maclear on the southern shore, because I had heard it was a cool place to hang out.

The bus heading south had lost most of its windows and they had been replaced with sheets of tattered plastic. It left late because two policemen had to apprehend a boiled lolly salesman operating on the bus without the driver's permission. One policeman approached from the back of the bus, another from the front, until the policeman at the front tackled the guy as he tried to run past. It was a spectacular collar – boiled lollies scattering everywhere and passengers swarming on them like a plague of locusts. The police dragged the hawker and his empty tray off the bus as he wailed, 'Wah! Wah! Wah!' I remember thinking if that was the way the Malawi constabulary policed a boiled lolly franchise, they were a force not to be messed with.

The bus stopped at the Adventist Health Centre on the edge

of town and picked up a group of people with their limbs freshly bandaged. The centre was clean and modern by African standards and I took heart that I may have played some part in getting it built. Not many people know this, but when I was ten I was one of the Seventh Day Adventist Church's best charity collectors.

Each year the Adventist Church has a charity drive called the Appeal for Missions. It's a drive that sees its congregation pounding the streets and asking for money to support health projects in Africa, Asia and the Pacific. The appeal comes with its own magazine that shows would-be philanthropists exactly where their money is going. The Sevs obviously believe in shock tactics because the way I remember it, the magazine was always filled with images of people horrifically disfigured by disease.

When I was a kid it wasn't just the adults who got to go doorknocking. The children were expected to contribute too. We'd toddle off down suburban streets with our magazines, receipt books and little yellow ribbons that indicated we were official collectors. I rather enjoyed it, even at ten, and especially when a bit of a competition started with my friends to see who could collect the most money. I used to think it was my sophisticated sales techniques or winning smile that was getting me the cash. But the more I thought about it that morning on the outskirts of Lilongwe, I think the people who gave me money may have been just trying to get a weird little kid in polyester and his sick snuff magazines off their front porch.

An hour out of Lilongwe the bus climbed up through granite mountains towards Didza, a pine tree and log cabin kind of town that was shrouded in mist. Here the hawkers sold boiled potatoes rather than the bananas sold in the lowlands. From Didza we descended to a scruffy savanna where the road formed the border with Mozambique. One side of the road was Malawi. The other side was Mozambique.

This area had seen fierce fighting during the civil war in Mozambique and the few buildings that remained were shattered and covered in either pro-Renamo or pro-Frelimo graffiti. If the bus stopped to pick up passengers only hawkers from the Malawi side approached to sell goods. The Mozambique hawkers, selling exactly the same stuff from exactly the same plastic bowls, sat motionless on their side of the road. There was obviously some sort of arrangement. The Malawian hawkers got the southbound traffic, the Mozambicans the traffic heading north. I found myself wondering if one side was more lucrative than the other.

The bus wasn't going to Cape Maclear directly but continuing south to Blantyre, so the driver dropped me off at the turn-off to the lake. He assured me that a minivan to Monkey Bay would come along shortly and that I'd be able to organise a ride to Cape Maclear from there. I had barely stepped off the bus when a young boy appeared at my side and asked me my name. I told him and seconds later he had whittled 'Peter' onto a wooden keyring carved in the shape of a fish.

I didn't want the keyring. It was the size of a small dog and, frankly, the craftsmanship was crappy.

But the boy was determined that I buy it. 'What can I do with this now?' he whined. 'What if another Peter *never* comes along?'

I assured him that it was quite a common name and he'd probably sell it within a week. I imagined him poking through his box of carved fish, digging passed the Fredericks and Karens and saying, 'Wait, I *know* I have a Peter in here somewhere.' It didn't matter anyway. As soon as I drove off in the minivan to Monkey Bay he whipped out a piece of sandpaper and started rubbing my name off.

Monkey Bay is the major southern port on Lake Malawi, but in one of Africa's smallest nations all that amounts to is a collection of dilapidated buildings, a post office and a general store. I didn't hang around. A small pick-up truck going to Cape Maclear greeted the minivan so I threw my pack in the back and rode on the tailgate, which had been lowered to accommodate more passengers.

The truck bounced along a red mud track that cut through jungle and across the mountains, struggling to get up some of the steeper inclines. It was slow and uncomfortable, and my legs dangled over the back, scraping the ground when we hit one of the many potholes. But I was as happy as I had been in Africa.

This was how I'd remembered it. The people on the back of the pick-up laughed easily with that big African laugh as we all clung on for dear life. Things were uncomfortable, and probably even dangerous, but rather than complain or swear, they saw the funny side of it. It was an inclusive laughter, too. Sure they laughed at me as I grasped manically for something to hold on to, but they were laughing at themselves too.

The pick-up arrived in Cape Maclear just as the sun was setting over the bay. It is a tiny village, right on the lake and overlooking the small offshore islands that form part of the Lake Malawi National Park. I found a room by the water and watched the last moments of the day from my veranda. Fishermen, returning home after a day fishing, dragged their wooden canoes onto the beach. Others sat repairing nets and joking about the day's catch. Children played in the water, pretending to spear fish with sticks. Mothers clanked pots as they prepared evening meals over wood fires on the beach. It was still and quiet, except for the sounds that carried eerily over the water. I went to sleep that night to the sound of murmuring voices and the lake lapping on the shore.

Lake Malawi is famous for its fish, in particular the fluorescent cichlids called mbuna. They are freshwater fish, but are as brightly coloured as any tropical fish, and Cape Maclear is one of the best places to go snorkelling among them. So I shouldn't have been surprised when Cape Maclear's notorious snorkelling touts latched onto me as I left my hotel the next morning. They followed me everywhere chanting 'Snorkelling? Barbecue fish dinner? Carving? Ganja?'

I thought I had shaken them when the owner of the restaurant in which I chose to eat breakfast refused to let them through the door. But these guys weren't so easily beaten and stood in the doorway chanting softly as I ate. I realised that the chanting was going to get very annoying very quickly so I organised for two of them to take me out onto the lake that afternoon. It cost me $US3, but it kept the other touts away for the rest of my stay so it was worth every cent.

The snorkelling trip was wonderful too. The guys paddled me out to one of the islands in a dugout canoe and I spent a couple of hours swimming among the rocks and submerged trees, marvelling at the mbuna.

When I came up for air one of the guys asked me how much I thought it was worth.

'Three dollars,' I said, knowing now that I'd got a real bargain. His mate smiled.

A group of fishermen had built a fire on the island to cook
fish and ugali (mealie meal) and they invited us to join them.
I used my hands to scrape out the ugali and dabbed it in a bowl
of tiny, crunchy fish to give it some taste. The guys paddled me
back to Cape Maclear right on dusk and took my money
without haggling for more.

❖   ❖   ❖

A quick telephone call to the Sudanese embassy in Lusaka the
next morning revealed what I had feared. The consul hadn't
heard back from Khartoum and suggested that I call again the
following week. I had hung around Cape Maclear ostensibly so
I could quickly go back into Zambia to get the visa, but now
that was looking less likely I decided to continue my journey
and head north towards Tanzania.

My idea was to catch the *Ilala*, the large passenger
steamboat that tootles up and down Lake Malawi every week.
It takes three days to get from Monkey Bay in the south to
Chilumba in the north, and my plan was to get off at Nkhata
Bay. The sensible thing to do would have been to wait for the
ferry in Monkey Bay. But the news from the embassy had put
me in such a funk that I decided to catch a van along the lake
shore to Chipoka, a small town further around the bay, just so
I was on the move again.

No good ever comes from such rash and irrational
decisions, and so it was with this journey. The van took forever to reach Chipoka and when it did I discovered that it
was even less extraordinary than Monkey Bay. The dock was
its most noteworthy landmark and it was little more than a
crane, a couple of P&O containers and a small brick shed where

passengers waited out of the sun, lying on concrete benches among their belongings. The ferry wasn't due until ten that night. By four I was already bored out of my mind.

The only place to get a meal in Chipoka was a lodge on the lake on the other side of the railway lines. A meal was as good a way as any to kill some time, so I asked a family to watch my bag and set off along a path through a maize field that I'd been told was a short cut to the lodge.

The path passed by the Millennium Sound Check Bar, a tiny drinking shack built under a baobab tree in a clearing beside the maize. A mzungo (foreigner) stood with his shirt off sucking on a large bottle of beer and watching a local grill offal on a makeshift barbecue. It was Paul, the Canadian guy who'd cheered me up with beers when I didn't get my Sudanese visa in Lusaka. I was flabbergasted.

'This is the only place in town with cold beer,' he said with a grin.

I was surprised by how happy I was to see him. I guess I'd had enough of travelling on my own and wanted a bit of company. And Paul was good company. He was older – about 50 – but that just meant that he wasn't too busy trying to be cool. He just wanted to have a good time and he had the kind of open charm that disarmed everyone, locals and travellers alike.

Chipoka Lodge was right on the lake and it looked like the kind of sad, rundown place that government departments in one of Africa's poorest countries would use for conferences. In fact there was a group of six people talking about something when we arrived. (I suspect they were busy declaring new corruption-free zones.) A waiter directed us to a table under a tree overlooking the lake and we each ordered a meal of grilled fish.

As we ate, three hippos came up for air with a snort about 200 metres from the shore. The waiting staff ran down to the shore banging their serving trays in an attempt to scare them away.

'What are they worried about?' asked Paul. 'They're just hippos.'

I had thought that way too once and had spent an afternoon throwing rocks at a herd of hippos in Lake Tanganyika in Burundi while I was waiting for a coup attempt in town to blow over. It wasn't until the manager of the nearby boat club ran over and shook me, telling me that hippos kill more people each year than lions do, that I realised the foolishness of what I was doing. They may look fat and harmless, but hippos are killers.

It was dark when Paul and I returned to the waiting shed. I needed to go to the toilet but couldn't figure out which one was the men's. They were no universal stick figures on the doors, just two words in the local language.

'Am I an amuna or an akuzi,' I asked a group of people near the door.

'*Amuna!*' they laughed.

Still, I was pleased when my torch lit up a urinal.

Just after eleven a spot of light appeared on the horizon and a ripple of excitement passed through the waiting shed. An old man with grey hair pulled out a harmonica, played a few notes, and then exclaimed, 'The steamer!' It pulled alongside the dock an hour later.

The *Ilala* was an old-style steamer. It had a long bow, three decks at the back and a funnel somewhere around the middle and it looked like the kind of vessel on which you'd expect to see Bogey behind the wheel. The people in the shed swarmed the lower decks, ignoring the gangplanks and simply clambering over the rails from the dock. The men went first and then caught the bags and small children that their wives threw at them. A man wearing a T-shirt that said 'Show Me Your Tits' led Paul and I to the cabin class deck. For an extra 1000 kwacha (around US$13) we could get our own cabin and have all our meals provided. And despite what his shirt said, we didn't have to get our gear off to secure it.

The next morning we enjoyed a full English breakfast in the saloon watching *Titanic*. The captain obviously had a sense of humour because at dinner another Titanic video was played, this time an HBO one made especially for television and starring Catherine Zeta-Jones.

Not that there was any danger of the *Ilala* sinking. The lake was like a bathtub for the two days we sailed on it. I spent the time leaning against the rails watching brown twisters dancing in the distance. (Apparently they were millions of flies spawning.) By the time we pulled into Nkhata Bay at three o'clock on the third morning the most dangerous thing that had happened was the bar running out of cold beer after Paul insisted it stay open all night.

The staff from the Njaya Lodge were the only ones to meet the ferry and their diligence was rewarded when all the foreigners on the ferry (there were about half a dozen of us) piled into their Land Rover and bounced our way out of Nkhata Bay, through the cane fields and up into hills to their resort 3 kilometres away. The cabins were rustic, with bare beds and mosquito nets, and we were shown to them by a guy holding a hurricane lamp. It didn't give out much light, so for all we knew the cabins may have overlooked a sprocket factory. Frankly, I was too tired to care.

Morning revealed that the cabins were perched pictur-esquely against a hillside. Mine hung right over the lake. A path wound its way up through beautiful gardens to a restaurant and bar and a huge deck with expansive views of the bay. I couldn't see the township of Nkhata Bay – it was on the other side of a headland to the left. Njaya Lodge was a magical spot with its own private beach, where there was nothing to do but laze around, read or swim.

Paul chose to drink. He found a shady spot on the deck and set about drinking as many beers and befriending as many people as he could. It was largely thanks to him that I soon had a vibrant social scene that included Frank, a French guy who ran a hotel in Madagascar, Christine, a pharmacist from Germany, and Ninette, a Dutch medical student.

Ninette had been in Malawi for three months doing the practical section of her medical degree. There was a severe shortage of doctors in Malawi so she had already been asked to perform more surgery than Dr Green does during an entire season of 'ER'. She wasn't just lancing boils either. She was tackling amputations and pulling out appendixes, pretty full-on stuff for a third-year student. 'Here I get to do things I never would back home,' she said.

She told me that the week before she had done her first spinal anaesthesia. It's a delicate procedure that involves injecting anaesthetic into the spinal column. If you get it wrong your patient could end up a paraplegic. 'It would be ten years before I would be allowed to do that in Holland,' she said happily.

I liked Ninette. She was brusque and forthright and keen to do things correctly. She felt that her English needed improving and asked me to correct her when she got things wrong. I think I may have been a little too enthusiastic because every time I corrected her she flipped me the finger. It became a running joke, but she was a proud girl, so I suspect that it really did annoy her when I corrected her.

Ninette spent most days at Njaya Lodge lying in a hammock studying for a surgeon's exam she was due to take. The textbook, *Advanced Trauma Life Support for Doctors*, was in English and the exam would be too, so she got me to ask her questions. She answered them correctly but had an annoying habit of pronouncing wound, as in injury, as wound, as in 'I wound up the clock'. When I corrected her she threw down the textbook and stormed off for a swim.

The next time I saw Ninette she was frolicking with Frank the Frenchman. She could also speak French so they chatted away merrily. She never gave him the finger, so I figured he never corrected her French.

And so the days passed. When the mindless relaxation or unappreciated English lessons got too much I'd walk into Nkhata Bay just for something to do. I'd wander through the markets, giving false names to the keyring carvers, or flick through the chitenges (sarongs), looking for the most ludicrous designs. Most featured traditional African patterns, but if you looked hard enough you could find ones featuring dartboards and decks of cards. My favourite was the one covered in pictures of mobile phones. I thought it was highly appropriate that the nearest your average Malawian got to this piece of modern technology was when they wore this chitenge as a skirt.

It would have been very easy to stay longer in Nkhata Bay. The weather was good. I had an active social circle. And Njaya Lodge was the kind of place you could wake up in one morning and realise that you were supposed to be back at work months ago. But if I didn't get going soon I would arrive in northern Kenya during the rainy season and the roads into Ethiopia would be impassable. So I booked a ticket on the bus to Tanzania that left from Mzuzu, a town 30 kilometres away, hoping that would force me to leave.

To celebrate I spent my last evening with my new-found friends down in Nkhata Bay at the Golden Dawg. The Golden Dawg was a video hall run by a young Indian fellow and boasted the biggest television in Africa (a 61-centimetre JVC hooked up to a DVD player). They played a different movie every night and the 'candy bar' sold ice-cold beer, fried chicken and hash cookies.

The movie that night was *Goodfellas*. We'd barely seen the first body stuffed into a boot before a giant communal spliff the size of a rolled-up newspaper was handed among the patrons. At one point the spliff's end flamed dramatically, flaring out the screen and threatening to ignite the hessian that hung from the walls. But disaster was averted, and when the spliff had been reduced to a smoking roach everyone settled in to watch the rest of the movie. The dramatic moment where Joe Pesci is killed was ruined when an English traveller with a thick cockney accent asked, 'Any of those space cookies left, mate?'

We walked back to Njaya Lodge as a group, a light breeze rustling through the maize fields and the stars twinkling above. As we walked and talked, I corrected Ninette's English and she gave me the finger but this time she laughed as she did it.

I had a last drink with my friends on the balcony over-looking the bay, but it was late and soon everybody went off to bed, leaving Ninette and me alone.

We watched the moon rise over the bay and she told me she had been a gymnast when she was younger. Quite a good one too – she could have gone to the Olympics. Then she told me she had not had a boyfriend for eight years. 'Boys are scared of me,' she said.

I didn't say anything, but I can understand why. She's an intimidating girl.

It started raining lightly and she snuggled into me to keep from getting wet. She looked up and smiled and we kissed. It was the first time I'd kissed a girl since the GND and it was nice.

She said I could come back to her room if I liked. 'I'll check if you've got testicular cancer,' she said without a trace of humour.

It kind of killed the mood.

Chapter 11

DAR ES SALAAM, TANZANIA

Kwenda mbio si kufika.

To run is not necessarily to arrive.

The bus taking me to Mbeya in Tanzania appeared out of the fog like a spectre just after midnight, looking like a vehicle from a Mad Max movie. It may have once been a normal bus, but now it was armour plated, jacked up and re-engineered to take anything African roads could throw at it.

The tyres were oversized to increase the vehicle's ground clearance so each passenger had to be pulled up onto the bus by the conductor, who stood in the door with an outstretched hand wearing a singlet and a Muslim cap.

The bus had started its journey in Lilongwe and was already packed solid. I'd bought a ticket in advance, and had been given a seat number, but I was not surprised to find my seat, K2, occupied.

The man already sitting in my seat refused to move. He had a ticket, and a reservation for the same seat, and wasn't going to move just because I was a mzungo. The conductor couldn't sort it out, either, so I resigned myself to spending the 12-hour journey to Mbeya standing. The aisle was packed so tight I figured I could sleep standing anyway.

It struck me that night that the atmosphere on a bus is totally different when you join it halfway through a journey. Bags that had been neatly stored in the racks above the seats were in disarray, their contents dishevelled from passengers searching through them for food or a jacket to ward off the cold. The floor was littered with food scraps, empty bottles and discarded wrappings. The air was thick with sweat, food odours and long-expelled farts. The mood of the passengers had changed as well. The excited anticipation that greets the start of a journey had been replaced by the dull, blank stare of people who wished it was already over but knew that there was still a long, long way to go. It only took me half an hour to get that same look.

A wall had been built across the front of the bus to segregate the driver from the passengers in the same way a cockpit does on a plane. This was where the conductor sat too, an inner sanctum for bus company employees from which the conductor only emerged to help people board and to deal with seat disputes. In my delirious state I imagined it was a wondrous place with plush reclining seats and complimentary food and beverages served by pretty girls in crisp, neat uniforms. So you can imagine how excited I was when the conductor opened the door and beckoned for me to enter.

The cockpit was not like I had imagined it to be. There were reclining chairs – three of them – but they were broken and tatty and already occupied. And the conductor in his dirty singlet was the closest thing to service staff. I was given the space between the seats, on top of the uncomfortably shaped engine cover. A sheet of cardboard was laid over it to protect me from the heat, but it slid like a toboggan on every corner. If I jammed my feet against the dashboard and my back hard against the back wall, I could stop myself from sliding, but only if I didn't fall asleep.

The other problem with my new seat was that I got a panoramic view of the road ahead. In cattle class all I saw was the armpit of the guy standing in front of me. Now I saw groups of cows standing in the middle of the road, a truck broken down and abandoned, and a pothole that looked like it had been created by a meteor. Each obstacle was spotlighted momentarily by the bus's headlights before disappearing again into complete blackness. I felt like I was being shown a slide show of how I was going to die.

The most horrifying image I saw that night was a sign that said 'Construction Activity Warning: Detour for the next 100 kilometres'. Now, I don't know about you, but I'm used to my detours going for a couple of hundred metres, maybe a kilometre at most. Not 100 kilometres. We lurched along potholed tracks, down embankments and across riverbeds to get around bridges that looked like they had been abandoned halfway through construction.

I tried to sleep. I really did. But every attempt I made was thwarted whenever the bus swerved or braked. I'd wake up in a tangle under the driver's feet staring at a horrifying snapshot of an obstacle I was making it very difficult for him to avoid. As we wound our way down the hills back towards the lake, the obstacles became more frequent. They waited around each bend, a strobe light of images, determined to guide us over the edge. I can't speak for the driver, but when we reached the Malawi–Tanzania border at dawn I was exhausted.

The border at Songwe is set in rolling green hills beside a river. A light misty rain was falling and even in the early hours it was already humid. The Malawi immigration post is beside a muddy village, separated from the dilapidated huts by a chainwire fence. A group of men stood on the village side shouting and waving money at us when we got off the bus. They were money changers and I inquired about their rates. I decided to wait until I got to the Tanzanian side to change money. The rate would be better there, I reasoned. After years of travelling it seems there are some lessons I have never learned.

The Malawi immigration office opened at 6 am, and considering how many passengers had been squeezed onto the bus we were processed quickly and efficiently. The border also marked a time zone. It was already seven in Tanzania but the border officials there kept more conventional office hours and didn't open until eight. I spent the time chatting with the Tanzanian money changers and discovered they had overly patriotic ideas about just how much their Tanzanian shilling was worth. At the rates they were quoting the country's massive international debt would be paid off within weeks.

The Tanzanian border officials were intent on being as quick and courteous as their Malawi counterparts. But they discovered that one of the passengers was trying to smuggle a motorbike into Tanzania and their mood darkened considerably.

One of the other passengers explained to me that while a tax was charged on fully assembled motorcycles, it was waived on motorcycle parts. In an attempt to avoid paying duty the owner of the motorcycle had pulled the bike apart and hidden the parts in different corners of the bus. The frame and engine were on the rack on top, the wheels and seat and other assorted accessories were spread about in the luggage compartment under the bus.

'He has done this before,' said the passenger. 'The Tanzanian customs are very angry with him and will not rest until they have found all the parts.'

A team of five Tanzanian customs officials scoured the bus searching for parts. They looked under the seats and rifled through bags and when they found something – a headlight assembly or rear mudguard – they yelled excitedly and held it aloft for the others to see. Soon there was a pile of motorcycle parts in the mud beside the bus.

'They will make him put it together,' said the passenger. 'If he can make a complete motorcycle he will be fined, maybe even jailed.'

As fascinating as watching a guy put a motorcycle back together with his bare hands was, I had a once-a-week train to catch in Mbeya. The different time zone had already put me behind schedule so I sought out the conductor and asked if we could leave the motorcycle guy at the border and get going.

'I shall ask, but I don't think the driver will agree,' he said frankly. 'The man is his brother.'

An hour later the driver's brother had the engine in the chassis and the front wheel attached, but was still a long way from assembling the bike completely. The Tanzanian customs officials had made their point, however, and the conductor peeled off a considerable number of notes from a wad of money to pay the 'fine'. The motorcycle and the parts lying around it were loaded back onto the bus and we were on our way again.

I was in East Africa proper now. The locals spoke Swahili as much as they spoke English (it was one of the official languages in Tanzania). And there were men lounging around in cheap suits drinking beer bought in bottles from tiny general stores. There were more substantial buildings too, farmhouses and sheds and quaint town halls, falling into disrepair but a reminder no less that this had once been a proud corner of the British Empire.

Now, for much-needed foreign currency, Tanzania relies on its national parks and game reserves. The country is blessed with some of the most famous and bounteous in the world. Ngorongoro Conservation Reserve and the Serengeti National Park are home to the largest ungulate herds in the world, boasting more wildebeest than you can point a stick at, as well as the last few black rhinoceros and African hunting dogs left in the world. Lake Tanganyika in the west of the country is the second deepest lake in the world, plunging to a depth of 1436 metres. And in the north is Mount Kilimanjaro, my ultimate destination in Tanzania and the highest mountain in Africa.

Here, near the border, it was tea country, a series of lush green hills covered in plantations. I didn't really appreciate it, though. I spent the journey watching for mileage markers and anxiously calculating an estimated time of arrival. The conductor noticed my concern and asked what time the train left Mbeya.

'About twelve,' I answered. I asked him what time he thought the bus would arrive in Mbeya.

'About twelve,' he said.

As it was the bus stopped at the turn-off for Mbeya just after twelve. It was continuing along the main road to Dodoma, the capital, so I'd have to get a taxi to take me the 5 kilometres to town.

I didn't have any Tanzanian money so the conductor gave me 500 shillings for the fare. 'If Allah wills it you will catch your train,' he said.

Allah must have had other plans for me because the taxi driver misunderstood what I said and took me to the Tanzania–Zambian Railway Authority (TAZARA) ticket office in town rather than the TAZARA train station another few kilometres away.

To be honest, I wasn't too concerned. Although I was already over half an hour late, I took heart in the fact that this train had started in Lusaka in Zambia the day before. If it was like every other train in Africa it would have easily lost an hour or two by now, even if it had left on time. I'd be able to buy a ticket and still have time to change money, have a meal and walk the 4 kilometres to the train station if I had to.

I walked up to the counter at the TAZARA office, slapped down my Visa card and asked the guy for a sleeper ticket on the train to Dar.

He told me that the train had already left.

I said that I knew it was *supposed* to leave at twelve, but both he and I knew that that was highly unlikely. 'When was the last time a TAZARA train left on time?' I joked. 'Last *millennium*?'

He didn't laugh. In fact, he seemed a little offended. 'It was only half an hour late,' he said.

Maybe I was in a state of denial, maybe it was the prospect of staying in a dusty little hovel like Mbeya, but I just couldn't accept that I had missed the train. I begged for him to call the stationmaster at Mbeya station and check with him.

'Why don't you just catch the train at Makambako?' he said. 'It is only 140 kilometres away and the train isn't scheduled to leave there until 16.36.'

I must have looked perplexed, because he explained his theory further. 'The train is slow; a minivan is quicker,' he said as if I were a moron. 'You will cover the distance to Makambako faster and catch up with the train.'

Now I know 140 kilometres in four hours sounds highly achievable – a similar journey back home, even on public transport, would take half that time. But the roads in Australia are infinitely better, the vehicles are better maintained and Australian transport companies don't insist on breaking world records for the number of passengers carried in a small Japanese minivan before setting off. When the van to Makambako finally departed that afternoon there were people hanging out the windows and less than three hours left to catch up with the train.

My chances of successfully running down the train were further diminished when the driver stopped at Chimala for a shag. Of course, I didn't know that was what the driver was doing. When he got out of the van and disappeared into a small brick house beside the main road I thought he was attending to another type of nature call. But when there was still no sign of him 20 minutes later I became concerned and asked the conductor what was going on.

'The driver is visiting his girlfriend,' he said. 'He shouldn't be long.'

I told him that I had a train to catch and he just shrugged his shoulders. None of the other passengers seemed too concerned. Some of them stared wistfully at the building as if they wished they had a girlfriend in the village too. The driver eventually emerged 40 minutes later. Instead of apologising and driving a little faster to make up for lost time, he drove around Chimala for ten minutes looking for more passengers. I think it was about then that I gave up on catching the train.

I was dropped off at Makambako railway station at 5.40 pm, well after the time the train was scheduled to leave. The ticket seller told me that the train hadn't come yet. In fact, it wasn't due until 11 pm.

I asked if there had been a problem between Mbeya and here and he shook his head. 'The train has not even *reached* Mbeya yet,' he said. 'The problem was in Zambia. Vandals stole the telegraph lines.'

I was stunned. I had just given myself an ulcer getting to Makambako when I could have been kicking back with a couple of Safari lagers at Mbeya station. (I could have also gone through life without being exposed to the mating habits of Tanzanian minivan drivers.) I wanted to call the ticket man in the TAZARA office in Mbeya and have harsh words with him, but instead I bought a second-class sleeper ticket to Dar es Salaam.

The train arrived just after eleven, emerging from the depths of the bitterly cold night with a hiss. I had spent the time waiting huddled in my sleeping bag, chatting to a guy in an orange coat with a fake-fur collar who assured me that

Makambako was the coldest place in Tanzania. There was no electricity at the station, so when we boarded the train our tickets were checked by a conductor carrying a hurricane lamp that he then swung in the general direction of our designated carriages. I found my bunk, cleared it of the sacks of clothes another passenger had put on it and settled in for the night. I had made the train, finally, and it felt good.

The next morning I discovered that the train's tardiness meant that we would be passing though the Selous Game Reserve during daylight hours. Selous is the largest park in Africa, covering an area of 55,000 square kilometres, with a complex of rivers that includes the Kilombero, Ruaha, and Rufiji. It is home to one of the biggest concentrations of large-maned lions and big-tusked elephants anywhere. The TAZARA train line runs right across the top of it.

I spent most of the morning in the dining car, sipping on Cokes and ticking off wildlife. Baboons, elephants, hippos, giraffes, impala, warthogs, wildebeest and antelopes—I spotted them all from the comfort of the train. And I made quite a show of pointing them out to those other passengers having difficulty finding them.

Without wanting to appear immodest, I must say that I'm pretty good at spotting wildlife. Some people are good at crossword puzzles. Others are experts at playing the money market. Me, I'm a dab hand at picking out a Thomson's gazelle lurking under a tree. That morning in the dining car I was so keen to impress people with my superhuman game-spotting abilities that I pointed out elephants and buffalo to them even if they had just come to the carriage for a sandwich and a cup of tea. I wanted them to say, 'Damn that boy's good.

I'd have never spotted that greater kudu.' Sadly, I think most of them left the carriage muttering, 'What was *that* guy's problem?'

Concerned that I was scaring away potential customers, the manager of the dining car asked me to leave, so I made my way to the first-class lounge, a carriage at the front of the train reserved especially for first-class passengers. The boy guarding the carriage from riff-raff asked to see my ticket, and on noting that it was only a second-class one wouldn't let me pass. I argued that I would have bought a first-class ticket if there had been any left and surprisingly he let me pass.

For those of you who are wondering what a first-class lounge is like on a train travelling between Zambia and Tanzania, let me just say that it is not unlike the lounge room in a shared student household. It has worn velour couches, grubby shag-pile carpet, faded curtains and cigarette burns on the laminated tables. The only difference was a bar at the far end where you had to actually buy the beers rather than simply nick someone else's from the fridge.

The only other passengers in the lounge were a young Australian couple from Perth. Andrew had long shaggy hair and struck me as a bit dopey. His girlfriend, Caroline, had blond dreads and blue eyes, and seemed much sharper and intelligent. They were both science graduates and worked for the CSIRO. I asked if they were working on salinisation – I knew that it's a big problem in the wheat belt of Western Australia – and they said no, they were working on sheep's farts.

'Actually we're trying to stop both sheep *and* cows from farting,' said Andrew.

I must have looked bemused because Caroline felt the need

to give me a proper, scientific explanation. 'Fifteen per cent of Australia's greenhouse emissions are caused by animal farts,' she said. 'We're working on a vaccine to cut it back.'

'If it works, Australia will meet the Kyoto accord,' said Andrew.

My tax dollars at work!

◆   ◆   ◆

By late afternoon we were approaching Dar es Salaam. Ten years before, almost to the day, I had arrived in Dar after a long and tiring train journey. Then I had been coming from Kigoma, in the far west of the country, on a 48-hour trip that ended up taking 72 hours.

Despite being exhausted I had liked Dar es Salaam. And that afternoon ten years later I found myself liking it again. It really doesn't have anything going for it. The harbour is not pretty and apart from St Joseph's cathedral there aren't that many grand buildings. But it is compact and exotic, with a real mixing pot feel created by the Indians, Africans, Muslims and Westerners all going about their daily business there. It is the largest city in the country, the largest port, the railway terminus and the seat of government and it still wears the scars of its days as a slave-trading capital and the centre of colonial intrigue between the Germans and the British. It is decaying and it is dank. But at least it's not Canberra.

The only sour note to my last visit was that people thought I was the 'White Dogman', a German guy accused of forcing his Tanzanian maid to have sex with a dog. It was the manager of my hotel who drew my attention to my resemblance to the guy. He showed me the story splattered on the front page of the

Daily News, Tanzania's English-language newspaper. All of a sudden I understood why, when I passed people on the rutted streets of Dar, they fell silent or pointed me out to friends, whispering behind their hands about my evil deeds.

Ten years later Dar es Salaam had embraced the cyber age. Connections were fast and cheap and every business seemed to be an internet cafe. My favourite was the T&M Beauty Salon and Internet Cafe. The rest of the country's infrastructure was up the crapper, but they were riding high on the information superhighway.

You could use the internet to make dirt-cheap international calls so I called the Sudanese embassy in Lusaka on the off-chance that my visa had been approved and I had to dash back to Zambia to get it.

Rose told me that they still hadn't heard from Khartoum and that I should call back next week. When I told her I was in Dar es Salaam she said I should visit the Sudanese embassy there. 'It might be quicker,' she suggested, before asking me how I was enjoying Tanzania.

The Sudanese embassy in Dar es Salaam was out on Ali Hassan Mwinyi Road in an old house that looked like it had been earmarked for demolition. I was ushered into a waiting room and given forms to fill in, before being allowed to see the consul.

He read what I had written on the forms then tried to make a phone call. There was no answer. He tried again and when there was still no answer, he grimaced. He asked me about my travel plans and when I told him that I planned to travel north through Kenya and Ethiopia he screwed up his face like he was going to pass wind. 'The process takes some time,' he said.

'Perhaps you can get your visa in Addis Ababa.'

He seemed like a genuine chap. And he seemed to be feeling my pain. But I sensed that still I was getting the old Sudanese two-step.

I decided to cheer myself up that night by eating at the Garden Restaurant, a pleasant place with outdoor seating and live music every evening. Listening to live music as you dined was very popular in Dar es Salaam. It wasn't authentic African music. The Indian restaurant next door to my hotel, for example, had a band that played 'soft' music every night. At the New Africa Hotel the Graffiti Band, featuring Nickolas, Edit and Lubja from Russia, played the hits of Abba. And at the Garden Restaurant that night, a guy with a guitar was murdering a whole selection of easy-listening classics. I ate a rather ordinary beef curry as he strangled 'I Don't Know Much' by the Neville Brothers and slurped down my crème caramel as he plodded through a number he claimed was a 'Roger Whattacker' song.

When he strummed the opening chords to 'Annie's Song' by John Denver – and the waitress asked me if I liked dogs – I decided it was time to go to Zanzibar.

Chapter 12

ZANZIBAR, TANZANIA

Asiye na mengi, ana machache.

Even he who has not many troubles has a few.

I think the thing I like most about Zanzibar – or Unguja, as it's known in Tanzania – is that it looks exactly like you expect it to. Stone Town is a tightly bound maze of medieval laneways, low stone buildings and intricately carved doors. On the wharves men who look Arabic or African or both hump sacks full of pungent spices onto dhows, old wooden sailing ships with triangular lateen sails. The loaded dhows, that haven't changed since medieval times, float past like wind-up toys, and the steeples of St Joseph's rise above it all for maximum picturesque value.

Zanzibar's history and, indeed, its present, were greatly shaped by its geography. The prevailing winds of the region placed it directly on the Indian Ocean trade routes, making it accessible to traders and colonists from Africa, Arabia and South Asia (Persians were among the first colonists back in the tenth century). Over the following centuries the island passed through the hands of the Omanis, the Portuguese, the Germans and the English. Like the native language, Swahili, it is a little bit Arabic, a little bit Indian and a little bit African. And it's one of my favourite places.

The ferry from Dar es Salaam pulled up alongside the dock and after clearing immigration and customs (even though I was still officially in Tanzania) I made my way to Stone Town, the medieval heart of the island. I stayed at the Flamingo Hotel, a modest establishment on the edge of Stone Town, near TV Corner, where a local posts the results of the English Premier League on a blackboard. I had stayed there before with two mates, Sean and Angelo. Apart from an extension on the roof it hadn't changed much in ten years.

Back then, tensions were high between us following the kind of small disagreement that occurs when you've been travelling together for far too long. (I think I made some comment about the way Angelo packed his bag. It was trivial but in Africa those kind of comments cause offence.) Most nights we would retire to our beds without saying much to each other. We'd simply lie under the mosquito nets listening to our Walkmans or reading. On our second night in Zanzibar Angelo started flapping about under his mosquito net, trying to get out of bed. I looked up from my book and asked him what was the matter.

'I've got the shits!' he said.

I thought he had a dose of the runs – the food *was* pretty dodgy on Zanzibar in those days – so I ratted around in my pack for a roll of toilet paper. On finding it I triumphantly presented it to him.

'No!' he said. 'I've got the shits with *you guys*!'

He had obviously been lying in bed stewing over the things that had happened over the two months we had all travelled together. The nicknames, the clash of ideologies, the unkind words about his Canadian girlfriend, the song we made up to the tune of 'Waltzing Matilda' when he dropped his sunglasses down an open pit toilet. On that steamy night in Zanzibar it all came to a head. He stormed out of the room and spent the night sleeping on the couch in the lobby. And the next day he packed his things and left for Nairobi.

Sean and I reacted by going to the Africa House Hotel to get drunk. It used to be the British Club in the days before independence, and had been largely abandoned except for the bar on the second floor overlooking the sea. It was *the* place to go for a cold beer at sunset. The veranda looked directly west over the water and the dhow captains thoughtfully sailed back and forth to provide picture perfect exotic snapshots.

On my first afternoon back in Zanzibar I went again to the Africa House Hotel and I'm pleased to report that it hadn't changed. The bottom floor was still empty and abandoned, the same decrepit chairs and tables scattered around the veranda. The barman still pulled beers straight from a chest freezer (they were so cold that they beaded with condensation immediately and the labels slipped off into your hands). And they still played Jive Bunny. What more can you ask of a drinking establishment?

After the sun had set I walked to Forodhani Gardens, the scruffy park that runs along the seafront opposite the old fort.

During the day it is home to souvenir sellers but at night it's transformed into a giant open-air kitchen. Hundreds of stalls with sizzling barbecues sell all sorts of seafood – prawns, marlin kebabs, squid. You simply point at what you want and it's cooked in front of you. There are no street lamps to provide lighting, just an orange glow from the candles or hurricane lamps on each stall. Each hawker tries to win your custom with either cheap prices or clever banter.

Moses got my business with both. 'May I tell you my stock?' he asked in English.

I stopped, impressed by his politeness, and he continued. 'First, may I assure you that it is fresh today. No stomach bugs.'

He described each item and after I pointed out what I wanted he flicked it dexterously onto the grill. As my dinner cooked he told stories about his family and his life. 'I am a Muslim,' he said. 'My name is Muhsin, but at school the English called me Moses.'

Zanzibar is a real melting pot of religions. Islam, Hinduism, Catholicism, even Zoroastrianism with each wave of colonists and settlers having left their mark on the island's spiritual identity.

Moses had grown up on Zanzibar. And like most Zanzibarians, he claimed to have known Freddie Mercury. The lead singer of Queen had been born in Zanzibar. His father was a Parsee who worked as a civil servant for the British colonial government. 'He was little Farokh back then,' Moses said. 'His family lived in the square behind the post office. His father was very fond of cricket.'

Moses was getting old now and was training his son to take over the family business. The son stood quietly to the side, watching his father carefully and occasionally turning the kebabs. He was a shy boy and it occurred to me he would need to develop a more gregarious personality if he was going to succeed. It was his father's friendly banter that set his stall apart from the others, and made tourists come back especially to him every night they were in Stone Town.

After two days wandering Stone Town, admiring the intricately carved doors and visiting the air-conditioned blue-tiled internet cafe to escape the heat and check my e-mail, I decided to venture out to the rest of the island. Public transport was slow and uncomfortable, so I thought I'd tool about on a Vespa for a few days instead.

I hired the Vespa from a mechanic who operated out of a greasy old workshop just around the corner from my hotel. Vespas were very popular on Zanzibar, especially in Stone Town, where the lanes were too narrow for anything else, and he had set himself up as a Vespa expert. There were Vespa parts scattered through the shop, and up the back, under a tarp, were three old ones dating from the fifties. Still, they looked like they were in better condition than the one he gave me.

The mechanic said that I needed a special Zanzibar motorcycle licence to ride the bike around the island so I gave him a photo and a dollar and he sent his young apprentice to arrange it.

While I waited a noisy crowd gathered outside the workshop. The mechanic put down his tools and went out to look, beckoning me to follow. The crowd were kicking and punching two men curled up on the ground.

The air was thick with testosterone and the crowd cheered whenever a blow was landed on the men. The men flinched, grovelling on the ground, covering their heads and trying to avoid the blows. The crowd parted to make way for a guy carrying a large tin on his shoulders. At first I thought he was going to drop it on the two, like the stoners in Monty Python's *The Life of Brian*, but instead he poured the contents, a thick black oil, all over them. The crowd then dragged them into the back of a pick-up truck, where they sat looking terrified. Occasionally someone would throw dirt at them or whip them with their belt. Weirdly, people were laughing.

A little fat kid standing next to me was laughing the hardest and I asked him what the men had done. 'They are thieves,' he laughed. 'They stole parts from the dock.'

Their mistake was trying to sell their booty to the guy who had shipped the parts to Zanzibar in the first place. I asked the kid if anyone had called the police.

'No,' he said. 'This justice is quicker. The men have been shamed in front of their family and neighbours. That is punishment enough.'

I told him that it seemed a bit excessive to me. The thieves had taken quite a beating.

'It is better this way,' he said. 'There are no human rights in our jails.'

The apprentice came back with my licence. It was a piece of paper with Arabic writing on it. The official-looking stamp was the only thing that gave it any credibility. For all I know it could have said, 'Peter Moore of Sydney, Australia, paid $1 for absolutely no reason.' After what I had just witnessed, however, I didn't want to be seen to be breaking any law. Or even a road rule.

Not that there seemed to be many road rules on Zanzibar.

I didn't have to wear a helmet and the ride out of Stone Town and onto the road heading east suggested that anything goes as long as you don't hit the cows and chickens that wander across the road with impunity.

I rode across Zanzibar that afternoon with 'Born to be Wild' by Steppenwolf on a constant loop in my mind. It didn't matter that I was driving past thatched huts and thick humid jungle on a seriously underpowered Vespa. I'd got my motor running and I was out on the highway – well, a pretty good secondary road at least. The only time my fantasy of being a devil-may-care easy rider dimmed a little was when I stopped and took shelter under a reed hut every time it rained. But hey, I was in the tropics. It rains *heavy* there, man.

By late afternoon I had reached Bwejuu Dere Beach on the island's east coast. After Angelo left us, Sean and I had spent quite a while in Bwejuu Dere. We only had a traveller's cheque for $US100 and the guy running the only guesthouse there, the Bwejuu Beach Bungalows, didn't have any change. We had to stay there until we had used up the money in accommodation, food and alcohol. Back then, even with heavy drinking, the money lasted for close to three weeks.

In that time our visas for Zanzibar expired, so I'd left Sean and gone back to Stone Town, on the other side of the island, to get our visas extended. The immigration office was out near the soccer stadium and it took the guy most of the afternoon to sort through a box and find the forms we had filled in on arrival. With a scribble and a stamp he gave us permission to stay another month.

It had been too late to go back to Bwejuu Beach so I'd stayed the night in Zanzibar Town. The Flamingo Hotel was full but the manager said I could share a room with an American girl if I wanted. She was paying a cheaper rate on the proviso that if someone else came along she had to share the room. I was that someone else, and from the way the manager winked at me, he felt as though he was doing me a favour.

The girl's name was Ellen and she was a self-proclaimed Jewish American Princess. With blond hair and blue eyes she was quite pretty, and smart and funny to boot. We spent the night chatting about books, in particular, the works of Thomas Hardy.

I don't know what it is about Thomas Hardy novels, but I love them. I've always suspected that I would end up with a girl who, if not exactly like Tess of the D'Urbervilles, would be an awful lot like her. I should point out that my image of Tess is a black-haired, blue-eyed, pale-skinned beauty with large breasts barely contained in one of those milkmaid wench outfits so popular in the 1800s. (You've got to remember that we didn't have Lara Croft when I was growing up.) Actually, I blame the New South Wales High School English curriculum for my troubled love life. What chance does a guy have of enjoying a mature, committed relationship when he was brought up on a diet of *Wuthering Heights*, *Sons and Lovers* and *Tess of the D'Urbervilles*?

Anyway, Ellen was a big Thomas Hardy fan too and was impressed that I had just finished reading *A Pair of Blue Eyes*, one of Thomas's lesser know works but, surprisingly, widely available in East Africa. I decided that Sean would be similarly enchanted with Ellen and I invited her to stay with us on the east coast at Bwejuu Beach.

Sean *was* happy. After a week at Bwejuu he and I had run

out of things to say to each other. With Ellen it was fun again. At night we'd sit on the beach together, staring at the stars and telling jokes.

On our last night in Bwejuu we bought a bottle of Tanzanian Scotch to celebrate. It was a startling shade of orange and because the bar had long run out of Coke we had to drink it with Fanta. It tasted as bad as it sounds, but on the east coast of Zanzibar in those days you were thankful for whatever you could get.

The Scotch loosened Ellen's tongue and she told us about her family for the first time. They were wealthy and expected her to marry a nice Jewish doctor, just like her sister had done. 'You know, when I feel my life is going too well, I go into a jewellery store and shoplift,' she said.

She said she did it to get back at her parents, although for what she didn't say. Her other plan was to marry an Indian pilot she had met in Mombassa. She didn't love the guy. She just knew that her father hated Indians. And she reasoned that because the guy flew for Air India she wouldn't have to see him that often. Throughout Africa she had been putting herself into dangerous situations, almost as if she wished something bad would happen. I wondered if she was doing that when she agreed to come over to the east coast with me.

That bottle of Scotch cleared our credit at the Bwejuu Beach Bungalows so Sean and I left the next day. Ellen decided to stay, and gave us a passionate hug goodbye. We made promises about catching up somewhere else in Africa – we invited her to spend Christmas with us in Lamu – but we never saw Ellen again.

This trip to Zanzibar had turned into quite a nostalgic one, so rather than fight it I decided to go with the flow and stay at the Bwejuu Beach Bungalows again. It had been extended since I was there last in anticipation of a boom that never came. I was the only tourist there.

That night I walked down to the deserted beach and sat in the same spot, just in front of the palm trees, where Sean, Ellen and I had sat each evening. The bar at the bungalows didn't have any Tanzanian Scotch, just an Esky full of imported beer, so I bought a can of Tusker lager and watched the moon come up over the water.

I found myself wondering whether Ellen had married the Indian pilot or if she'd ever been caught shoplifting. In the end I decided that she was probably back in New York, maybe up state, in a pretty Cape Cod house, just like the one in the family photos she showed us. And she'd have two neatly dressed kids with blond hair and blue eyes who she'd read Thomas Hardy stories to at night.

I felt a small pang of a yearning inside. It wasn't for Ellen. I don't think I could cope with a wife with random shoplifting impulses. But maybe for the life I imagined she was living. The home, the hearth, the family, the *stability*. I thought that staying at the Bwejuu Beach Bungalows would be a happy nostalgic trip but it had left me feeling a bit empty. Ten years on, I was in exactly the same position as I was back then. Poor and rootless, but with less hair.

❖   ❖   ❖

The next day I trekked my way north on the Vespa towards Nungwi. I took a short cut along a road that passed through nutmeg, cinnamon and cardamom plantations and discovered that Piaggio had not designed Vespas with off-road trips in mind. I lost control of the bike and spent ten minutes extricating it and then myself from a muddy puddle. A policeman pulled me over to look at my licence (it was legit!) and asked me if I had crashed. I said no, desperately trying to think of some other credible reason as to why the bike and I were covered in mud, but he didn't ask. He just shook his head and tutted and let me go.

In the years since my last visit to Zanzibar Nungwi had become the premier beach resort on the island for independent travellers. It's easy to see why. The beaches are clean and sugar white. Accommodation is cheap and rustic. And there are beach-side bars and restaurants to suit every taste. Where Bwejuu had been deserted Nungwi was buzzing with life.

A group of overlanders were in town – they had left their truck on the mainland and were on a five-day excursion to Zanzibar – and had taken over the bar right on the water. I spotted Zoe among them looking as sarky as normal, and waved hello. She seemed fairly happy to see me – you couldn't tell with Zoe's deadpan manner – and took great delight in showing me her spots.

'They just came up the other day,' she said. 'I have no idea what caused them.'

I asked her if she'd been swimming in Lake Malawi. She had, so I suggested that it might be bilharzia. Ninette, the Dutch doctor, had told me that one of the first signs of the disease were the red spots left by the parasite burrowing into your skin.

'Shit!' said Zoe. 'Did she tell you how to get rid of it?'

She had, actually. After snorkelling in Lake Malawi I was a little anxious about contracting bilharzia myself. Ninette recommended a dose of praziquantel. She was planning to take it anyway, without having a test for bilharzia first. She claimed it didn't have any side effects. Ninette had written a 'prescription' for me in the back of my notebook based on my weight – 1600 milligrams in the morning and 1600 milligrams in the evening. Comparing our weights and doing a little mathematics, we worked out the dose Zoe should have on the back of a beer coaster.

She gave me a kiss on the cheek. 'Thanks,' she smiled. 'You've probably just saved my life. Or at least my liver. Can I buy you a beer?'

Accepting the beer probably constituted payment for medical services rendered and no doubt I should have looked into liability insurance to cover me should Zoe die. But I thought what the heck. The girl still owed me for all the Bacardi Breezers I bought her in Zambia.

The next morning I got up at dawn and went for a swim. As I floated on my back young schoolgirls in long shawls, their heads covered in the Muslim manner, walked along the beach to school with their books tucked under their arms. Ancient dhows, with their tattered lateen sails flapping in the light breeze, floated by serenely. And the water was a pleasant temperature, just on the right side of refreshing.

It was idyllic and, quite honestly, I would have liked to stay there, running down a sizable tab like I'd done in Bwejuu a decade before. But I had only hired the bike for three days. It had to be back in Stone Town that afternoon.

And besides, it was time to climb Mount Kilimanjaro.

Chapter 13

MOUNT KILIMANJARO, TANZANIA

Painamapo ndipo painukapo.
Where it slopes down is where it slopes up.

I don't know exactly why I wanted to climb Mount Kilimanjaro. On my last trip to Africa I climbed Mount Kenya, the second highest mountain in Africa and a good 696 metres 'shorter' than Kilimanjaro, and it nearly killed me.

I made that climb with three friends who I will refer to as Stuart, Neil and Tracy, primarily because those are their names. We had decided it would be a good idea to climb a tall mountain after spending a night in a seedy Nairobi bar drinking beer and writing limericks about each other. Not the way Sir Edmund Hilary would have planned one of his expeditions, to be sure, but then we weren't attempting to climb Everest.

The climb started disastrously when we chose to walk the 30 kilometres from Chogoria to the national park gates. A man in Chogoria had kindly offered to drive us to the gates in his Land Rover for $US50 but we thought he was trying to rip us off. He wasn't – the road was atrocious and incredibly steep. It took us all day to reach the gates and when we did we were buggered.

Three days later we got to Point Lenana, the highest peak on Mount Kenya that you can reach without equipment. At 4986 metres, it was quite an achievement. Especially when you consider that only the day before Stuart had shit his pants and Tracy had been wandering around in a daze, her lips blue from altitude sickness, muttering about penis implants.

I was ten years older now and, if anything, even less prepared to scale a mountain of any substance. I didn't have any wet weather gear or even anything that would keep me particularly warm. My shoes were more like runners than boots. And I hadn't exactly been in training. I had just spent the last week in Zanzibar lazing about on tropical beaches. Still, I was in a positive frame of mind, and I figured that had to count for something.

I had my first glimpse of Mount Kilimanjaro from the window of my bus to Arusha. The sun was setting and the mountain rose above the sisal plantations, its snow-capped top clearly visible and bathed in pink. It looked better than all the postcards, posters and coffee-table books it graces; more ethereally beautiful, more *conical*. It also looked bloody high. I knew it was 5895 metres high – I'd read that in my guide-book. I just hadn't realised that 5895 metres was *that* high. Mount Kenya had hidden its stature behind ridges and folds.

Mount Kilimanjaro rose as a single entity from the flat plains of north Tanzania, not even attempting to hide its naked elevation.

Although Moshi was the closest town of any size to Kilimanjaro, I had decided to use Arusha as my base. Arusha is just another dusty East African agricultural town servicing the coffee, cotton, pyrethrum and sisal farms that surround it. But there are more tour companies there than in Moshi and I hoped to use the extra competition to secure a better deal on my Mount Kilimanjaro expedition.

Two things struck me as odd about Arusha immediately. The first was the split personality of the old Arusha Metropolitan Cinema. At lunchtime it hosted the Hosanna Music Hour where patrons 'could come into God's presence with praise and worship'. In the evenings it showed movies like *Sex and Zen*, *American Masseuse*, *Erotic Zen* and *Wet Nurses*. I didn't even want to think about whose presence they came into during those.

The second thing was the sheer volume of tour touts working the streets of the town. Its cracked and broken pavements were thick with them and quite frankly they were the most ferocious and persistent touts I have ever dealt with.

I couldn't walk two metres without being accosted by a tour tout. Worse, they worked in teams so you didn't get a moment's peace. The first tout would try his best to sell me on a tour and when he didn't win me over with his promises of three-course meals and expert guides he peeled off and let the next guy seamlessly sidle up and try his luck. If he lucked out, a third would try. Then a fourth, a fifth and a sixth.

They also mixed up their offers. If I didn't show any interest in the six-day Kilimanjaro trek they'd try a three-day safari in the Serengeti, or a luxury tented tour of Ngorongoro Crater. The only constant was that when I asked a tout how much a Kilimanjaro tour cost they'd tell me what the tour included – park fees, accommodation, all meals, guides, porters – but they'd never tell me a price. I had to agree to go back to their office before they'd do that. And that was something I would never do.

There were times when I wanted to wander the streets of Arusha unmolested by tour touts – most of the time, funnily enough – but shaking them was an almost impossible task. Simply telling them to bugger off was the least successful tactic. Most had been abused by people with a more colourful vocabulary and a more intimidating physical presence than I. And insisting that they told me a price before we went any further had only limited success too. They'd go silent for a while, but when I tried to walk away they followed, starting their spiel all over again.

I found the most successful ploy was to pretend that I didn't speak English. It took a good deal of effort – it's more difficult to pretend you don't understand your own language than you'd think. And the touts are so used to people ignoring them it takes a while for them to realise that you don't understand them. When it finally dawns on them that it is a lack of comprehension that you're conveying, not the expected indifference, they'll try any other language they speak – usually Italian, German, Spanish or French (the more persistent will even try Russian or Afrikaans). When that fails they resort to the same tactics I use when I am having trouble being understood in a foreign country – speaking loudly and slowly to me in English. But after that, you're home free.

I wasn't being difficult just for the fun of it – although it *was* fun. Arusha is full of dodgy tour operators and countless tourists have been fleeced. A court case against one of them was underway while I was there. A Mr Clarence Mutta was being charged with 'false promises' after arranging a Serengeti tour for some Germans and then shooting through with their money. The Arusha Tourist Bureau has a black business card holder full of the cards of the shonky and unlicensed tour operators. There are hundreds of them and that's just the ones they know of.

In the end I decided to use the tour company attached to the hotel I was staying in. I figured if anything went wrong I wouldn't have to go far to find them.

I decided to take the Marangu Route. It's less scenic than the other routes but it's the easiest. The six-day trek would set me back a staggering $US600 (the bulk of it going in ridiculously expensive park fees) so I wanted to make sure I did everything to ensure I'd get to the top. And a track that was so easy they called it the Coca-Cola route sounded fine by me.

My $US600 also got me a ride from Arusha to the park gates at Marangu in a beat-up Peugeot 504 with a sticker on the front windscreen that read 'Mother Mary Pray for Us'. I don't think Mary was listening because over the course of the 120-kilometre journey we were stopped five times by the police.

Each 'bust' followed the same routine. The policeman waved our car over and then started scribbling furiously into a plain paper notepad, making quite a show of taking down the registration number and the driver's licence details. Then he'd 'fine' the driver 20,000 shillings (about $50). The driver would plead, 'Help me out my friend,' and the cop would eventually settle for 2000 shillings. The driver would peel off a wad of notes and the policeman would make a show of ripping out the page he had been scribbling on, screwing it up and throwing it on the ground. Judging by the piles of scrunched up paper, these policemen were doing rather well for themselves.

'Writing, writing, writing,' bemoaned the driver. 'They are *too* hungry.'

My guide for the trek was Daniel, a stocky little guy with eyes like a bull terrier. He was waiting for me in the carpark, along with my porter and cook for the climb. They sat on a stone wall, sucking on cigarettes, looking like thugs from a bar rather than seasoned climbing professionals.

As they sorted through the supplies we had brought in the car I wandered down the hill to a small general store for a Coke. We were taking the Coca-Cola route – it would be remiss of me to start the journey without drinking one. There was a poster on the wall for the 'Great Gospel Crusade with Stephen Zanzibar'. It quoted Isaiah 38:1 – 'Set thine house in order for thou shalt die!' It was just the sort of thing I needed to read before setting off to conquer the highest mountain in Africa.

An hour later I set off to conquer the highest mountain in Africa wearing a pink fleece that looked like it was a cast-off from a Sheena Easton film clip. The tour company had supplied it – the fleece was the mountain-climbing gear they promised they would lend me when I told them my own stuff was inadequate. It was inadequate, too, and the colour was bright enough to snap synapses, but I didn't care. I had noticed a sign at the gates that said we were already at an altitude of 1980 metres. That meant there were only another 3915 to go.

The first day was easy. It was a short four-hour walk to Mandara Hut (2700 metres) through coffee plantations and lush rainforest where lichen hung picturesquely from the trees, thicker than usual because of the cool winter weather. I was in such high spirits that I went and checked out Muandi Crater, which had been created by a meteor millennia ago, while the cook prepared my evening meal of chicken and rice. I was up early the next morning after sleeping in one of the A-frame huts built by Norwegians as part of an aid program, rubbing my hands together and raring to go.

The scenery on the second day was a little more varied. The rainforest was behind me and the path crossed tussock grassland and heather and a vast moorland that wouldn't have looked out of place in Scotland (except for the giant lobelias that rose from the earth like huge phalluses – that was very African). The track got a little steep at times, but I had a porter carrying my bag so I covered the 14-kilometre walk to Horombo Hut (3720 metres) without raising a sweat. I'd already gained an extra 1740 metres in altitude. I went to bed that night thinking that this mountain-climbing caper was a piece of piss.

I think I must have angered the gods of Kilimanjaro with such thoughts – or at the very least with my pink fleece – because late on that second night things went horribly wrong. I woke up just before midnight, my teeth chattering. I was shuddering with cold and had to put on all the clothes I had with me to get only slightly warm. Then, in the early hours of the next morning I woke bathed in sweat and burning up with a fever. I was convinced I had malaria.

At breakfast Daniel said that I was acclimatising to the higher altitude. We were now close to 4000 metres above sea level, he said. My body was bound to react in funny ways. But

I wasn't suffering from headaches, shortness of breath or dizziness. I had a fever then chills, I had stomach cramps and I was shitting through the eye of a needle. His diagnosis of altitude sickness couldn't explain that.

That day was an acclimatisation day, an extra day at Horombo Hut to allow my body to get used to operating at such high levels. I had added it to the tour in an attempt to make doubly sure that I made it to the top. I had imagined it would be a lazy day where I kicked back in a bunk reading. I spent it dashing to the toilet every ten minutes.

The diarrhoea was an unpleasant and unwanted intrusion. I'd been in Africa for over four months and hadn't been sick once. Now when I needed health and wellbeing I could feel my strength and energy draining from me.

One of the other climbers staying in my hut gave me some anti-diarrhoea tablets, so I was able to walk out to the saddle later that afternoon as part of my acclimatisation. The Saddle is a vast desert of scree that stretches between Mawenzi peak and Kibo peak, the tallest. It's a spectacular sight, the snow-capped cone rising from a harsh grey desert, but I was more excited by the fact that I had only to duck behind some bushes three times in the hour it took Daniel and I to walk there.

The fever struck again that night and now I was *convinced* that I had malaria, maybe even falcipram malaria, the fatal one. My *Rough Guide to Travel Health* said if I even suspected that I had falcipram malaria I should put the book down and get help immediately. Two per cent of falcipram malaria cases result in death, usually because of delayed treatment. The clock was already ticking and I was halfway up a mountain.

I told Daniel that I wanted to go back down the mountain and get tested for malaria but he wouldn't have it. 'It is because you haven't been eating,' he scolded. 'The cook told me you didn't touch your breakfast!'

I hadn't eaten my breakfast because I knew I'd be shitting it out again.

Although he didn't say it directly, I suspected Daniel was worried about his tip. He'd spent the whole trek to this point telling me anecdotes about happy customers showing their appreciation of his superior guiding skills with displays of largesse. The American industrialist who promised him a Cadillac. A German woman who had put his children through school. The Englishman who bought him new hiking boots. (It is instructive to note that he didn't have any such story about an Australian!) He was worried that if I didn't make it to the top – or worse, turned around on only the third day – he wouldn't get a tip at all.

So I spent the fourth day staggering like a drunk across the scree to Kibo Hut.

We arrived at Kibo Hut (4700 metres) just as the rescue ranger stationed there was being wheeled away on the rescue cart. He had come down with malaria and a porter from one of the other climbing groups was wheeling him down the mountain. I wanted to give Daniel an 'I told you so!' look but he refused to catch my eye. Instead I made my way into one of the dorms, bumping against the walls as I did, and collapsed onto a bed, exhausted.

The wooden frames of the bunk beds didn't help my fragile state of mind. They were covered in graffiti like 'Never, ever again!', scribbled by Marius from Denmark, 'You won't die but you'll wish you did,' scratched by Ruth from Canada, and the most sobering one – 'Get out while you still can!' – left by Thomas of Austria.

Daniel came into the room and told me to rest. 'We will start the final ascent at midnight,' he said. 'Try and get some sleep.'

The theory was that by leaving at midnight we would reach the summit just as the sun rose, casting its golden rays across the savanna that stretched out below. As I drifted off I tried to imagine this sight as a kind of motivational tool. But I was kept awake by an Australian girl lying in the bunk next to me clutching her head and groaning, and leaning over every few moments to vomit on the floor. She was suffering altitude sickness and her guide sat beside her rubbing her back and talking to her softly. After consulting with Daniel he decided to take her back down the mountain. She was in such a bad state that the guide had to do up her shoelaces for her. I did not regard this as a particularly good omen.

Midnight came sooner than I wanted. I hadn't slept much – a strong wind howled and slammed against the walls, waking me any time I drifted off to sleep. My mind was clear – that wasn't the problem. But the fever attacks I had suffered the nights before had sapped me completely of my energy.

Daniel came to the door with a grim look on his face. It had snowed as we slept. It would be more difficult to find and follow the trail, and the trekking would be harder too. I would have to drag one foot in front of the other through about 30 centimetres of fresh snow now. I put extra socks on and then covered my boots in plastic bags, hoping that my feet would stay warm and dry. But my feet were still cold and the extra socks made my boots tight and uncomfortable. As we trudged off just after midnight, a light snow falling, I realised how dreadfully inadequate my pink fleece was.

The path climbed vertically from the hut and it became immediately apparent that to this point the climb had been a doddle. The Coca-Cola route became a little more potent here – I think someone had spiked it with a gallon of JB – and the final steep ascent to the summit was more like a ladder than a path. After an hour I could still see the lights of Kibo Hut behind me but I was already struggling to drag one foot in front of the other. I tried not to look up – it was too discouraging. I just kept my eye on Daniel's feet in front of me.

We zig-zagged our way up the mountain towards a rock that didn't seem to get any closer. When we finally reached it, I ate a chocolate bar, but the act of chewing it expended more energy than the hit it gave me. It is a fair indication of just how fragile my mental state had become by this point that I began singing 'Try again' as motivation. Sadly, singing about dusting myself off and trying again in my best Aaliyah voice didn't seem to help.

I think that's when Daniel realised that I wouldn't make it. When I asked him how far it was to the top he stopped lying and told me that we were only about halfway there. We had passed Hans Meyer Cave but the path would only get steeper from here.

My heart sank and with it went my will to go on. In my mind's eye we were close to reaching the top. I was staggering like a boxer who had taken a savage blow and I was sweating profusely, even though it was bitterly cold. I continued for another half hour before sinking to my knees and giving up. In altitude terms we were only 100 metres from the top but the circuitous route meant that the summit was still an hour away.

The walk back to Kibo Hut wasn't any easier. Suddenly the snow was conspiring to trip me up. There was a sharp pain in my big toe as it pushed against the front of my shoe. I could see the lights of Kibo Hut below again but now they didn't seem to be getting any closer. Even the thought of the can of Coke I'd saved to celebrate couldn't motivate me.

I got back to the hut in just over an hour, ripped all my clothes off and collapsed into bed. Just after dawn, Daniel woke me. I wanted to sleep longer, but he insisted we needed to get going. I went to put my boots back on and noticed that the toenail on my big toe had been completely dislodged. I could slide it up and down and if I pressed on it a goocy red liquid seeped out from under the nail.

I think it was then that I realised just how unprepared I had been for this climb. Coca-Cola route or not, Mount Kilimanjaro is a mountain that deserves more respect than I had given it. It's the highest mountain in Africa, for Christ's sake. What made me think I could turn up in the middle of winter and just stroll up it in nothing more than a bright pink fleece?

Sadly, I wasn't alone. The mountain was crawling with people of all ages, shapes, sizes and levels of fitness. Some thought it would be easy, mainly folk from mountainous countries like Austria, wearing sensible mountain-climbing gear. But most, like me, seemed to have a sneaking suspicion that they had bitten off more than they could chew. They'd ask everyone coming back down the mountain whether they made it or not. Then they'd compare themselves to that person. Did they look fitter? Were they better or worse equipped? But by that stage it's all academic anyway. You've paid your money and you're taking your chances. The fact that you've shelled out $US600 makes you repress the sobering statistic that 80 per cent of the people who attempt to climb Kilimanjaro don't make it.

Of course, there's a whole industry in Tanzania supporting this idiocy. The tour companies, the porters, even the government charging extortionately high fees, all want you to think it's easy.

Daniel spent the entire walk back to Mandara Hut angling for a tip. I told him I was Australian. It's in our constitution that we don't tip.

He thought I didn't want to tip him because I didn't reach the top and was at pains to show me that it was largely my fault. I hadn't eaten everything put before me. I didn't smoke (apparently 80 per cent of the people who make it smoke). Really, when I thought about it, he said, it was a miracle that I got as far as I did. The inference was that it was a miracle largely of his making. Maybe years of guiding had shown him that I was the kind of climber who needed to be *annoyed* to the top.

When we reached Mandara Hut, it was still light, so Daniel wanted to push on to the national park gates at Marangu. I wanted to stay. I was tired and besides, I'd paid for a hut for the night and I wouldn't get my money back if I didn't. Realising I couldn't be convinced otherwise, he tried to get me to give him any tips I may be shelling out. The porter and the cook would be going back to their villages, he said. Couldn't I pay them now? I told him that *if* there were any tips, I would hand them out back at the office in Arusha. He got angry and buggered off in a huff, leaving the cook to take me to the carpark the next day.

I ended up walking back down to the gate with a middle-aged American guy called Ed. He hadn't made it to the top either, but then he hadn't planned to. He was happy enough to get to Horombo Hut and hike up to the Saddle and look at the peak from there. I asked him how much he was tipping his guide and was shocked by how high it was. It was three figures and in a hard currency. He asked me how much I was going to fork out and I said probably the same amount, but in Tanzanian shillings. I told Ed that I just didn't come from a tipping culture.

'You don't tip your barber?' he asked, shocked.

I shook my head. 'Nup.'

'Your barman?'

'Nup.'

He was flabbergasted. He asked if I tipped my drycleaner, my greengrocer, my milkman or my doorman (I never even had one of those).

I just shook my head and said, 'Nup, nup, nup and nup.'

He told me that my dilemma was totally out of his realm of his experience and that there was nothing he could do to help me.

When I got back down to the park gates the next day Daniel was waiting with a car to take me back to the hotel in Arusha. I gave him his tip, which I think was unexpected because he jumped excitedly around the carpark like a puppy. He was so happy with his tip, in fact, that he offered to lie so I'd get the complimentary 'I made it to the top of Mount Kilimanjaro' certificate the national park authorities handed out to those who'd said they'd made it.

I didn't take it. A piece of paper saying I had reached the top wouldn't change the fact that I hadn't. Instead I spent the car trip back to Arusha contemplating the climb and trying to put a positive spin on it. Perhaps I could take something philosophical away from it, maybe that I'd given it my best shot and that was all that mattered.

Somehow that didn't ring true. I'd given my relationship with the GND my best shot and I still felt lousy about that failing. And if I couldn't get a visa into Sudan and had to terminate my journey somewhere in Ethiopia I'd be devastated by that too. It was better, I thought, to blame it on outside forces. Like malaria.

But before I could press on through northern Kenya and deal with the vagaries of Ethiopia there was a more urgent task to attend to.

I had to get that bloody Aaliyah song out of my head.

Chapter 14

NOWHERE IN AFRICA

Usijifanye kuku mweupe.

Do not pretend to be a white fowl when you're only an ordinary chap.

I arrived in Nairobi, the capital of Kenya, and immediately got tested for malaria. I had failed to climb Mount Kilimanjaro and I wanted a better excuse to give people than that I was just too buggered to do it.

The pretty nurse at the Sarit Medical Centre in the suburb of Westlands couldn't understand why I was so disappointed when the results of the test came back negative. 'It doesn't mean you *don't* have malaria,' she said, trying to cheer me up. 'The parasite could be still in your liver. In six hours you could be very, very positive. It's just that it isn't showing up at the moment.'

I took some heart from the fact that she told me that if I got the chills or fever again I should see a doctor immediately.

I had travelled to Nairobi on a beat-up minibus that struggled through the edges of the Serengeti, dodging the odd buffalo that wandered lazily onto the road. Kilimanjaro was clearly visible for most of the way, its white peak taunting me, a few zebra and giraffe scattered picturesquely in the foreground.

On my first visit to Kenya the mere sight of a zebra had sent me delirious with excitement and saw me shelling out more than I should have for a five-day safari in the Masai Mara, the country's premier game park. Like most first-time visitors to Africa I wanted to go on an *authentic* African safari and, I've got to admit, the first couple of lions I spotted were exciting. But soon the big cats became like the cathedrals of Europe – just another pile of stones – or, in the case of the lions, fur and bones.

I was also a little disillusioned by the fact that with a million and a half acres of African savanna to choose from, the drivers of the vans insisted on following each other. From a distance it looked like all the vans were somehow connected to each other. If one veered to the right, the others would too. If another peeled off to the left, the others would quickly follow. Finally, when it came time to stop, the vans formed a perfect half circle around whatever animal was unlucky enough to be spotted. It was like being on safari with the Kenyan National Precision Driving Team.

Of course, what the drivers were hoping for was a kill, the holy grail of an African safari, where you witness a lioness getting off her butt for a couple of minutes to run down and eat something. The closest we got was an ocelot pouncing on a field mouse, and as disappointing as that was, enough film was exposed for the good folk at Kodak to breathe a collective sigh of relief, knowing their jobs were secure for another year. I decided to give the safari a miss this time.

I was staying at the Iqbal, a hotel that is legendary with travellers for no apparent reason. It is on the wrong side of River Road, in an area so bad that the locals call it the Third World, and has a security guard on the door 24 hours a day. My room was clean and cheap, though, and filled with music from the cassette shop below the window. I'd wake to the strains of Dolly Parton Christmas carols and then shower in another part of the hotel that was next to a cinema used for gospel revival meetings. Let me tell you, there's nothing quite like soaping under your arms to a rousing 'Hallelujah!'.

Nairobi hadn't changed much since my last visit ten years before. The touts still wandered up and down Kimathi Street looking for customers. The beggar boys still spoke perfectly enunciated English. Postcards with pictures of animals shagging were still the most popular with tourists. And the greasy chip shops still offered lunchtime specials of sausages, chips and a soft drink for less than a dollar. What pleased me most, though, was that the locals, no matter how poor they were, still wore suits.

At the risk of being dragged off to a sanatorium, I'd like to let the record show that I actually don't mind Nairobi. It has a dreadful reputation – travellers call it Nairobbery – and the area I was staying in was a horrible, muddy, noisy mess. But some parts, like Kenyatta Avenue when the jacaranda trees are in bloom, or the outer suburb of Karen, with its stately homes, are quite lovely. And while I know 90 per cent of the population of Nairobi spend all their waking hours inventing new scams to part gullible tourists from their money, I've only ever met charming friendly folk.

I even like the matatus, the Kenyan minibuses with names like Death Star 2000 and blaring music played at deafening levels. They had been the same ten years earlier and it struck me on this visit that matatus were the original doof-doof-doof vehicles.

By African standards Nairobi's a pretty easy place to get things done. Most countries have an embassy there so it's a convenient place to stock up on visas (there's even an Australian embassy – believe me, that's saying something). And by African standards, the banking system is sophisticated. Neither Ethiopia or Sudan would have facilities for me to get a cash advance on my credit card, so Nairobi was the last place I could get some US cash together before heading north. In Nairobi it was just a matter of walking into a bank, slapping down the credit card and buying some dollars.

The downside is that Nairobi is the kind of place you tend to get stuck in. On my last visit to Kenya I spent ten days there arranging visas, drinking in bars and arranging more visas. In a way it's a bit like the Hotel California. You can check out of Nairobi any time but unless you get on the right matatu you may never leave.

It was the same this time. I found myself propping up bars with colourful local identities or perusing local magazines with stories about sex romps with goats, which had been laid out carefully on blankets on the broken street. At other times you'd find me refusing kind offers from scruffy young men to discuss politics and have their friends, flashing fake police cards, agree not to arrest me on treason for the reasonable sum of 200 shillings. But what really kept me in Nairobi this time was the siren song of international film obscurity.

My call to the silver screen had come in the form of a note stuck up on the notice board in the foyer of the Iqbal. 'Wanted,' it read. 'Caucasian males 20 to 50 as extras in movie directed by Academy Award–nominated director. Shooting starts Monday. 3500 Ksh [$US50] per day. Call MTM Film Production for more details.'

I rang the number excitedly and spoke to the company's Kenyan production assistant, Dan. He explained that the movie was a German production and it was being directed by Caroline Link. She'd been nominated for the Best Foreign Film Oscar in 1998 for a film about deaf mutes called *Beyond Silence*, he said breathlessly. It sounded to me like Dan was already figuring out what to wear when this one got nominated.

The movie was based on a book by Stefanie Zweig called *Nowhere in Africa* that Dan assured me was *very* popular in Germany. It told the story of a German–Jewish farmer in Kenya thrown into a British internment camp during World War II. There was some kind of love triangle as well, but Dan told me not to worry about that. They needed people to play British soldiers and German prisoners. In fact they needed lots. Could I come out to Muthaiga for casting? And bring any friends I might have?

Casting was held in a large mansion that the production company had commandeered as home and headquarters for the German cast and crew. I had imagined that the casting would be a rigorous affair in front a panel of people, including, perhaps, the director herself. They would ask me to give them my best German or British accent and to twirl around in front of them a couple of times. In the end casting was nothing more than joining a long line and filing past a bored woman who arbitrarily decided whether I was soldier or prisoner material. After a cursory glance she decided that I was a prisoner.

I had wanted to be a soldier. They were allowed to play with guns and were given a number-one buzz cut immediately. I hadn't had a haircut for a couple of months so being shorn would have been a welcome perk, especially if they gave me a *Pearl Harbor* Josh Hartnett. As prisoner material, sadly, all the make-up department had to do was trim my sideburns and comb my hair over in a very unappealing manner. I hadn't seen anything like the haircut they gave me on any barbershop posters in Africa. The *Stripes* Bill Murray was obviously never a big hit with the young urban African.

The wardrobe department was in the basement of the mansion. A severe German woman sat among racks of garments and doled out clothes that looked like they had been rejected by the Salvation Army. I needed two outfits – a set of civilian clothes for my arrival at the internment camp and a khaki outfit for everything thereafter. Picking out my prison clothes was easy – the wardrobe mistresses simply found a set of khaki shirt and shorts that fitted me. Choosing my civilian clothes, however, proved more problematic. I was forced to try on a number of outfits, all as terrible as each other, before the woman eventually settled on a pale brown ensemble that made me look like an extremely dull accountant.

'Hmm,' I said, looking at myself in the mirror. 'I might keep these after the shoot.'

I was joking, of course. (No, really, I was.) But the big, scary wardrobe mistress didn't see the funny side. 'Zey vill be returned immediately after ze shoot!' she snapped, giving me the kind of look that men with an S & M fixation pay good money for.

My name was written on a tag and pinned onto the outfits so I could pick them up at the set. The wardrobe mistress spelt my name wrong and I made the mistake of correcting her. (Hey, she was German. In my experience things like spelling were quite important to the good folk of Deutschland.)

'Vy does everyone care about zer name spelling,' she said, shooting me a withering glance. 'You are *only* extras.'

I very nearly retorted that I was sure she'd want her name spelt correctly on the movie's credits, but she was bigger than me so I didn't.

A Toyota Coaster minibus was sent to pick up the extras at the Kenya National Theatre at six o'clock each morning of the shoot. We were a motley bunch of backpackers, expatriates and white Kenyans who, on the whole, looked more suited to a Guy Ritchie 'sowf' London robber flick than a sensitive portrayal of life in an internment camp. I quickly befriended the dodgiest looking of them, a young Aussie guy from Perth called Dave, deftly picking him as a prisoner because he had a *Stripes* Bill Murray haircut as well.

The location for the first day of shooting was Kabete Approved School, a rundown boarding school with unkempt hedges on the outskirts of Nairobi. We were dropped outside a huge marquee where the gruff wardrobe mistress pointed us towards piles of clothes and dealt with the people who couldn't find theirs because their names had been spelt wrong. After changing we were directed towards a marshalling area where Film Unit Catering Kenya (FUCK) were doling out breakfast to everyone. I was chuffed to spot Geoff Crowther, the legendary author of Lonely Planet's first *Africa on a Shoestring* guide tucking into a plate of bacon and eggs. I couldn't tell from his hair what role he had been cast in – he was balding – but by the look of his clothes, he was a German prisoner too.

After breakfast we were led to the set, a faithful reproduction of a World War II internment camp with high barbed-wire fences, long canvas tents and watchtowers. The perimeter was dotted with soldiers, black and white, their rifles trained on the 120 prisoners. It had a kind of 'Hogan's Heroes' meets *Out of Africa* vibe happening that screamed international box office hit to me.

A big 35-millimetre camera was set on a platform in the middle of the set and it was from here that the director, Caroline Link, gave us our instructions using a megaphone. She was a small woman with an easygoing demeanour, and I was relieved when she assured us that she believed a quick shoot was a good shoot.

The first scene involved greeting our wives and children when they came to visit us in the camp. They were arriving on the back of trucks and our job was to rush up to the trucks, scramble up the sides and cry out the names of our wives and children. When we found them an emotional reunion of hugs and kisses was to ensue. Easy enough, you'd think. But there was a problem. We hadn't been allotted wives and/or children.

This seemed to disturb my new Aussie mate, Dave, immensely. As the trucks revved outside the gate and we waited for the director to yell '*Action!*', he became more and more agitated.

'What if there aren't enough wives?' he said, shifting his weight from one foot to the other. 'We're going to look like a right pair of fuckin' poofs!'

Fortunately two girls on the back of the nearest truck, facing a similar dilemma themselves, had already picked us out as their husbands. As we milled around the back of the nearest truck, they climbed down with as much dignity as they could muster before rushing over and throwing their arms around us.

Mid embrace, Dave looked over to me with a sheepish smile on his face. 'Shit, we've done all right for ourselves!' he grinned.

We certainly had.

When the director called '*Cut!*' we introduced ourselves to our 'wives' properly. My wife was Mags, an Irish girl with long red hair and freckles. Dave's missus was an English girl called Sarah, who had her hair pulled back in a hair net. Both had boyfriends, of course, and both boyfriends were on the set as soldiers. But they were fun, intelligent girls and on each take we would try to make our reunions all the more extravagant and emotional.

The scene had to be done five times before the director was happy with it. I was happy there wasn't any more – Dave had got a little too passionate with Sarah on the last take and I thought her boyfriend was going to come over and club him with the butt of his rifle.

The other scenes shot that day largely involved us wandering around the camp arm in arm with our wives. Despite Ms Link's best efforts to stick to her 'fast-shoot-good-shoot' mantra it soon got boring so Dave and I decided to liven things up by trying to get in as many shots as possible. We'd watch where the camera was being set up, listen as the director gave the main actors directions, and then figure out the best way to walk across the line of the camera. And when we did, we would point to something in an exaggerated gesture, so that when friends and family watched the DVD they could easily pick us out. I half expected the director to yell 'Cut!' and scold us angrily in German, but she never did.

As the day progressed Dave and I became more and more audacious with our 'acting'. One scene involved the main character talking to his wife at a table laid out with glasses of blackcurrant juice. The extras were supposed to mill around in the background, with one or two walking up to the table to get a drink. When Dave wandered up to the table to get drinks for the four of us, he made sure he got as close to the actors as possible, and by the third take he had worked up enough courage to linger a little and take a sip. By the fourth take he was taking a sip and then screwing up his nose in disgust. By the fifth he was coughing and spluttering. The director never said a word, but the rest of us had to stop ourselves from laughing.

I was determined not to be outdone by Dave. I organised an elaborate mock execution during a particularly poignant scene where the wife of the main character told him that she was in love with another man. The back perimeter fence of the camp would be just in shot, so I got Dave to blindfold me and give me a cigarette while three of the guards pretended to shoot me. The scene was shot six times and the director didn't say a thing once.

On the bus back to town Dave and I agreed that it was the most fun we'd had in a long time.

There was no filming the next day – the director was shooting scenes that didn't require extras – so I used the opportunity to try and sort out my visa for Sudan. I rang the embassy in Lusaka to see how my application was going and was disturbed that Rose was surprised I was ringing from Kenya.

'I shouldn't be telling you this,' she whispered conspira-torially. 'But the consul is ignoring your application. He has not even sent it to Khartoum.'

I was stunned. I had spent over $40 dollars calling the Sudan embassy in Lusaka and the guy was just pulling my chain. I felt like asking Rose to put me through to him so I could abuse him, but at close to $5 a minute that would have been an indulgence. Instead I thanked her for all the help she had given me and hung up.

I walked out of the telephone centre feeling betrayed. The consul had assured me that there was a 90 per cent chance I'd get a visa. Now there was only Ethiopia between Sudan and me and I was back to square one.

The news didn't get any better when I visited the Sudanese embassy in Nairobi. They refused to give me a visa point blank. 'We don't issue them here,' snapped the receptionist, a sharp-featured Indian woman. 'Too many Westerners going in and stirring up trouble in the south.'

I guess I should have been happy that the Sudanese embassy in Nairobi was at least being up front and honest. They didn't ask me to fill out forms to send off to Khartoum. They didn't even tell me to try somewhere else. They just said no.

To be honest, I was more alarmed at the reasons the receptionist gave than the fact they wouldn't give me a visa. In my heart I still held onto the faint hope I would get a Sudanese visa in Ethiopia, that somehow the consul there would take pity on me and say, 'Oh all right, you big lug!' But if there was a decision to stop people going in for security reasons I'd be pushing shit up hill. The latest issue of *Time* magazine concerned me too. It had a cover story about fundamentalist

Christians smuggling guns and Bibles into the south of Sudan. What if this trouble meant that I wouldn't be able to get into Sudan, full stop?

My mood lightened when I got back to the Iqbal and found a note tacked onto my door from Canadian Paul. He'd finally left Malawi and was waiting for me with a cold Tusker lager at the Modern Day and Night Green Bar.

The Green Bar, as it is affectionately known, is a legendary place on Latema Road. It's neither modern nor green, but it is open day and night. In fact it's open 24 hours a day, 365 days a year and until recently didn't even have a front door. It's also home to the rougher element of Nairobi and in this part of town that was pretty rough.

It wasn't the first time I had been to the Green Bar. On my first trip to Nairobi I spent an evening there listening to a Kenyan guy who insisted on giving me tips on how to please the ladies. 'You do not do it straight away,' he advised. 'First you must make them hiss. Hiss like a snake.'

I nodded my head and hoped that he would pass out before he got any more explicit.

He didn't. He was intent on passing his knowledge on. 'I should know,' he said. 'I have seen a woman with the lights on!'

I told him I was going to the toilet and sneaked out the door while he wasn't looking.

Paul was holding court with a bunch of drunken bar girls and when he saw me come through the door he waved me over with a big Canadian 'Yo!'. In the same instant he beckoned for the barmaid to bring me a beer. She was a scary-looking woman who opened beer bottles with her teeth.

'Peter!' Paul said in his booming voice. 'Meet my new friends!'

His new friends were all young women who sat sipping soft drink or chewing miraa, a mildly narcotic plant popular in these parts.

'This is Betty,' he said, introducing a pretty, but clearly out-of-it-girl. 'She's from Mombassa.'

Judging by the spangly little lycra number Betty wore she was a working girl. If I had to put money on it, I'd say they all were. But having travelled with Paul on and off throughout Africa, I knew that his interest in them had nothing to do with their chosen profession. Like all good real estate agents, he was a people person. He just liked people and he liked talking to them about their lives. He didn't judge these girls or treat them any differently from the other people he'd met in his travels. That was one of the things I liked about him.

Every now and then a drunken guy would stagger over and demand a cigarette or a beer from us. They were like the guys I had met in Khayelitsha and Soweto – aggressive, bitter and disillusioned. They didn't have money, they didn't have a job, they had no sense of worth. And they were angry – really angry – that the girls had a way of earning money.

A cute little girl with a tight butt and perky little breasts tottered into the Green Bar and plonked herself down. She was clearly under the weather, from what I wasn't sure, and she was new to Nairobi. She had just come from the Friends Corner Bar across the road.

'They should call it Enemy Corner,' she slurred before throwing up beside the table. She wiped her mouth daintily, telling Paul and I that she had only been in town for six weeks and that she sent the money she earned back to her mum to help support her younger brother and sister.

The girls realised that neither Paul nor I was interested in availing ourselves of their services and drifted off periodically to other darker, danker corners of the bar looking for customers. The guys here snarled at them and treated them like shit, taking them off to back rooms for what I imagined would be angry, impotent exchanges. Soon only Betty was left on our table and she was asleep.

I mentioned the movie to Paul and told him that he should try to get work as an extra too. With his shiny bald head and white moustache he'd make a great British colonel.

'I think I will,' he said. 'But first I want another beer.'

❖   ❖   ❖

At the Kenya National Theatre the next morning, the woman in charge of ushering the extras onto the Coaster bus told Paul that she didn't think that they needed any more extras, but that she would take him out just in case. 'If they don't want you, you'll have to make your own way back,' she said.

The set that day was an old building at the back of Westlands belonging to the Ministry of Agriculture. A large hall had been turned into a cinema where the prisoners would watch a newsreel announcing the end of the war. I went off to get changed. Paul was taken to casting. The next time I saw him he was in full colonel regalia. As I'd suspected, the casting people had loved him.

The cinema was tiny and stuffy and as we filed in the director encouraged anyone who smoked to light up a cigarette. Beer was handed out as well, in brown glass bottles with old East Africa beer labels.

'And they're paying us as well?' smiled Paul, cradling the beer.

The director, Caroline Link, wandered through the extras and shuffled us around to suit her vision of what the cinema should look like. She walked straight past Dave, but stopped and told me and a few other prisoners to remove our shirts and sit in just our white singlets. Cool! A white singlet would be easier to spot when the movie came out.

Just as I was congratulating myself on my bit of luck, she saw Paul and stopped dead in her tracks. 'You must sit nearer to the camera,' she said. 'You must be seen!'

Paul raised his eyebrows and smiled. First day on the set and the bastard had already upstaged us.

That last scene was fairly chaotic. We had been instructed to shout at the Germans when they came on screen and with the beer flowing people began to get a bit silly. There was lots of 'For you ze var ist over!'. When Caroline Link finally called '*Cut*!' everyone was pretty legless. She went to the front of the theatre and thanked us all for our participation. The movie would be out in Germany in December, she said, and the following Easter in the UK. I fancifully imagined the credits: '. . . and introducing Peter Moore as Prisoner 86.'

Of course, even with all the hard work I had put into getting my face in front of the camera, I realised I could still end up on the cutting room floor. I asked Paul to take a photo of me with the director as proof just in case.

Eventually I joined the queue outside to collect my 'wages' from the paymaster. Three days of fun, all meals provided and 7500 shillings to boot.

'I wish I'd come earlier,' said Paul. Dave and I didn't. He would have stolen the whole show.

The ride home took longer than normal. There had been an accident on a roundabout near Westlands between a petrol tanker and a taxi. The tanker had blocked the roundabout entirely and traffic was forced to drive over the middle of it to get through. It was chaotic and there was no sign of any police. Three hundred metres down the hill we passed a group of policemen pulling over matatus and extracting bribes to use as beer money. Paul was shocked, but I just shrugged. That's just Nairobi.

The next day I changed my shillings into US dollars and checked out of Hotel California Nairobi. Spookily I'd been there for ten days, just like my first visit.

Chapter 15

NORTHERN KENYA

Kujikwaa si kuanguka, bali ni kwenda mbele.

To stumble is not to fall down, but it is to go forward.

If you ever find yourself in Nairobi heading north towards Nanyuki and you are given the choice between travelling in a Peugeot 504 and anything else, may I suggest taking the anything else option? I made the mistake of putting my life into the hands of a Peugeot 504 'taxi' driver and I have never been quite the same since.

I had planned to catch a bus directly to Isiola, a town in northern Kenya with road connections to Ethiopia. Indeed, I wasted a good deal of a morning wandering around the backstreets of the Third World trying to find it. But the bus to Isiola had long stopped running and the journey now had to be made in two legs – from Nairobi to Nanyuki and then Nanyuki to Isiola.

Still, I didn't *have* to catch a Peugeot 504. When I finally tracked down the muddy street corner where the transport to Nanyuki congregated I was presented with two options – a minivan that still had to find seven passengers before it would leave and a white Peugeot 504 that only needed one and promised to be much faster anyway. As it is never a good idea for a backpacker to stand still in the one spot in Nairobi with all his possessions for too long, I chose the Peugeot.

The journey through the highlands north of Nairobi is one of the prettiest you can make in Kenya. It's a journey that takes you through cool, green hills dotted with tea plantations and backstopped by a snow-capped Mount Kenya. Kenyans in cheap, ill-fitting suits lounge beside the road, sometimes alone, sometimes in groups, bracing themselves against the cold. Their children play with toy cars fashioned from wire beside them. Unfortunately I was too busy 'driving' to enjoy it fully.

You know how, when someone drives really badly, you end up driving along with them? Well, that was what I was doing. I sat beside the driver operating an imaginary set of pedals, applying the brakes when I thought they should be applied rather than the ten minutes later that he did. I intensely scanned the road ahead with panic as he overtook on blind curves, waiting, for what little good it would do, to react in an instant to the slow, overloaded truck that inevitably lumbered around the corner in the opposite direction. It was exhausting work.

Amazingly, none of the other eight passengers seemed particularly perturbed by the driver's proclivity for weaving across unbroken lines at high speed. They sat watching the world whiz by with expressionless faces, not even flinching when lorries passed, their horns blaring, spraying dirt from the verge they were forced upon by our driver's reckless antics. They didn't even blink.

A sweet girl called Nancy sat behind and tapped me on the shoulder to announce each town we came too. She was nicely dressed in crisp, clean clothes but had a slight whiff of body odour. 'We are now entering Thika,' she said. And later, 'That is the road to Embu.' I raised my eyebrows slightly and smiled weakly with each announcement and she seemed happy enough with that. When she declared that we were finally entering Nanyuki, she asked where I was staying and was shocked when I told her that I was just passing through.

'When will you be back?' she asked, alarmed. She seemed genuinely disappointed when I said, 'Never!'

Nanyuki is a small agricultural town right on the equator. It celebrates its association with this bit of geographic trivia by naming every business in town after it. There is the Equator Pharmacy, the Equator Hotel, the Equator Video and Music Centre and the Equator Butcher Shop. There was a time when this sort of thing would have interested me. I probably would have stayed a few days to search out any equator moments, conducting experiments to see if water really did go down the plughole in different directions on the different sides. But I wanted to reach Isiola that night and there was a minivan leaving for the town pretty much immediately.

Kenya is different when you get north of Nanyuki. The farms with rolling green fields and the patchworked slopes of Mount Kenya recede and are replaced by a dry savanna of acacia trees and yellow grass. Instead of being neat and cool, it becomes scruffy and hot, the kind of sweaty heat that has you sliding across vinyl bench seats and into the lap of Peugeot drivers whenever they take a corner hard. And there are a hell of a lot more police roadblocks.

There were checkpoints before and after every town. Northern Kenya is a notorious stomping ground for the shifta, Somali bandits that roam the countryside, helping themselves to money, livestock and the occasional International Aid Agency Landcruiser. Even so, I felt it was a little optimistic of the police to pull over a minivan on the off-chance that a Somali bandit with an AK-47 slung over his shoulder might be on board. As it turned out, they were just after a bit of beer money and the quickest way to get hold of that was to pull over a minivan, check it for defects and then 'fine' the driver for carrying too many passengers. It's part of the reason the Tusker Brewing Company is one of the most successful businesses in Kenya.

Just after the turnoff to Meru, however, it started getting ridiculous. Upset that his colleagues were getting all of the action, a rogue policeman had set up a roadblock 500 metres before the 'official' one. It was his way of making sure that he got first bite of the cherry, and the police at the latter roadblock were not impressed that our driver begged off poor, claiming he'd given the last of his money to their colleague. I worried that we might get caught up in some sort of inter-constabulary turf war but it was a last hurrah. From there the towns, and the roadblocks, became less regular, and the landscape became scruffier and more godforsaken. At its most godforsaken it became Isiola.

The bus station in Isiola is on the outskirts of town, a brisk 2-kilometre walk from the town centre. Actually the term 'town centre' is probably overselling Isiola. It is merely a dusty road lined by low-level buildings that house shops selling supplies for the surrounding districts. My guidebook said that there was a bus from Isiola to the Ethiopian border, but a quick conference with the assorted drunks and layabouts outside the town's general store ascertained that the bus had stopped running years before.

Just as I was about to ask them if there were any trucks heading north a young guy bounded up and breathlessly introduced himself as Ali. He had spotted me from the other side of the road and was determined that my white arse, and any commissions that it might bring, was his. 'Do not trust these men!' he said, catching his breath. 'They are chokric' (thieves).

I told him I didn't trust anyone, not even him.

He was shocked. 'But I am a Muslim man!' he protested.

Like that mattered when there was a commission to be made. Still, he spoke English well and seemed enthusiastic, so I told him I wanted to go to the Ethiopian border.

'The buses stopped years ago,' he said. 'No, you must catch a lorry. I will help you find one. A fast modern one!'

I didn't see how the age of the truck would make much difference. All vehicles travelled in convoys north of Isiola – the shifta bandits were particularly active there – so surely a truck could travel only as fast as the slowest vehicle in the convoy. My logic clearly baffled Ali because he looked at me as if I was quite mad.

I checked into the Jamhuri Guest House. A sign saying 'No alcohol or prostitutes allowed' hung over the entrance, reminding me of the strong Muslim influence in Isiola. Then I went back on the streets with Ali to find a truck.

'Do you like Craig David?' he asked as we walked along the dusty street, dodging piles of rubbish.

I said he was all right and Ali gave me the same look he gave me when I espoused my convoy–speed theory. 'His songs are so wonderful!' he exclaimed, his eyes lighting up. 'I cannot even decide on my favourite song. Sometimes I like "Walk Away" best. Other times it is "Seven Days".'

It always amazes me how quickly music travels these days. Here I was in a fly-blown town in northern Kenya discussing the latest in R'n'B soul. It wouldn't have surprised me to see the local barber offering a Craig David 'Seven Days' haircut.

Ali's other passion was miraa (also known as khat), the leafy twigs and shoots of a plant that the locals chew as a stimulant and appetite suppressant. 'The red tips are the best,' he said. 'They cost 300 shillings for a kilo. The best is grown on the hills near Meru.'

It seemed everyone in Isiola chewed miraa. Most were originally from Somalia and were at least nominal Muslims, so miraa was an acceptable stimulant in a culture where alcohol is not allowed (hence miraa's growing popularity not just in the Horn of Africa but in Arabic countries to the north and west). Most started chewing around noon, and by mid-afternoon they were alert and wired. By early evening, however, the buzz had gone and the chewers crashed, sitting droopy-eyed, still chewing out of habit, their teeth and gums blackened by the stuff.

Ali believed miraa should be chewed more, and instead of gum. 'If you swallow gum you will get ulcers,' he pointed out. 'With miraa there are no side effects.' Apart from rotted teeth, a numbed mind and the demeanour of a zombie, of course.

Like all narcotics, there was a ritual to chewing miraa, and a plethora of theories on how to get the best high and make it last longer. Ali's theory was to chew it drinking a Pepsi. Unfortunately, a bottle of Pepsi was more expensive than the miraa. 'I always punch a tiny hole in the lid,' he explained. 'I can't drink it so fast and it lasts two days!'

We reached a corner near the petrol station and Ali made a few cursory inquiries among people chewing miraa there. The general consensus was that there were no trucks heading north. 'You will have to wait a few days,' Ali said.

A goat wandered across the road and stripped what few leaves were left on a stunted tree beside us. In a town like Isiola, a few days was an alarming prospect. I bought Ali a Coke, unopened, as a token of thanks for his help and returned to my hotel room.

The manager was sprawled out on a mattress in the courtyard, seemingly asleep, but stopped me as I passed. 'A truck driver has just checked into room 10,' he said. 'I think he is heading north.'

I knocked on the door and the driver answered it, dressed only in a pair of yellowing jocks. He was just going as far as Marsabit, a town about halfway to the border, but said I'd be able to get another truck heading to the border at Moyale from there.

'The truck is leaving at 5 am tomorrow,' he said. 'Be at the petrol station by four.'

By 6 pm, the communal miraa crash had hit and Isiola was somnolent. I ate a stringy piece of chicken in an empty restaurant and decided to go to bed early. At 10 pm I was woken by a knock at my door. It was Ali. A friend who he didn't introduce stood beside him, chewing and nodding his head like one of those novelty dogs people put on their dashboards.

I figured Ali had heard about the truck and was here to tell me about it. 'Don't worry,' I said, rubbing the sleep out of my eyes. 'I know about the truck. The driver is staying in that room over there.'

'I have not come about trucks,' he said, shifting nervously from foot to foot, his stoned eyes vacant. 'I want to discuss miraa.'

I told him there was nothing to talk about. Thanks to him I now knew the red tips from Meru were the best.

'No, not that kind of discussion,' he slurred. 'I want you to buy me some.'

I'd been waiting for this. One of the pitfalls of accepting help when you're travelling, especially in poorer countries, is that often payment is expected. Even if – no, especially – if they've been no help at all. I told Ali that he didn't help me find a truck, and besides, I'd already bought him a soda.

'Not as payment for helping,' he said. 'As a friend.'

I told him he wasn't my friend. Before he could protest I said that real friends don't wake up other friends in the middle of the night for money for drugs. (Even as I said it I thought of at least half a dozen occasions when that has happened to me, but that wasn't the point.)

Ali shifted uncomfortably, not sure what to say. His friend stood there nodding like a madman, seemingly agreeing with me. I closed the door and heard them shuffle off a few minutes later.

❖   ❖   ❖

The truck heading north was a beer truck. And it was the only vehicle heading north that day. We weren't going in a convoy. We'd just have a few soldiers accompany us. I clambered up. I liked starting journeys before dawn. It reminded me of my childhood, when my dad would bundle us into the back of the Valiant.

On the outskirts of town we stopped at a military checkpoint and picked up our two armed guards for the journey. They sat on top, up front, right above the driver's cabin. Their guns were cocked and ready and silhouetted against the full moon. The rest of us sat huddled on top of the beer crates, using whatever baggage or jackets we had to prevent the pointy ends of the Tusker beer bottles from sticking up our arses. There was a ripple of excitement when we stopped at a shop a little further along and half a dozen foam mattresses were tossed on top.

We were greeted by a spectacular sunrise, the blood-red sun bursting over a vast plain dotted with acacia trees. Little plastic bags of miraa were produced and soon everyone was chewing, even the soldiers. Another passenger fished out a tape player and soon we had a soundtrack, a squally Arabic-sounding whine that was at first offensive but eventually, when a Tusker bottle went up my arse, strangely matched my mood.

We got our first flat tyre at Sere Olivi, and while we waited for the offsider to repair it, the driver came up and offered me a cup of tea from his thermos. 'I heard those men disturb you last night,' he said.

'All part of being a mzungu,' I replied.

He nodded sympathetically before wandering over to give the offsider instructions.

We were now in a wild barren area that was home to the Rendille tribe. They were tribesmen of the African coffee table book variety who dressed in loincloths and brightly coloured beads and wore their hair slicked back and coloured red. We passed girls with elaborate bead necklaces and stretched earlobes herding goats, and men who walked along the road in groups. More often than not, the men were miles from any sign of civilisation and the passengers yelled out for them to jump as we passed. The Rendille men obliged, popping into the air with a smile. The passengers thought it was a great laugh but it struck me as a little patronising and malicious. I told them they shouldn't make fun of other people's customs.

'They love to jump,' said the boy with the tape player. 'It brings them joy.'

The Rendille seemed to have a lot in common with the Masai – they had a penchant for coloured beads and they led a largely pastoralist existence. But any attempt on my part to find out more about their culture when we stopped to deliver beer was met with a wall of silence. They were aloof – or shy, I wasn't sure – and seemed content to keep their distance from civilisation, only coming to town to buy supplies. Getting any useful information from the other passengers was just as fruitless. They regarded the Rendille as little more than a weird group of people who would bounce at their bidding.

It was a long, slow and hot journey to Marsabit. Most people sat on the battens that the canvas cover was thrown over, pulling the cover back just enough for them to dangle their legs below. At first I sat with them, but when I began to get sunburnt I moved below, sitting on the dwindling supplies of beer and hiding from the burning sun in their shadows.

Everyone was chewing, chewing, chewing, reaching into their pockets, desperately looking for more miraa. I got bored and started looking at people's shoes and trying to put faces to them. Mr Biro – he'd drawn patterns on his shoes with a pen – was the boy with the tape player. Mr Knock-off Reebok was the old guy with grey hair. Mrs Knock-off Nike was the large lady who kept snuffling cake. Mr No Shoe Laces, disturbingly, was one of the soldiers guarding us.

It struck me that catching a beer truck had not been the fortuitous break I had first thought it was. The truck stopped to make a delivery at every town between Isiola and Marsabit. And between those towns the driver drove at mind-bendingly slow speeds in an attempt to protect his precious cargo.

Then there was the matter of the cargo. Beer. Quite the bandit magnet, I would have thought. I had already spotted a number of what I regarded as suspicious circumstances. A car abandoned in the middle of the road, a jack under it and the rear wheel missing. Three guys milling beside the road, miles from even the slightest sign of civilisation. A guy sitting on a camel, watching the truck pass. And rocks placed in the middle of the road. To me any of these could have turned into hostile ambush situations but not one of them piqued the interest of our guards. They sat chewing miraa, oblivious to the potential for banditry.

I think the folk of Marsabit were more aware of the risks we had faced to get there. When the truck crawled into town just as night fell, townsfolk came out of their houses and cheered our arrival. Kids ran beside the truck laughing and whooping. At first I took the celebrations to mean that the safe arrival of the beer truck was something of a rare event. Then I noticed the men of the town following us, hoping to pick up work helping to unload, paid in beer of course. The men were happy to see the beer but the women of Marsabit weren't. They stood in doorways, looking fearful about the torment a drunken husband would bring.

The driver dropped me off at JJs, the fanciest hotel in town. I got a room with a framed picture of Jean-Claude Van Damme on the wall. There was a quote on the picture – 'A man who is incapable of making a mistake is incapable of anything' – and I wondered if it was a line from one of his movies or just someone at the printer with a sense of humour.

The manager of the hotel was an Indian and he didn't like my chances of finding transport to the Ethiopian border at Moyale. 'It has been raining recently, so the road is in bad condition,' he said. 'Many trucks cannot make the journey.'

I was astounded. Since Nanyuki the countryside had been bone dry. I found it hard to believe that conditions would change so dramatically over the next 250 kilometres.

The manager agreed with me, the rainy season *had* already passed. But the road, churned up during the rainy season, had not been graded since and had dried into an impassable mess. 'There is a truck trapped 30 kilometres north from here,' he said. 'It got stuck in the mud and by the time help came it had dried. Now they must wait for the rains to come again.'

I asked the manager why the buses had stopped running and he said it was because there wasn't any money to be made. 'With trucks a passenger is an added bonus,' he said. 'The truck is going to Moyale anyway. A passenger is just beer money.' The manager suggested that I go down to the cheap hotels and bars where the truck drivers hung out when they were in town.

All the trucks were dark and abandoned, and the drivers at various stages of inebriation in the bars. Most had passed out, and those that hadn't simply stared straight ahead, periodically bringing a glass to their lips.

A patron at one of the bars overheard my inquiries and beckoned me over with a drunken flourish. He was going to Moyale too and pointed to a truck parked just outside the door. 'It is leaving at 5 am tomorrow,' he slurred. 'But you better be early. It is the first truck to Moyale in a week so there are many passengers.'

I very nearly asked him which piece of human flotsam was the driver but decided that some things are better not known. Instead I went back to my room, and under the watchful – and unexpectedly wise – eyes of Jean-Claude, set my alarm for four.

❖   ❖   ❖

Marsabit was covered in a thick fog the next morning. I left the hotel, without waking the security guard, and stumbled to the truck. There was already quite a crowd gathered. Many had slept beside the truck, and now they were standing and shuffling, waiting for the driver to wake up. He was passed out, sprawled across the steering wheel in the cabin of his truck. He woke with a start just before five to find a crowd staring in at him expectantly. He took his hand off his groin like it had just given him an electric shock.

His truck was not ideally suited to taking passengers. It was a light-weight Mitsubishi Canter packed solid – with what I never found out – a canvas tightly pulled over the top. Space for passengers was limited and anyone getting a space would have to sit on top, their feet under the rope for grip. It was up to the driver to decide who got one of the few spaces and he cast his eye over the assembled crowd as if he were apprising livestock at an auction.

Price was not mentioned during the process. Getting chosen was the priority and it was quite nerve-wracking. I stood there, waiting to be chosen, knowing that if I wasn't I'd have to spend a week waiting for the next truck. With only two spaces left the driver gave me the nod and I clambered up onto the top with a whoop. My joy was tempered a little when a woman broke into tears at having missed out.

The trip to Moyale was as long and slow as the trip from Isiola to Marsabit the day before. There was nowhere to hide from the burning sun so I sat, unprotected, turning an alarming shade of red. The scenery was more Arabic now, and we passed long lines of camels sauntering west towards Lake Turkana, the only place within hundreds of kilometres with enough water to sustain life. The truck staggered like a drunk along the road, which was in as bad a condition as the manager of JJs had said it was. With each lurch a passenger was nearly tossed from the roof.

We came upon the truck trapped in the mud, also just as the manager at JJs had said. It was as if the truck had mistakenly driven into a pit of brown cement that had then immediately set. We stopped here to change a tyre so I wandered over and took some photos of the stuck truck. The other passengers got rather agitated at me and I wondered why. Were they worried that the word would get out: 'The main arterial road between Kenya and Ethiopia is a piece of shit'? Or worse, someone now had incontrovertible evidence? I think most people in the world already take it as a given that any road between these two countries would be in rather bad shape. My photos were hardly going to be front page news.

I don't know if it was a socio-economic thing – this truck ride had cost slightly more than the one the day before – but my fellow passengers didn't chew much miraa. They chewed on twigs instead, using the masticated ends to clean their teeth. They poked the sticks around their mouths with the intensity of an Osmond flossing and whenever we came to villages they bought new twigs from kids with straight, shiny white teeth, walking adverts for their own products.

Noticing my interest, one of the passengers bought me a twig and showed me how to prepare it. He stripped about a centimetre of bark off and then motioned for me to chew the revealed stem until it became fibrous. Then he indicated for me to rub it over my teeth in the manner of a toothbrush and then, when the exposed stem wore out, got me to chew it off and start the process all over again. My guidebook said there was a naturally occurring anti-decay agent in the twigs, but I think they need to work on some minty flavours. My twig tasted muddy and, well, twiggy, and I ended up with a mouth full of fibrous pulp.

By two we had reached Moyale. It is a large town, set in the hills, a scattering of tin-roofed buildings. An administrative centre with a largish hospital and a collection of government buildings, Moyale is quite the sophisticated urban centre compared to what we had passed through to get there. The roads are sealed and there is even an airport, a strip cut out of a field. A small twin-engine plane was sitting on the runway, readying for takeoff.

Not for the first time I questioned the sanity of my choices of transport options. It had taken me three days of very hard travelling to get to Moyale from Nairobi, yet by air, the Kenyan capital was less than an hour away. It was a question I found myself asking again as we drove through the centre of town and I was slapped across the face by a power line stretched across the road that the truck drove under.

I think I must have been in denial because I decided that it was civilisation that was dangerous.

Chapter 16

SOUTHERN ETHIOPIA

Kufa kikondoo, ndiko kufa kiungwana.

To die like a sheep (uncomplainingly) is to die
like a gentleman.

I walked down the hill towards the Ethiopian border with a
spring in my step. It already felt more exotic, even on the
Kenyan side of Moyale. The shops lining the road were covered
in the squiggly script of Amharic, a Semitic language that
evolved from the liturgical language of the Ethiopian Orthodox
Church and the official language of the country. They had set
their clocks to Ethiopian time, a bizarre 12-hour system that
starts just after daybreak (6 am to everyone else) and ends at
dusk (6 pm). So while it was 2.30 pm in the afternoon by world
clock standards, to Ethiopians it was 8.30. I was happy to be
somewhere that was so skewwhiff about something as globally
fundamental as time.

The Ethiopians, however, didn't seem as pleased to see me. While the local folk were allowed to pass after getting a lazy nod from the guard sitting beside the border with an assault rifle resting on his lap, I was stopped and taken inside a building for special treatment. My visa was checked and double-checked by a variety of people and I was given three different forms to fill in. On completing the forms my bag was searched thoroughly and an explanation for each item demanded. Then I had to wait for 40 minutes to be 'interviewed' personally by the border chief.

Frankly, I had been expecting better treatment. Ethiopia's legendary long-distance runner, Haile Gebreselassie, had just won gold at the Sydney Olympics, beating his arch rivals, the Kenyans, in spectacular fashion right on the finishing line. It was a famous victory, and the people of Sydney had taken Gebreselassie to their hearts, treating him as a hero for the rest of his time in the city. I had hoped that generosity and kindness had been noted in Ethiopia and made a point of mentioning that I was from Sydney when I was ushered in to meet the man in charge of the border.

'Your country has rejected my application to emigrate,' he said flatly. 'My only hope now is New Zealand.'

Hmmm. Bad call. I'd be unhappy with the New Zealand option as well. Worse, I had disturbed him from filling in the form. The New Zealand immigration application was on his desk and he was still deciding whether to claim refugee status or not.

'What are your intentions in Ethiopia?' he asked brusquely. I told him that I was a tourist and he asked me if I had any maps. I showed him my Lonely Planet guidebook and after scouring its maps he seemed satisfied that they were suitably inaccurate and that I wouldn't be using them to open a southern front on behalf of Eritrea.

Then we sat in silence for ten minutes, the only sound the ticking of the clock on the wall, before he stamped my passport and tossed it at me. 'You may go,' he said gruffly.

It was one of the most intense border crossings I have ever made.

Unfortunately, the border official's attitude reflected that of everyone else in Moyale. When I walked up the main street of the Ethiopian side of the town in search of a cheap hotel, young children and adults alike pointed at me and yelled in a rapid-fire staccato, 'You! You! You!'

I was used to being called out to. In Indonesia you can't walk 5 metres without someone yelling, 'Hello Mister!' And throughout East Africa I'd heard 'Mzungu!' more times than I care to remember. But on getting my attention, people calling out to me in those places would smile broadly and wave. Here, when I turned to meet the calls, I was greeted with angry, hostile stares.

Aggression, it seemed, was part and parcel of everyday Ethiopian life. When I clambered onto the bus to Addis Ababa at 4.30 the next morning I walked into a brawl between passengers not just for seats, but for the space above, below and between them. Punches were thrown, head butts exchanged and bodies pushed heavily against the seats – and that was just between the women. I found a seat and meekly sat in it, expecting at any moment to be taken in a headlock and dragged roughly into the aisle.

My hopes that the tarmac would lead to a fast and easy trip

to the capital were dashed early on too. The route from Moyale to the capital was notoriously popular with smugglers and was lined with makeshift roadblocks, manned by police keen to extract bribes from the passengers who had stowed enough plastic bowls, kitchen utensils and colanders to fulfil Tupperware's orders for a year. One woman was so incensed at the extravagance of her 'fine' that she struck one of the policemen with a plastic ladle. She was dragged off the bus and forced to sit outside the police post until the bus drove off, leaving her and her three sacks of contraband behind.

I wasn't running plastic kitchen utensils into the country – I hadn't realised it was such a lucrative racket – but the police at these checkpoints still considered it their patriotic duty to drag me off the bus and interrogate me. This consisted of repeatedly asking me if I was with the CIA, hoping that by the fifth time they asked the exact same question I would break down and confess. Instead I explained that Australia was a land of cuddly animals with no need of CIA-type shenanigans.

It was not a wise line of reasoning. The police pointed to the picture of the kangaroo on the Australian coat of arms on my passport and said 'Skippy!' as if it was proof that I was involved in some sort of international conspiracy. 'Skippy', the aged Australian TV show, was still popular in Ethiopia and these guys figured a kangaroo that could save a small boy from down a ravine could just as easily be pressed into service for a little espionage and intrigue. Luckily, I didn't have a kangaroo in tow, so more often than not I was allowed back onto the bus before all the other bribes had been extracted.

At first we passed through scenery that was very reminiscent of Kenya, a dry savanna of flat-topped acacia trees and parched yellow grass. But soon the bus climbed into mountains where there were fir trees among the eucalypts and round huts with thatched roofs, topped by ornate metal crosses. The huts were surrounded by small tilled fields and smoke from cooking fires seeped through the roofs. The crops were mostly maize and only enough to support the farmers' families, but among them were plots of coffee and miraa, the two main cash crops of Ethiopia. Men lazily herded cattle along the road, while women in bright kangas struggled along with piles of firewood or buckets of water on their heads. As elsewhere in Africa, it was the women doing all the hard work. These were not the famous Omotic or Nilotic tribes – they were further inland, avoiding civilisation. These were simple folk who had followed the road south from the crowded north looking for somewhere to scratch out a living.

As midday approached it became hot and stuffy in the bus, so I reached up and slid open the window to let in a breeze. The man sitting behind me immediately reached up and closed it. I opened it again and he closed it just as quickly.

I sat there not sure what to do. I didn't want to make a scene, but it was like an oven in that bus. Sweat was streaming down every passenger's face, including the guy closing the window. We were on tarmac, so it wasn't as if dust would come in, so I reached up and opened the window again. The man behind reached up and closed it, this time a little more aggressively.

A murmur went around the bus and everyone turned to watch what was happening. I reached up and slide the window open again, but before I could move my hand out of the way, my nemesis slammed it shut, catching my finger between the glass and the frame of the window.

I can't tell you how much it hurt. I shook it and sucked on it, as you do, and when I looked at it to assess the damage there was a blood blister under the nail of my index finger. I swung around to show it to the guy, pleased that in doing so I could flip him at the same time. He shaped up, thinking I was going to hit him. I wasn't, I just wanted him to see what he had done. But he wasn't going to back down.

A guy sitting across the aisle intervened. His name was Eyasu and he could speak English. 'In Ethiopia the simple people believe evil comes through the window,' he explained. 'This man thinks he will catch a disease.'

The 'simple' man wasn't sure what Eyasu was saying to me or how I would react to it. He sat alert, his fists raised, ready to fend any sudden move on my part.

'He can leave the fucking window shut,' I said. 'But I want an apology for this!'

I thrust the injured finger right under the guy's nose so he could see what he had done. Eyasu translated quickly and nervously, but the guy still shaped up as if he thought I was going to hit him. Eventually his wife spoke to him and he reluctantly reached out and shook my hand.

'That's all I wanted,' I said, turning back to face the front. Everyone on the bus laughed and I suddenly felt foolish for making such a scene. I enjoyed a minor victory half an hour later, though, when the window slammer's wife reached forward and slid the window open herself. It seemed she'd rather take her chances with the germs than die of heat exhaustion.

My hopes of reaching Addis Ababa that day were dashed when the bus stopped for the night in Dila, still over 300 kilometres short of the capital. Eyasu explained that buses weren't

allowed to travel at night in Ethiopia. It was too dangerous –
not because of bandits but because most buses didn't have
working headlights. Our bus would set off for Addis Ababa
again at 4.30 the next morning. The fact that it would still be
dark at that time was seemingly lost on the driver or whoever
it was who decided we needed to make such a ridiculously
early start.

My stay in Dila was unremarkable except that it was the first
place I experienced injera, Ethiopia's national dish. When the
injera was laid before me in the dining room of the hotel I was
staying in, I thought the woman had mistakenly left the
dishcloth under my meal. As it turned out, the spongy grey
thing under the bowl of diced, spicy lamb *was* the injera. A sour
pancake, it had the unfortunate distinction of tasting as you'd
imagine a dishcloth to taste.

I was the only person who ate that night and figured the
restaurant's reputation for preparing sour, unappealing injera
was well known among Ethiopian bus travellers. The next
morning Eyasu sat next to me on the bus – I think he was
trying to prevent another window war – so I asked him why he
hadn't warned me.

'Injera always tastes like that,' he said. 'Everyone else is
fasting for Easter.'

Easter is a big deal in Ethiopia, because Ethiopia is pre-
dominantly Christian. The Ethiopian Orthodox Church is one
of the oldest Christian sects and Ethiopia was the second
country in the world to pronounce Christianity as the state
religion. It was introduced to the country in the fourth century
by two brothers from Tyre. When it was cut off from the rest of
Christianity by Muslim advances in the seventh century, it

relied on an Ethiopian monastery in Jerusalem for contact with the outside world, and absorbed a lot of Jewish influences along the way. (Many devout Ethiopian Christians, for example, worship on the Saturday Sabbath.) The Church has long enjoyed a dominant role in culture and politics and holidays like Christmas and Easter are seen as ways of reinforcing that.

During the two months before Easter Sunday Ethiopians don't eat meat, eggs or milk products. It is a variation of Lent and I wondered if the fasting was causing the short-temperedness and aggression I'd been witnessing. After all, it was Easter Friday. It had been a long time between omelettes.

'On Sunday there will be a great feast,' Esayu said. 'That's why these people all have animals.'

I hadn't noticed it before, but nearly everyone on the bus *was* carrying a live chicken. Esayu told me that he had a sheep on the roof. I guess I had travelled on so many Third World buses in my time that I took the presence of livestock as a given. I asked Eyasu why they didn't wait until they got to Addis to buy the Sunday roast.

'The prices are inflated in Addis,' he said. 'A chicken that costs 16 birr in Dila costs 30 there. My sheep cost me 50 birr in Moyale. It would cost 200 in Addis.'

Eyasu hadn't been home for two years. By returning home with a sheep for the feast he was hoping to show his family that he had made something of his life.

Just after Lake Asawa, a pretty stretch of water surrounded by low, blue hills, we stopped at a series of villages for no other reason, it seemed, than to allow the passengers to buy more supplies for the Easter Sunday feasts. One village sold eggs. One sold pineapples. Another sold chickens and peanuts. Our arrival in each new village caused a frenzy as every passenger clamoured at windows, thrusting grubby notes at the hawkers outside. That day the stretch of road was the world's longest supermarket aisle.

About 100 kilometres short of Addis we hit a straight stretch of road and the driver decided to make up for the time lost stopping at all the villages for food by pushing the bus to a speed that made the panels shake. The road was now lined by eucalypts but they were nothing but a blur as we flashed by.

I am always heartened by how many eucalypts there are in the world. They are probably our most successful export, a reminder that there are some things from Australia that the world will quite happily take. Unfortunately, there is no direct economic benefit from this success.

I once came up with a plan to rid Australia of its foreign debt by introducing an international eucalypt tax. As I saw it, they were our trees and the world should pay for them. It wouldn't have to be a high tax, there were millions of trees. But I soon dismissed the plan as unworkable. For one thing, it was mainly poor countries that introduced them as a fast-growing source of firewood, and I suspected they would default on their obligations. Also, if my scheme proved successful other countries would follow suit and any income Australia made on eucalypts would be lost on a hefty jacaranda, elm and liquidambar tax. I decided it was best to let sleeping arbours lie.

I was roused from my thoughts by a series of loud clunking noises on the roof. I couldn't be certain, but it sounded an awful lot like hooves. 'Is that your sheep?' I asked Esayu.

He looked alarmed. 'I thought I tied it down thoroughly,' he said. 'I hope it hasn't chewed through the rope.'

The clunking got louder and skittered along the roof. Esayu got up and followed the sounds up the aisle towards the back of the bus, craning to look out the windows and up to the roof. There was one final clunk before the sheep flew off the back of the bus in a manner that suggested that it had jumped. It landed in the path of an oncoming van. The van didn't have time to swerve, but the sheep rolled out of the way like Jackie Chan in a *Rush Hour 2* outtake. Esayu called for the driver to stop, and when he did, he jumped out and ran back down the road clutching both sides of his head.

Remarkably, the sheep was still alive. Even more astounding, it was able to walk back to the bus, Esayu pulling it along by what was left of the rope. He lifted it back onto the top of the bus and then sat beside me, shaken. 'It is fine,' he said unconvincingly. 'There is only a scratch on its leg.'

That year Good Friday fell on 13 April. I told Esayu that Friday the 13th was called Black Friday in my culture and that it was considered bad luck.

'Yes, Black Friday,' he nodded solemnly. 'It *has* been a black Friday.'

My heart went out to Esayu. This feast was so important to him. He wanted everything to be perfect. Still, I couldn't help envisioning him arriving home with a dead sheep, assuring everyone it was still alive, just like a Monty Python sketch.

'It's not dead!' I imagined him saying. 'It's pining.' Except his sheep wouldn't be pining for the fjords, it'd be pining for Moyale. I looked at all the animals on the bus and it struck me that by Sunday they'd all be dead. Maybe the sheep knew its number was up and wanted to go out this way – on its own hooves, not with a knife across its throat.

The bus approached Addis Ababa just as the sun began to set. We would have arrived earlier except for a series of flat tyres that saw us stopped beside the road for an hour or so. Esayu got off at a scruffy crossroads on the outskirts of town, and as he did he arranged with the driver to drop me off near the hotel I had chosen from my guidebook.

'God bless you this Easter, Mr Peter,' he called up to me from the road, his sheep, still alive, standing beside him and looking up too. As we drove away he set off down the dusty lane to his family, the sheep limping slightly on its gammy leg.

'God bless you, Esayu,' I whispered to myself.

I had chosen to stay at the Tropical Hotel because it was central and my guidebook described it as a 'clean cheapie'. What my guidebook didn't say was that it was also Ethiopia's most heavily patronised brothel. It had just gone seven on Easter Friday night when I arrived and the place was jumping. Obviously the Easter fast did not extend to cheap booze and fast women.

The manager led me through the bar to the rooms out the back, a line of cells along the back wall of the compound. He showed me a room, and it seemed okay, so I said that I'd take it.

'Only you can't have this one,' he said. 'It was just used for fucking!'

He opened up the room next door and gave me a key. I wondered why he hadn't just shown me that room first, but quickly decided that I was too buggered to care. I had been travelling non-stop from Nairobi for five days now, getting up at 4 o'clock each morning to catch transport. I was tired and dirty and just wanted to sleep. Even the sound of loud sex in the rooms around me couldn't disturb me from one of the deepest sleeps I'd had in a long time.

Chapter 17

ADDIS ABABA, ETHIOPIA

Usiende kukata tikiti kabla hujapata ruhusa ya kusafiri.

Don't purchase a ticket before you have been
permitted to travel.

I wanted to like Addis Ababa. At 2400 metres above sea level it
is the third highest capital in the world and has that ethereal
atmosphere that all high places have. It is surrounded by hills
covered with eucalypts and the city centre is compact with a
kind of Soviet bloc exoticness about it. That first Saturday
morning the sky was blue and the temperature cool and I was
rather taken by the sight of young boys herding sheep through
the centre of town.

From the moment I left the Tropical Hotel compound,
however, it quickly became apparent that the entire population
of Addis Ababa was convinced that I was there to give them
money. The 'You!You!You!' of Moyale and Dila was amplified

and intensified, but in the capital it was also followed by an aggressively thrust-out hand and a demand for birr.

Now, I know Ethiopia is one of the poorest countries in the world. It has suffered famine and just before I arrived had concluded a debilitating war with Eritrea. But I had travelled through Malawi too, another of Africa's poorest countries, without being hassled for money once. In Addis I couldn't go 2 metres without being hit upon for cash. And it wasn't just the beggars and street kids either (although they were as persistent and aggressive as you'd imagine). Everyone, from all walks of life and every strata of society, was up for a bit of monetary action from a visiting foreigner.

I'm not exaggerating. I went up to the Hilton on that first morning to change money and was accosted by a well-dressed guy coming out of a pastry shop. He was still wiping the crumbs from his face when he spotted me and stuck out his hand, crying, 'Birr!' For a moment I thought that he was just taking the piss, but he was serious, and got quite angry when I refused to give him any money. I began to suspect that after the success of Live Aid, sponging might be a national sport.

While I was at the Hilton I decided to take advantage of a current phone book and concierge that could speak English to find out where the Sudanese embassy was. My plan was to hit the place first thing Tuesday, but the concierge, a tall pretty girl in a neat blue uniform, told me that because Sudan was an Islamic country the embassy opened on Saturdays. She scribbled down the address and I waved down a taxi at the roundabout just down from the hotel. It had a bumper sticker that read 'Repelling aggressors is our culture'. And so is hassling for money, I thought.

I was nervous about going to the Sudanese embassy. Sudan was the next country on my itinerary and if I couldn't get a visa in Addis I was stuffed. The overland route to Eritrea was closed, the border patrolled by UN troops trying to enforce a shaky cease-fire. And the option of going to Djibouti, the tiny French port-country at the top of Ethiopia on the Red Sea, and finding passage on a boat going to Suez was highly unlikely too. If I didn't get a visa in Addis I'd have to fly straight to Cairo.

My visit didn't start well. I was searched at the gate and when I arrived at the visa section, a little hut at the back of the embassy compound, the consul was shouting at a group of Ethiopians who had come to apply for visas. I couldn't tell what they had done wrong, but the consul was clearly upset. He was a small man with wiry grey hair that stuck out like Einstein's and a little grey moustache, and the vein near his temple was bulging. When I entered the room he turned sharply to face me and snappishly demanded what I wanted.

'Fill this form in and come back Tuesday,' he barked.

I wanted to ask him whether that meant I would get a visa or whether I was being merely considered, but his demeanour suggested that it wouldn't be wise. He reminded me of the Soup Nazi from 'Seinfeld' (in my mind I had already christened him the Visa Nazi) so I decided to do what Jerry did to get his lobster biscay – follow instructions precisely and not ask any questions. I did take heart from the fact that the consul made no mention of sending my application to Khartoum for approval.

I walked back to the Tropical with butterflies in the pit of my stomach. This was it, my last chance. If I didn't get my Sudanese visa here I would have to fly to Cairo and my plan to travel overland would be in tatters. I'd miss out on catching the ferry from Wadi Halfa to Aswan on Lake Nasser. I wouldn't get to see the Valley of the Kings near Luxor. And I'd be in Cairo ahead of schedule, my trip over well before I wanted it to be. I guess that's why when two young guys up near Churchill Road invited me to come back to their place for a glass of tej later in the day, I accepted so readily.

Tej is the local honey wine and Addis Ababa is famous for its tej scams – my Lonely Planet guide to the country had devoted a whole column to it. Unsuspecting tourists are invited back to houses, plied with tej (a drink that isn't as pleasant-tasting as it sounds) and then charged an extortionate amount for what they have drunk. It should have been obvious that was what these two guys were up to but such was my state of mind that I really believed Kebede and Abede when they said that we were going to a special Easter celebration nearby hosted by the granddaughter of Haile Selassie.

'There will be dancing and singing,' said Kebede. 'And lots of tej.'

The 'celebration' was in a neat bungalow set behind metal security gates, and consisted of Kebede putting on a tape and three bored-looking girls shuffling clumsily to God-awful music.

'They are tired,' apologised Kebede, correctly guessing that I was not overly impressed. 'It is Easter, so they have danced very much!'

It wasn't until a vase of tej was placed in front of me and the prettiest of the girls snuggled up against me and asked if she could have some that I realised what was going on. I consider it one of my finest moments of haggling that I was able to talk them down from the initial asking price of 100 birr to 5 birr and a heart-felt curse of 'You fucking Aussie motherfucker!'.

◆   ◆   ◆

On Tuesday I went back to the Sudanese embassy. The Visa Nazi told me that I needed a letter of recommendation from the Australian embassy before he would even consider my application. Why he hadn't told me that on my first visit I couldn't imagine. But his response when I told him there wasn't an Australian embassy in Addis Ababa gave me a pretty good idea. He said he didn't care.

I've always found that it's the countries that no one wants to go to that make it the most difficult to obtain a visa. People aren't exactly lining up at the local Flight Centre to get the cheapest fare to Khartoum. Nor are they asking the pretty girl down at Thomas Cook about Red Sea holiday packages at Port Sudan. Yet this guy was making me jump through hoops as if Nicole Kidman and her single girlfriends were holidaying in Sudan that year.

If I had mentioned to my mother that I was thinking of going to Sudan she would have reached instinctively for my forehead to see if I had a temperature. My closest friends would have organised an intervention, worried that I was going off to join a weird religious militia and that the next time they'd see me was on a news report, being dragged off to Camp X-ray in shackles. Yet this guy was carrying on like I should consider myself lucky to be even *considered* for a Sudanese visa.

Getting a letter of recommendation wasn't as difficult as I first thought it would be. The nearest Australian embassy was behind me, back in Nairobi. And I wouldn't come upon another one until I reached Cairo. But there was a Canadian embassy in town, a neat white building with manicured lawns, and for Aussies that's close enough.

You see, Australia has a reciprocal agreement with Canada. When a Canuck gets caught on trumped-up drug charges in a tiny Pacific island the Australian embassy bails them out. When an Australian traveller needs a letter of introduction in Ethiopia the Canadian embassy bails them out. It's all part of being members of that wondrous thing, the Commonwealth.

A lot of people question the relevance of the Commonwealth these days, especially when they see the presidents of tiny African nations living it large at meetings paid for by our tax dollars. But to them I would simply say three words – The Commonwealth Games. Imagine the cost to society of having to support the second-rate athletes who have been able to garner a career of sorts because they won gold in an event that would have otherwise been dominated by the Americans, Russians and Chinese.

The Canadians weren't doing me any favours on the cost of the letter of introduction though. It set me back a staggering $78! The price included a reprimand from a tall woman with Alanis Morissette features for wanting to travel in Sudan at all. There was a war in the south of the country between the Muslim government and Christian rebels, she lectured. And the route I planned to take was a war zone and the playground of bandits. She held the letter just out of reach and wouldn't give it to me until I promised not to travel at night. I left the Canadian embassy duly chastened and considerably poorer but with the letter in my hand. When I dropped the letter off at the Sudan embassy on the way back to town, I cheered myself by imagining the Visa Nazi clicking his fingers and saying, 'Drats!'

I arrived back at my hotel and found a man pissing against the wall of my room. He wasn't being malicious. All the toilets were full and he had a pressing need. Nevertheless, I decided it was time to leave the Tropical. Since the end of the Easter fast it seemed like most of the male population of Addis Ababa had dropped by to celebrate by shagging a bar girl, and the simple act of getting to my room had become an obstacle course of embracing and/or copulating couples.

The day before I had run into Paul and Marjo, a Dutch couple I had seen once or twice along the trail up the east coast of Africa. They were staying in a hotel up near the Piazza called the Wutuma. It wasn't much more expensive than the Tropical and it didn't have a bar. They were certain I would get a room.

I caught a minivan up Churchill Road past the plinth-shaped Marxist monument and the souvenir shops towards the Piazza. There seemed to be more people walking back towards the city than usual, but it was just after two so I figured they were workers returning to their offices after lunch. Just before the big roundabout, surrounded by Coke billboards and still 500 metres short of the Piazza, the driver did a reckless U-turn over a median strip high enough to launch Evel Knievel and started heading back towards town too. I yelled for him to stop and was unceremoniously dumped beside the road, before the van squealed off, its wheels smoking and spinning.

I put my pack on, still shaking my head, and turned to look up Churchill Road. Hundreds of people were running down the hill in a panic. A couple of hundred metres behind them was an angry mob waving chunks of wood and firing guns into the air.

It was like a cartoon. The frightened people streamed around me like I was a rock in a river. I stood dumbstruck by what I had walked into, unable to turn and run too.

Just as the mob approached a young guy grabbed me and shook me from my inertia. 'Quick, come this way!' he said, taking my arm and dragging me into a mudbrick building beside the road. He slammed the door behind us and I moved to the window and cautiously peeked out.

The mob had set upon a Toyota pick-up truck. The driver hadn't been able to turn around quickly enough, and was dragged from the cabin to be kicked and punched. A group of bare-chested young men, their shirts wrapped around their waists, rocked the pick-up from side to side until it overturned with the sickening sound of crunching glass and scraping metal. Then they set it on fire, whooping as the flames quickly consumed it. It was the sort of thing you see on CNN and it was no more than 5 metres away from me.

'Get away from the window,' hissed the young guy, realising that I was mesmerised by what was going on. 'They might not be happy to see a white man.'

It was only when I turned away from the window that I realised that we were in a coffin shop. Crudely made coffins were stacked against the walls, their lids leaning against them like macabre surfboards. A smallish coffin sat half-made on a bench beside some tools, a pile of sawdust sitting below it. There was a small room at the back of the shop and Mebratu, the young guy who had saved me, beckoned for me to follow him. It was the carpenter's bedroom, with room for a single bed and little more, and this was where I hid with the carpenter, Mebratu and five other people who had taken refuge in the workshop. The air was thick and pungent from our sweat. The clamour outside was deafening, but we sat in silence.

'The students are angry,' whispered Mebratu. 'Not just with the government but anyone who is rich.' The driver of the Toyota had been in the wrong place at the wrong time.

Soon we heard sirens, first in the distance, then closer. Then came the sound of gunfire. The police had begun shooting at the rioters. The little old woman beside me started rocking backwards and forwards on her haunches and wailing.

'Her son goes to that university,' explained Mebratu. 'She thinks he will be killed.'

When the gunfire was right outside the shop and the rioting at its most intense, I began to wonder how much protection these crumbling walls would give me from a stray bullet. I wasn't frightened. Strangely, it was more of an intellectual exercise. I wondered whether I should hide in one of the coffins just in case the rioters had spotted me going into the shop and came looking for me.

Then I was struck by a bizarre thought. What if a stray bullet shot me through the coffin? I would die and my body would already be in a coffin. They could patch the hole in the coffin and bury me straight away. The detached way I had all these thoughts indicated just how far out of my usual realm of experience it all was.

After half an hour the gun fire dissipated and the sound of the fighting seemed further away. Mebratu went to the front of the workshop and peeked through the window. 'The students have gone,' he called back. 'We should go now.'

The little old woman stayed behind. She was still rocking on her haunches and wailing, convinced more than ever that her son was dead. Outside a crowd had gathered around the burnt wreck of the Toyota, fascinated, as I had been, by its destruction. Mebratu and I set off up the hill towards the Piazza, broken glass crunching under our feet.

Churchill Road, one of Addis Ababa's busiest thorough-fares, was empty. The tiny soft-drink stalls that sat on each corner were either shuttered or lying on their sides. There was glass and rubbish everywhere. It was like Sunday morning in The Rocks in Sydney before the garbage trucks have been.

The mood was still very dark. A group of young guys milled on the corner, scowling, and they yelled angrily at me as I passed. 'American! American!' they accused as if I was somehow to blame.

Mebratu spoke to them in Amharic and they seemed a little mollified. 'I told them you were Australian,' he said. 'They have seen your Skippy on television.'

The Wutuma was shuttered when we arrived but Mebratu pounded on the metal door and they let me in. I offered him money for helping me, but he refused.

As he ventured back out onto the street, he turned to me. 'It is still dangerous,' he said. 'Be careful.'

I spent the rest of the afternoon sitting in my room listening to the echo of gunfire around the streets and across the city. It sounded thin, almost laughably innocuous, just tiny pops and cracks. But the sound was deceptive. People were dying and the Piazza was being trashed. I'd been told that the students were protesting about government spies infiltrating the campus to weed out those harbouring liberal thoughts. But the anger and the violence I'd seen seemed to be directed more towards those with power, wealth and privilege.

That night in the dining room all the guests staying at the Wutuma gathered and told tales about their close escapes from the angry mobs. Paul and Marjo, the Dutch couple, had taken shelter in an internet cafe, checking their Hotmail account as a car outside burned. A Canadian guy had been walking downtown when a well-dressed woman grabbed him and implored him to 'run to the Sheraton!'. He took her advice and spent the afternoon eating pizza and drinking beer by the pool, running it all up on his credit card. I had hidden in a coffin shop. We laughed at each other's tales. It had been exciting, a bit of an adventure, a story to dine out on when we got home.

Just as I finished telling my story an English girl was helped into the hotel by two Ethiopian men. She was smeared with blood and mud and her clothes were torn. Her name was Caroline and she had arrived in Addis by bus just as the riots had started. She hadn't realised why taxis drove by her, refusing to stop, so she started walking towards the Piazza, where the worst of the rioting was underway.

A mob spotted her and set upon her. They beat her and tore at her clothes. Some of the men started pulling down her pants to rape her. Another group were furiously trying to open her pack and it burst open, spraying clothes and toiletries everywhere. In the mad scramble for goodies, the attackers were distracted long enough for Caroline to get up and run. A passing motorist, his own car under attack and blood streaming from his head, picked her up and brought her to the Wutuma.

She was still in shock and told her story with a weird grin. 'Shit,' she said, rubbing her leg. 'I think I've been stabbed.' She lifted a tear on her pants, revealing a puncture wound on her leg.

Paul and Marjo took Caroline back to their room and helped her clean her wounds. The rest of us sat in shocked silence, reassessing what we'd been through that day. What if Mebratu hadn't been with me? What would have stopped the guys that accused me of being American from beating and robbing me? And what if the angry mob had got hold of me instead of the Toyota ute? I think we all realised what a fine line we walked in these countries and how quickly things can turn ugly and dangerous.

The next morning things were quieter, but still tense. The university was closed, but the manager of the Wutuma was sceptical that it had been the students that had caused the problems anyway. 'The students may have been protesting,' he said. 'But it was the street people who caused the riots. They would have used it as an excuse to make trouble.'

I wandered up to the Piazza where most of the trouble had been. Any shop that had not been shuttered in time was smashed and looted. All the illuminated signs that hung over doorways were shattered and the umbrellas from an outdoor cafe were upturned and slashed and sitting in the middle of Adwa Avenue. A few brave shop owners were sweeping glass and rubble from their doorways but they didn't have customers.

At one o'clock that afternoon I tried ringing the Sudanese embassy but the phones weren't working. The telephone exchange for the Piazza district had caught on fire when a car was overturned and burned beside it. Even though I had been specifically instructed to ring, I decided to visit the embassy instead.

When I walked into his office, the Visa Nazi looked up at me angrily. 'I told you to call!' he snapped. 'Ring me tomorrow!'

I tried explaining about the phones, about the exchange burning down, but he wasn't interested. I hadn't followed his instructions precisely and I was being made to pay for my insolence. I didn't push it any further. I was worried he would snap, 'No visa for you!' I walked back to the hotel wondering if I was ever going to get a Sudanese visa, or even get out of Addis.

I must admit that my feelings towards Addis had improved since I had left the Tropical. The beggars weren't so much of a problem now either. I had learnt a few words of Amharic that seemed to work – yellem (I don't have) and bakka (enough). Even so, after close to a week of Easter scams, moaning bar girls and student riots I had well and truly had bakka.

Caroline, the English girl, was sitting alone in the dining room when I got back. The few possessions she had left and things other travellers had given her were stuffed in a collection of plastic bags at her feet. The British embassy had told the Ethiopian government what had happened to her and they were going to put her up in one of the better hotels in the city. She had even been taken to meet the Minister for Tourism.

'He gave me this coffee table book on Ethiopia,' she said, pointing to a heavy volume sitting on the table. 'I haven't even got a bag to put it in.'

I was worried about her. She was still in a daze. I wasn't sure that being alone in a hotel room, no matter how luxurious, was exactly what she needed right now. It would have been better for her to stay here at the Wutuma, where people could keep an eye on her. But the taxi arrived to take her to the hotel before the others returned to help me convince her to stay.

The next day I borrowed the hotel manager's mobile phone and called the Visa Nazi. He was pleased that I had followed his instructions and told me to come and pick up my passport immediately. I thought it meant I had the visa, but I couldn't be sure. I'd been told to pick up my passport by a Sudanese embassy before, back in Lusaka, and then that was only to give me my money back.

When I arrived at the embassy the Visa Nazi was down at the gate talking to the guard. He motioned for me to follow him and I tried to make small talk about the weather as we walked up the gravel drive towards his office but he just ignored me. He unlocked his office, sat behind his desk and asked me when I planned to enter Sudan. I said in about a week and he grunted. He pulled out my passport, scribbled a few dates on the visa sticker that had already been put in it, and then handed it to me.

I'd been playing this scene in my mind all week. At first I thought I'd flip him. Another time I had a little speech figured out where I told him what a wanker he was. But before I could do any of that the Visa Nazi did something that really surprised me. He shook my hand. I think it had all been a test to see if I would lose my temper, get all Western and start demanding my 'rights'. I had obviously passed the test.

I'd like to say that I felt elated but I didn't. I just felt tired. The tension that had been building since I visited my first Sudanese embassy back in Lusaka had finally eased, but it was replaced with exhaustion. To be honest, I think I was more excited about being finally able to leave Addis Ababa.

Chapter 18

LALIBELA, ETHIOPIA

Kichango, kuchangizana.

Everyone should contribute when a collection is made.

The Addis Ababa bus station is in the Mercato district, about 2 kilometres from the Piazza and the hotel I was staying in. It is home to the largest market in East Africa, a sprawling labyrinth of stalls selling everything from AK-47s to the kind of plastic kitchen utensils that accompanied me from the border at Moyale. Like the Piazza it was badly hit by the riots, and that morning I rode in a taxi through the worst of it, past burned-out cars and looted shops and along a road covered in broken glass that glittered like diamonds in the beam of the taxi's headlights.

My bus north to Bahar Dar was scheduled to leave at 4.30 am. The strictly enforced 'no travelling at night' rule meant that every other bus leaving Addis Ababa that day did too.

Their drivers backed them in and out of tight spaces for no other reason, it seemed, than to prove that they could do it. And their touts latched onto gormless passengers and convinced them that where they really wanted to go was the destination serviced by their particular bus. It was an anarchic expanse of putrid mud and cacophonous buses, and a cloud of noxious fumes hung low over it, but I found the energy of the place at such an early hour intoxicating. Of course, I could have just been giddy from the fumes.

I found the bus going to Bahar Dar and settled into a seat that I shared with an Ethiopian family who hadn't been planning to go north at all. They sat silently, tears streaming down their faces, the mother occasionally dabbing her children's faces with a damp cloth. I wondered what had upset them before I realised that my eyes were stinging and my cheeks were wet to the touch too. It wasn't because we were all emotional to be leaving Addis (although I was!). It was the effects of the toxic fumes from a hundred revving bus engines.

As dawn cast a grey pall over the chaotic bus station, the bus's conductor wandered down the aisle, taking each passenger's ticket back and refunding our money. At first I thought it was some kind of silly Ethiopian jape and that the conductor would eventually hand my tickets back and say, 'Just joking, we'll be heading off in about ten.' But it wasn't a joke. The government had commandeered the buses for military purposes so there were no buses running out of Addis Ababa that day. To cap off the morning a pickpocket tried to rob me as I got off the bus and when I got back to the Wutuma I discovered that my room had already been given to another guest – an author, the manager breathlessly announced, on a BMW motorcycle. I'd get a room when, or if, someone else checked out.

The author was Ted Simon, the guy who wrote *Jupiter's Travels*. It chronicled his adventures riding around the world on an old Triumph Tiger and now he was retracing that journey 25 years later on a BMW for a new book. He looked a little greyer and more portly than on the cover of his book and he was walking with a limp after coming off his bike in Sudan.

I found Ted sitting in the hotel dining room eating breakfast. I had nothing to do while I waited for a room so I talked to him about his last book, *The Gypsy in Me*. It was about a walk he did from Germany to Romania, tracing his father's roots, and had come out around the same time as *The Wrong Way Home*. I was interested to hear how it went.

'Not too well,' he admitted. 'My readers prefer it when I'm on my motorbike.'

I didn't tell him that I also wrote travel books. I have learnt the hard way that no good comes of it. A mate of mine used to run the author events at Gleebooks, a small independent bookshop in Sydney, and he invited me along to dinner with Bill Bryson when he was in town. Bill and I are published by the same company, in fact we share the same editor in the UK. It was a very pleasant evening in a small Indian restaurant, about half a dozen or so of us, and towards the end of the evening Bill began talking about his new laptop. I startled him when I said that Alison, our mutual editor, had told me that he was a bit of a Luddite.

I think he thought I was a stalker. He asked me how I knew Alison, worried, perhaps, that I had been sifting through his garbage and had come across private correspondence about his next book.

When I told him that she was my editor he looked even more shocked. 'What do you write?' he asked. 'Are you a *novelist*?'

I was wounded. I told him I wrote travel books and reeled off the titles – *No Shitting in the Toilet*, *The Wrong Way Home*, *The Full Montezuma* – hoping that he might recognise one, but he only looked even more perplexed. 'I'll have to get Alison to send me some copies,' he said diplomatically.

I had fantasised that the likes of Bill Bryson, Paul Theroux – and even Ted Simon – were all looking nervously over their shoulders, worried about this new young gun travel writer from Down Under. But it seemed I wasn't even a blip on the radar. That morning I decided to let Ted Simon think I was just a fan of his work – and one that had heard of his gypsy book.

'I haven't got any copies,' he said, thinking I was angling for a signed edition. 'But you can have this book. I've finished it and I'm trying to cut down on weight.'

It was *The Sign and the Seal* by Graham Hancock and it was indeed a weighty tome. It followed the author's quest to find the final resting place of the Ark of the Covenant, a search that took him through the parts of northern Ethiopia that I was about to travel through. I thanked Ted, and thinking I was about to get a bit gushy, he begged off, saying he had to meet the minister of tourism for lunch. One of the perks, I guess, of selling over half a million books.

The next morning I was down at the bus station before dawn again. I found the bus to Bahar Dar, bought a ticket and sat in my seat, swallowing lethal doses of carbon monoxide and praying to a picture of an Ethiopian saint just above the driver's seat that the army wouldn't commandeer the bus again. Ethiopian saints are obviously more obliging than most other deities I have asked for help, because as dawn crept upon us the bus shuddered out of the bus station and crawled up into the hills of the northern suburbs of Addis Ababa. Finally, after a week of begging, blagging and bullets, I was leaving the Ethiopian capital.

As well as the usual Third World accoutrements of bald tyres, broken seats and suspect radiator, the bus came with its own onboard priest. He wore a flowing orange robe, an ornate headpiece not unlike the pope's, and the sort of chunky crucifix necklace Greek lads like to have nestled in their chest hair at discos. He spent most of the journey walking up and down the aisle reading to passengers from a small battered Bible. Each passenger got a different verse and was expected to cough up a donation when it was finished. If the passenger's concentration wandered, or they refused to look at the priest, hoping that he would leave them alone, he rapped the metal frame of their seat with a gnarled wooden staff until he had their undivided attention.

The priest must have divined my short attention span from somewhere near the front of the bus, because he started rattling on my seat before he had even begun reading. Then he punctuated each word with a rap and a glare, and if I looked away, wouldn't continue until I held his gaze again. I couldn't understand a word he was saying, of course. That didn't matter. He was of the old school where mindless subjugation was more important than understanding. When he finished reading to me I gave him a grubby 5-birr note, hoping that my generosity would earn a nod of thanks and he'd move on, but instead he rewarded it with another, longer, Bible text. When he finally went on to the next passenger I put on my Walkman and pretended to sleep, just in case he stopped on his way back down the aisle.

We were passing through a different Ethiopia, now. Unlike the dry and barren south, the north was a prosperous region of patchwork fields full of healthy crops of maize and wheat and rolling pastures where animals grazed. It was a region that looked as productive and fertile as any place I had been to and a world far removed from the desolate country of drought and famine I knew from television reports. It seemed Ethiopia's curse was not a lack of arable land. Like the rest of Africa, it was the burden of greedy and corrupt politicians.

The begging was just as intense and constant as in the capital, though, except here they dressed it up with religious trappings. The priest used every stop as an opportunity to stock up on provisions, regaling the owners of small stalls with Bible texts until they gave him what he wanted. At Debre Libanos, a pretty spot of rolling farmland, a group of men who looked like Mafiosi had set up a roadblock, demanding money from every passing vehicle. The two biggest ones boarded our bus and wandered up the aisle, soliciting individual donations from passengers. When a passenger questioned them about what they were actually donating to, the men pointed to a hastily assembled shrine beside the road (it featured a poster of the Virgin Mary which was stuck on a pile of rocks and a few flowers) and glared until the passenger fumbled around in their pocket to find some loose change.

The travelling was as slow and difficult as elsewhere in the country. The road was sealed, but the driver conspired to drive as if it wasn't, piloting the bus at a pace more appropriate for a road festering with potholes. The passengers were just as strident about keeping windows closed, so after we wound our way down the Blue Nile Gorge and then back up again to Dejen, the bus was awash with the pungent smell of vomit. And as night fell, we stopped at the small crossroads town of Bure, even though Bahar Dar was less than 150 kilometres away. That didn't mean we could sleep in, though. The driver was outside the hotel we all stayed in, revving the bus and honking the horn at 4.30 the next morning.

By ten the bus was in Bahar Dar and I decided I liked the place immensely. It sits at the bottom of Lake Tana, Ethiopia's largest lake, and the proximity of such a large expanse of water has an agreeable effect on both the town and its people. The main road along the lake front is wide and lined by palm trees, and pom-pom wearing horses pulling carts clip-clopped merrily among the few cars and trucks that drove along it. The people seemed relaxed and content and smiled at me rather than demanding money. It was the first place I had been to in Ethiopia where I didn't feel compelled to catch the next bus out.

I was greeted at the bus station by a young guy called Ababil, who declared that he would be my guide to, as he put it, 'the wonders of Bahar Dar'. He wore the standard tout uniform of worn jeans, T-shirt and baseball cap, and I was sure that if I asked him he'd admit to being a little partial to listening to Craig David. But unlike most touts, Ababil believed in transparency. 'I will not lie to you,' he said solemnly. 'I will take 10 per cent on your hotel room and any tours that you do. Others, they will take 20.'

The wonders I had come specifically to see were the monasteries of Lake Tana. The monasteries date from medieval times and are found on islands scattered across the lake or on isolated peninsulas along it. They were frequently used as safe havens for treasures and sacred relics during troubled times, and even today house stunning collections of old illuminated manuscripts and relics. In *The Sign and the Seal*, Hancock claims that the Ark of the Covenant had been kept briefly at one of the monasteries, Tana Cherkos, on its way to its final resting place in Axum.

The only way to visit the monasteries is by boat, and unfortunately for Ababil I was befriended by a Korean engineer called Song-yun in one of the town's pastry shops. He had hired a boat for the afternoon and asked me to come along with him, for free.

The boat left from a dock in front of the Ghion Hotel, a crumbling hotel with garden bungalows that at one time must have been quite posh. The boat had seen better days too, and puttered out through the reeds and onto the lake with the dexterity and energy of an old man using a Zimmer frame.

Song-yun was returning home to Seoul after working in Ethiopia for seven years and was on a whistlestop tour around the country to see the things he hadn't found the time to see during his contract. He'd already spent the morning visiting the former palace of Haile Selassie and the Blue Nile Falls so our itinerary wasn't too audacious. We went out to the Zege Peninsula and visited Beta Giorgis and Beta Maryam, the monasteries there, and then stopped off at the island monastery of Kebran Gabriel on the way back.

I was particularly taken by the frescoes on the walls of the monasteries at Beta Giorgis and Beta Maryam. They adorn the outside walls of the Holy of Holies, a central enclosure within the monastery's church that only priests are allowed to enter, and they are colourful and vibrant like a comic book. Except here it isn't the exploits of Spiderman that are chronicled, but rather those of the mutant freaks of their day, the Ethiopian saints.

There was St Tekla Haimanot, a chap who prayed for seven years standing on one leg. Saint Gebre Kristos was a bloke who knocked back the perks of being a prince to take up a life of chastity and a dose of leprosy. Abuna Samuel was partial to riding about on a lion. And of course, the country's patron saint, St George, was out and about and slaying dragons. I looked at the frescoes, tracing the stories and deeds of these good Christian saints and thought of my sister. She worries about the effect of Harry Potter on her kids' young minds. What would she make of this stuff?

For crosses and illuminated manuscripts you can't beat the monastery at Kebran Gabriel. It sits at the end of a long flight of stone stairs at the top of a hill, which dominates the small island. The height affords uninterrupted views of the lake, picturesquely framed by the stone arches of the monastery's church, giving the place a distinct 'other-worldly' feel. It has a wonderful collection of icons, manuscripts, crowns and crosses that are kept in a small mudbrick hut that has to be unlocked by the 'curator', one of the monks. He blocked the door with a piece of wood so we couldn't enter and then presented each precious item to us, waving his hand over the crosses and manuscripts in the manner of the scantily clad girls on 'The Price is Right'.

Song-yun was overwhelmed. 'Too many treasures!' he said.

Ababil was waiting for me at the hotel when I got back. He was disappointed that I had found a boat without him and devastated that I hadn't paid for the trip at all. Transparent or otherwise, the way touting works in Ethiopia he had seen me first and was therefore entitled to a cut of everything I did, whether he arranged it or not. Desperate for any kind of kickback, he tried to talk me into going with him to Tis Isat Falls, a spot near Bahar Dar where the Blue Nile drops 42 metres over a lava barrier. I shocked him by refusing.

'They are very beautiful,' he pleaded. 'They are surrounded by paradise.'

I went instead to the internet cafe on the edge of town. I had spotted it from the window of the bus when I arrived in Bahar Dar. It had 'Internet Cafe' painted above the doorway and inside there were a few tables and chairs and a display cabinet with a small number of sad-looking pastries. The computer terminal, however, was not immediately apparent.

'Internet Cafe?' I asked.

The guy behind the counter nodded his head. I asked if I could *use* the internet. He shook his head. Thinking that he may have misunderstood me, I asked where the computer was. He shook his head again. Finally, a girl tucking into an eclair at one of the tables interrupted and explained. 'It is called the Internet Cafe but there is no internet,' she said.

Apparently the owner liked the name. He thought it made his cafe sound cool and modern. I would have to wait until Gonder to check my e-mail.

I should have made my way directly to Gonder. It is the last major town on the road towards Sudan and only four hours from Bahar Dar by bus. My one-month Sudanese visa was going to start within a couple of days whether I was in Sudan or not, so the sensible thing to do would have been to quickly make my way to the border and be sure I crossed on the day that it did. But I hadn't seen the rock churches of Lalibela yet. And while it was a little out of my way, the churches – hewn from slabs of monolithic rock and covered in intricately carved reliefs – were the main reason I had wanted to pass through Ethiopia anyway.

My bus journey to Lalibela was long, hot and tiring and extraordinary for only two things: the burned-out tanks beside the road – from which war, I wasn't sure – and the fact that the bus didn't plunge over a ravine. There was nothing immediately extraordinary about Lalibela though. It looks like just another isolated village sitting high in dry, barren mountains. The only thing that suggests something more rarefied is an all-pervading silence that bears down from the empty countryside. The sound of a voice, the bleat of a sheep, the tinkling of a bell, seems to hang a little longer in the air there.

I found a bed for the night at a pretty hotel with rustic rooms that looked onto a flower-filled courtyard. I had barely settled in before there was a young man in a neat suit at my door. He introduced himself as the National Tourist Office (NTO) representative for Lalibela and offered his services as a guide. I asked him how much he was charging and he said whatever I saw fit.

The guy was obviously having trouble picking my financial status. I was staying in a reasonable hotel but I looked ill-kempt and penniless (two days on a hot, crowded bus will do that to you). Telling me to pay whatever I saw fit was his way of seeing how much he could get away with.

I'm sorry to say that I got a little gnarly with the guy. I saw his dithering over price as another manifestation of the

Ethiopian handout mentality. And because he struck me as an articulate and intelligent man with a good command of English, I let loose all the anger that had been building up in me since the first Ethiopian stuck out his hand and said, 'You!You!You!' I told him that as an NTO official it was part of his job to know the proper price of a guide. I told him that the old 'whatever you see fit' caper was just a way of trying to squeeze more money out of foreigners. I told him that by using it he was no better than a beggar on the street.

Sensing that I had an awful lot still to get off my chest he made his excuses and left. 'A plane is coming soon,' he said. 'I must be at the airport to greet foreign guests.'

And, I suspected, try and rip them off. I'm sure they wouldn't be as belligerent as me.

In the end I chose a young guy with acne to guide me around the churches. Not only was he the least aggressive of the touts trying to get my business, he had a pretty cool name as well. In Ethiopia, your name tells a story. His name was Habtamu, which means 'you are rich'.

'Just before I was born my father got a new job and they moved into a new house after years of being poor,' he explained. 'So they called me "You Will Be Rich".'

Most of the churches at Lalibela are behind an unassuming compound wall just down the hill in the centre of the village. The rest, including the chapel of St George, are on the outskirts of the village, just beyond the football field, only a short walk away. They don't tower over the village but are hidden in the rocky shelves the village is built around. If I had been on my own I would have walked right by them, past the women selling vegetables on tattered blankets and beyond the men repairing shoes that were well past saving, until I got to the vast empty mountains that surrounded the small settlement.

That they are monolithic is the most impressive thing about them. Instead of being made from blocks of rock, they are hewn out of the rock in one piece, entirely below ground level. There are 11 churches near the town and each of them is carved in a different style. They are arranged in two main groups, which are connected by an underground passageway. The largest of the churches, Bet Medhane Alem, is 33 metres long, 23 metres wide and 10 metres deep. That's a hell of a building to whittle out of a slab of rock.

It is thought that the churches were created during the 12th or 13th century. Regardless, their incredible craftsmanship has led to some fanciful theories about who actually made them. According to an Ethiopian legend, they were built by angels. Graham Hancock speculates in *The Sign and the Seal* that it may have been red-headed Templar Knights who knocked them up. Most historians agree that most were carved during the reign of King Lalibela, but the different styles and techniques used to make them suggest that they may have been built over a longer period than that.

Like the monasteries on Lake Tana, each church has its own collection of relics, guarded by priests. You enter, marvel at the ornate carving in the church then slip the priest a birr or two so he unwraps a cross or a portrait. If you're lucky he'll even pose for a photo. My favourite priest was the guy at St Michael's. 'One moment please,' he said when I asked if I could take his photo. Then he popped on a pair of sunglasses to protect his eyes from the flash.

My favourite church, of course, was St George, or Bet

Giyorgis, to give the place its proper name. Unlike the other churches, it is on its own and out in the open. At first glance it looks like an ornately carved stone crucifix in the middle of a moat and surround by peppercorn trees. But as you get closer and you look into that moat, you realise that the crucifix is in fact the roof of a three-storey church. A church carved straight down into a slab of rock. The amount of work involved in creating it is astounding.

From St George's Church, Habtamu and I returned to the main compound and made our way back to the town along a secret passage that wound its way through boulders and overhanging rocks. Tiny cells just over a metre high and big enough only for a bed and a desk have been carved into the rock. The cells don't have windows so the wizened monks and nuns who live in them sat hunched over in their tiny doorways studying the scriptures. It was positively medieval. The dusty path emerged finally on the scruffy outskirts of town, where less pious characters drank tella, a potent mix of garlic and hops, from Merta Marmalade tins.

When dusk approached I went back to St George's Church alone and sat on the branch of a peppercorn tree that had fallen on its side. I wanted to watch the sun set behind the mountains, to see the shadows lengthen across the craggy valley and the colour of the stone change in the different light. It was peaceful and lovely and I felt content for the first time in Ethiopia.

Of course, a foreigner sitting on his own in Ethiopia doesn't stay alone for long. Within minutes two young boys had joined me on the branch. One sat quietly, content just to be close to a foreigner. The other boy fancied himself as a bit of an English speaker and insisted on pointing to things and naming them.

'This is a stone,' he said pointing to a stone, and then, after pointing to a tree, 'This is a tree.'

I smiled weakly, hoping that if I didn't praise his English abilities he would tire of the game and go away. It didn't work. He pointed to dogs, cars, houses and ants. And when he ran out of things to point to he stood up and jiggled. 'This is a boy dancing!' he cried.

Just as I was about to break my silence and say, 'And this is a boy getting a clip around the ear,' two men approached and demanded to know what I was doing. I recognised one of them from earlier in the day – the guard from the church. The other, judging by his robes, was a priest. He seemed extremely agitated and poked the guard and motioned for him to speak to me. 'The chapel is closed,' the guard said. 'Please leave.'

I said that I was just watching the sunset. I was near the church, but not in it. The entrance was three storeys down, for God's sake, and I clearly didn't have any abseiling gear with me. The guard translated what I was saying to the priest, who grew apoplectic with rage. The guard repeated that I must leave.

'Tell him I am watching God's handiwork,' I said pointing to the sunset. The guard hesitated, sensing that my comment might make the priest break a commandment or two, but I insisted he tell him. The priest spoke calmly to the guard and I thought I had swayed him with my divine argument.

'He said he will call the police if you do not leave,' the guard said.

I wasn't really surprised. There had been a lot of theft from churches in Ethiopia. Only a month before a Belgian guy had been caught at Addis Ababa airport trying to smuggle out a 15th century Lalibela cross.

When I gave up and walked up the hill the guard called after me. 'The priest says come back tomorrow at 6 am for a special service!'

I couldn't. I'd be on my way to Gonder.

❖   ❖   ❖

My guidebook described Gonder as Africa's Camelot. Like everything in the Lonely Planet guidebook to Ethiopia, it was a little strong on the hyperbole. Sure, there are some old ruins of a castle on the hill, but I defy anyone to arrive at Gonder's crappy bus station, wander through the down-at-heel market district and check into the Ethiopian Hotel and feel like they had just stepped back into an Arthurian legend.

To be fair to Gonder, I was just passing through. I was already past my nominated entrance date for Sudan and my visa was ticking. I spent an afternoon wandering around the ruins but that was all I gave it. Perhaps its Camelot-ness is something that is revealed over time.

There was no direct bus to Metema, the Ethiopian town on the border with Sudan. I had to catch a bus to Sheyday and then get another one from there. The Ethiopians were building a new road as part of a joint initiative with Sudan, and frustratingly we travelled beside it most of the way to the border. It was straight and smooth and looked finished, except for the boulders that had been placed across it at strategic places to discourage people using it. A banner in Gonder had declared that it would meet up with a similar road from Gedaref in Sudan before the end of the year.

I'm not sure how Metema will cope. It isn't so much a town as a dusty road lined by shops, bars and restaurants. It took me half an hour to track down the immigration officer and when I did he refused to stamp me out of Ethiopia until the next morning. I pointed to a bunch of Sudanese guys who were crossing the border in their white flowing robes, giving him a nod as they passed.

'They have come to Metema to drink,' he said with a shrug. 'It is forbidden to drink alcohol in their country.'

He gave me directions to the only hotel in Metema. It was a collection of mudbrick cells containing soggy straw mattresses. In an attempt to give the place a little bit of glamour the proprietor had named each room after a Hollywood action star. I got the Sylvester Stallone Rambo III suite. (My first choice, the Jean-Claude Van Damme Double Impact room, had already been taken by a family of Sudanese refugees.) The room only cost me 5 birr, but even that was too much.

The hotel didn't have a bathroom. If I wanted to wash I would have to use the public shower next door. It was a rattan room with a bucket with a hole in it on the roof. It cost 1 birr. As I showered a young boy scampered up and down the side of the room to fill the bucket with water. It was the most uncomfortable bathing experience I have ever had, and in my agitated state I dropped my bar of soap. I watched in alarm as the gunk at the bottom of the shower swallowed it up with a disturbing 'glooomp'.

I was beginning to think I had been cursed. Perhaps I should have been a bit more generous while I was in Ethiopia after all.

Chapter 19

KHARTOUM, SUDAN

Subira ni ufunguo wa faraja.
Patience is the key to tranquillity.

When I crossed into Gelabat the next morning the Sudanese men who had come over to Metema the evening before were stumbling back bleary eyed after a night on the tiles. Sadly, I was sober, and I immediately began to wonder if all the trouble I had gone to get into Sudan was worth it. If you added up the costs of the telephone calls to the Sudanese embassy in Lusaka, the letter of introduction from the Canadian embassy and the visa itself I had spent over $US150 just to get to this point. All I seemed to be getting for my money was a shanty-town on a dry riverbank.

I was distinctly underwhelmed. The only buildings of substance were a customs building, a police station and an immigration compound. Every other structure was built from reeds so it could be easily dismantled, moved or simply abandoned. There was a market but I had seen everything they were selling cheaper and in better condition on the other side of the border in Metema. Judging by the lax attitude of the border guards on either side (people crossing just yelled and waved as they passed by) it would be just as easy to simply pop over and pick up a little something for dinner in Ethiopia instead.

The border marked the divide between Christian East Africa and Islamic North Africa, however, and that was immediately apparent in the different dress code in Sudan. On the Ethiopian side everyone wore the standard African uniform of second-hand clothes from the West – T-shirts with pictures of Leonardo DiCaprio and Kate Winslet on the front, faded jeans, trousers and jackets with patches. But on the Sudanese side they chose to wear galabayyas, the flowing white robes I've always associated with the Middle East. The people were still dark skinned, with typical African features, so it felt like stepping onto the set of Lawrence of Arabia, but with Denzel Washington playing Lawrence, not Peter O'Toole.

Further south the distinction was much less clear. A civil war raged as Muslims and Christians battled for control of the country as they have done during much of Sudan's history. Now, rather than getting support from an imperial nation keen to shore up control of the Nile as they had with the British, the Christians were sponsored by Bible-wielding fanatics from the Deep South of America, keen to save souls and raise some extra cash. The Muslims, on the other hand, were backed by a corrupt government desperately clinging to power, a far cry from the Mahdiyah, whose main aim back in 1883 was to clear the country of infidels.

Like most Muslims, the Sudanese were hospitable. When I popped in to see the immigration officer he invited me into his hut and gave me a cup of tea. He was still dressed in his nightshirt and possessed a painfully high-pitched voice. 'Welcome to Sudan!' he screeched with a smile. 'How are you enjoying your stay?'

Considering that my stay in Sudan to that point had consisted of walking a dusty 500 metres to his office, I said that it was not bad at all.

'It will be a few hours before the truck arrives,' he said. 'If you like, you can sleep in my bed until it gets here.'

His bed was in his office and although I'd have to put up with his screeching it was a tempting offer. I'd had a dreadful night's sleep in the Rambo III suite – the entire insect and small mammal population of Metema had been anxious to make my acquaintance – but I wanted to explore Gelabat to see if there was more to it than met the eye.

There wasn't and I ended up sitting in a makeshift shelter made from sticks and sheets of plastic drinking lukewarm Pepsis.

The Pepsis had cost me 100 dinars, about 50 cents, which was much better than the price I thought the guy was trying to charge me. The government had recently replaced the old Sudanese pound with a new dinar at a rate of 10 pounds to a dinar, but most shopkeepers still quoted prices in pounds. So when the guy told me that the Pepsi I had just drunk cost ten times more than I thought it should I was a little alarmed.

It is a testament to the kindness and honesty of the people of Sudan that the shopkeeper did not take advantage of my confusion. Instead he reached into my wallet and pulled out a

100-dinar note, saying '1000 pounds' clearly and slowly so that I understood how things worked in his country. I promptly ordered another Pepsi.

After my third Pepsi I wandered back to the immigration office. It was already oppressively hot and a group of people hoping to catch the truck to Gedaref sat in the shade cast by the compound wall. They were all black Africans, except for one man dressed in a white robe, with a black beard and strong Arabic features. His head was wrapped in the red and white chequered scarf favoured by Yasser Arafat. The young street boys tugged on my shirt and pointed to him. 'Mzungu!' they said.

It was the same word they used for me. In their eyes we all looked the same.

The guy's name was Ahmed and he was from Yemen. He had caught a boat across the straits from Aden to Djibouti and had travelled overland through Ethiopia to the border. After ascertaining that I wasn't American or British he told me that he was going to Khartoum 'on business' and would be flying back from there to Yemen. He spoke English perfectly, so I asked him why he hadn't just flown to Khartoum in the first place. My journey through Ethiopia from Moyale had been hellish; it would have been worse from Djibouti. Ahmed became evasive and simply said that he could not afford to fly until he had visited his 'associates'.

At ten an old Bedford cattle truck bounced into the village, an event that stirred Gelabat's somnolent inhabitants to life briefly. The prize seat in the cabin was secured by a fast-thinking woman who pushed an old man out of the way to get it. He had to join the rest of us in the back, exposed to the blazing sun.

The immigration officer, still in his nightshirt, came out to wave us goodbye. 'The driver will take you directly to the immigration office in Gedaref,' he squeaked at me. He had only sighted my passport – I had to officially register when I got to Gedaref. 'He assures me that you will be there by late afternoon.'

I hoped so. After five months on the road I was beginning to feel weary with travel. I was on the final leg of my journey now. A ride on a truck, a bus, a train and a ferry and I'd be in Egypt and only eight hours away from my final destination. The Sphinx, on the plains of Giza, in the same spot my grandfather had stood close to 60 years before. I wondered how tired I'd be feeling then.

When the good folk at the Bedford trucking company assembled that truck back in the sixties, I'm sure they didn't give much thought to the comfort of passengers riding in the back. The flat metal tray, with wooden planks around the side, suggested that they had designed it with other less demanding passengers in mind, the sort who were happy enough to hang their heads over the railing to catch the breeze and have somewhere to put their four hooves.

The driver didn't concern himself too much with our comfort either. The truck was loaded high with sacks of charcoal and bundles of firewood. I set off for Gelabat wedged into the back left-hand corner with a sizeable piece of wood sticking up my arse. Then, on the outskirts of the village, we stopped at an army checkpoint, where a half a dozen hessian sacks full of beans were thrown on top of me.

It became quickly apparent that the Sudanese were dragging the chain on their half of the Gonder to Gedaref superhighway.

Every couple of kilometres I'd spot a half-hearted attempt to grade a road through the scrub and an abandoned grader nearby. The grader operator and his roadworking mates were always somewhere about as well. They sat in the shade of the grader or a tree nearby, drinking tea, unanimously adamant that it was too hot to work. The banners back in Gonder that had boasted a year-end completion date for the Gonder to Gedaref highway were looking a trifle optimistic on this side of the border.

Even the road it was replacing was worse than its counterpart on the other side of the border. For most of the morning the truck followed a track that disappeared among the scrub periodically, leaving the driver to guess where he should have been going. And when it did become the approximation of a road again, it was potholed and rutted from the recent rains. The truck lurched along like Frankenstein and I became more intimate with a piece of firewood than I had ever really wanted to.

The heat was so intense that it made my skin crackle so I reached into my bag for sunscreen. Skin cancer awareness is obviously not a top priority for the Sudanese government because the other passengers watched fascinated as I applied my 150+. They stuck out their hands for some too and began applying it, watching me for guidance and laughing at the smear of white that it left across the bridge of their black noses. It was a great icebreaker and I'd like to think that in my own little way I've helped bring down the incidence of skin cancer in eastern Sudan.

By early afternoon we reached the next village and stopped at an army outpost, where we lined up to show a soldier our passports. The driver figured this would be a good time as any to clean the carburettor and got himself into all sorts of strife when he stripped the thread on three of the nuts and tore the gasket. He grew more and more frustrated, cursing and throwing his tools into the dirt. The passengers turned from watching and without saying a word wandered into the small village nearby.

Ahmed beckoned for me to follow. 'The driver will be some time,' he said. 'Let us have some tea.'

There was a strong army presence in the village. Soldiers in fatigues and carrying assault rifles wandered the dusty streets, sweating and looking like they had just come from heavy fighting. They didn't look at me – Ahmed said they were look-ing for rebels – but their presence reminded me that I was travelling through dangerous territory.

The tea shop was a modest shack with a dirt floor and a collection of low beds 'sprung' by long, criss-crossing strips of cowhide. I followed the lead of Ahmed and the other passengers and reclined along a bed on my side, my head held up by my cupped hand. A large woman so mannish that a colourful kanga pulled over her head like a cape was the only sign of her femininity brought us sweet tea in small silver pots. Everyone waited and watched me take my first sip, and smiled when I nodded that it was good.

An hour later the driver joined us. Ahmed told me that he hadn't fixed the truck yet, he needed a part before he could, and had come to the tea shop to have a cuppa and compose his thoughts. He reclined on one of the mattresses, but had barely taken one sip before he jumped up and fossicked under a bench on the far side of the shack. He had spied a piece of tin and held it up like it was a gold nugget found by chance. He could use it to make the part, said Ahmed. Half an hour later we were on our way again, after one of the passengers insisted on paying for my tea.

I was amazed by how much friendlier the people in Sudan were. In Ethiopia people were constantly demanding money from me. Yet here, people were buying me things. The tea was ridiculously cheap, but that wasn't really the point. They regarded me as their guest, not their bank manager, and were determined to make me feel as welcome as they could. Which was lucky really. Over the course of the next six hours our truck broke down at least a dozen times, mostly, as luck would have it, near a road-side tent selling tea. When it broke down right on dusk, the driver gave up and we slept on the back of the truck, heading off again when he got the truck going at dawn.

The next day was a carbon copy of the first. What should have been a six-hour journey had turned into an odyssey of heat, dust and mechanical failure. At sunset we reached a police checkpoint, still some way from Gedaref.

'The driver says we will be there in half an hour,' Ahmed assured me. We weren't, of course. We were stopped motionless on a dirt road in the middle of nowhere and the driver had the bonnet up. And worse, it was dark.

The Canadian consul in Addis Ababa had been quite adamant that I shouldn't travel through this part of Sudan at night. I sensed a certain agitation in the other passengers too. The night before we had slept out in the open, but we had been in a village. Now, we were miles from civilisation in an area that rebel groups were known to roam. Our only saving grace was that our truck was pretty slim pickings. Most passengers only carried a vinyl bag of meagre possessions. And I'm sure bags of charcoal or bundles of firewood held little appeal for a roving band of rebels. They could have commandeered the truck to use as transport, I suppose, but my guess was that these guys wanted to win a war, not get caught within the next couple of hours.

The driver was clearly spooked though. When a group of passengers lit a fire in the middle of the road he made them put it out. I took out my sleeping bag and lay down beside the road, luxuriating in the space and stretching out limbs that I'd feared had seized up.

Ahmed came up to me and excitedly pointed out flashes of red light in the distance. 'It is gunfire. Semi-automatics by the look of the flashes,' he said.

I wanted to ask him how he could tell what kind of weapons they were, but the driver got the truck going and we drove off, slowly and without the headlights on.

I had long given up hoping that each glow on the horizon was Gedaref. Without fail it would turn out to be a tiny pissant village full of hurricane lamps and generated power. Instead I rested my head against the wood, each bump causing it to slap against the boards, hoping that somehow I might get to sleep and wake in Gedaref.

Just as I finally dozed off, using my arm as a pillow, Ahmed shook me awake. 'Gedaref!' he said, pointing to a large glow of light on the horizon.

I regard what happened next as proof that I have done something very, very bad in a previous life. With Gedaref within sight, beckoning us like a beacon, the driver turned right off the main road and bounced down a track *away* from the town. For the next hour we wound our way through scrub, Gedaref getting further away. Just after midnight we stopped in a small dusty village of walled compounds.

'Gedaref?' I asked with a whimper.

'This is a village on the outskirts of Gedaref,' said Ahmed. 'It is too late to enter the town so we have to stay here.'

I'm ashamed to say I lost it. I used the 'f' word more times than I'd care for my mother to know. And I refused to sleep on the mats laid out in the compound, saying I'd rather just take my bag and walk into town. It was not one of my proudest moments. And it was made worse when the Sudanese thought I was complaining about the quality of the accommodation. With typical generosity they offered me the only bed in the place. I didn't take it, but their open-handedness made me realise what an idiot I was being. I asked Ahmed to apologise for me and to explain that I was just a little tired and cranky.

The compound belonged to the truck driver and the way we were quickly accommodated suggested this wasn't the first time he'd used it to put up his passengers. His wife brought us plastic containers filled with water, straight from the refrigerator and ice cold. I have never tasted anything so sweet in my life. I had calmed down, and the other passengers joked about my little performance. I laughed too, lying back on my mat and looking up at the stars in the sky. There was a cool breeze and the stars looked close enough to touch. I drifted off to sleep knowing that there were a lot worse places I could have been. I'd spent the two previous nights in them.

The next morning we were driven into Gedaref and dropped off at the local Aliens Registration Office. While the everyday citizens of Sudan had been friendly and generous to a fault, the people who worked here were cantankerous and officious. It took three hours and $37 for me to officially enter Sudan, including close to a dollar just to photocopy my passport. To add insult to injury I had to listen to a painfully inept army marching band practising in a dirt field beside the compound while I waited.

Gedaref is on the main highway between Khartoum and Port Sudan, the most important road in Sudan and one that is kept in excellent condition. So although it was three times further from Gedaref to Khartoum than from the border to Gedaref, the journey was over in a matter of hours. It was a hot journey, though. So hot that the plastic flowers the driver kept in a small vase at the front of the bus had wilted.

The bus approached Khartoum at dusk. Ahmed the Yemeni sat beside me and pointed out the remains of the 'pharmaceutical' plant the Americans had destroyed in retaliation for the US embassy bombings in Nairobi and Dar es Salaam in 1998. The Americans said that the plant was being used to produce chemical weapons. 'Bin Laden's factory,' he said with a grin.

Not for the first time I wondered what Ahmed was doing in Sudan and why he had such an intimate knowledge of the world of rebellion and international terrorism.

After the long, torturous trip from the border I wanted to splash out on a decent hotel in Khartoum. I felt like I had earned it, but it had been impossible to get a cash advance on my Visa card in Ethiopia or Sudan, so I was limited to the few US dollars I had left. Of course, I could have stayed at the Khartoum Hilton. It was bound to take credit cards. But at $US150 for a hot shower, a comfy bed and bland, barely edible food it was a bit of an extravagance. My budget for my entire stay in Sudan was less than that. The residual effects of the truck ride, however, had me seriously thinking about it.

In the end it was taken out of my hands. As we got off the bus Ahmed asked where the minivans to the centre of town left from, tracked one down and negotiated the proper price for both of us. It was a slow and uncomfortable journey and I took this as fate scolding me for even considering such an extravagance as a night in the Hilton. I consoled myself with the thought that I hadn't lost face in front of Ahmed. If I'd gone to the Hilton he would have lumped me in with the rich Americans he seemed to have a problem with.

As it was he was shocked when I was prepared to shell out $US12 on a room with airconditioning and a satellite TV at the Danah Hotel. 'It is too expensive for me, my friend,' he said. 'I must find something cheaper. Good luck with your travels.'

As I luxuriated in my hot shower, an English Premier League match on the TV in the background, I wondered again what Ahmed was doing in Khartoum and how it was that he would be flying back to Aden rather than returning overland again. I just hoped that I wasn't dragged in by ASIO and shown his mugshot one day.

◆   ◆   ◆

I liked Khartoum. The architecture reflects its time as a British army garrison, an Islamic centre of learning under the Mahdists, and now as the administrative and economic capital of the republic. There are signs too of more turbulent times – you can view a gunship from 1885 when the Mahdists razed the town and killed General Gordon.

In many ways it struck me as a smaller, less hectic version of Cairo. Dark men swished by in flowing galabayyas and turbans on their heads. Women scurried by, covered head-to-toe in capes. At dusk families strolled along the Sharia el-Nil, under the neem trees, watching the lateen-sail boats bobbing along the Blue Nile. Small stalls sold delicious kebabs for less than a dollar and refreshing ice-cold lemon drinks for half that price again. My only complaint was that I couldn't stay longer. Transport through the north of the country and into Egypt only left once a week and my little side trip to Lalibela meant that my Sudanese visa only had two weeks left on it.

With so little time up my sleeve I needed things to go smoothly. In a country where everything is slow and unreliable, I had to count on everything going like clockwork. I had to get a ticket on a once-a-week train to Wadi Halfa and hope that it didn't take more than 50 hours to get there. Then I had to secure passage on a once-a-week ferry whose departure my guidebook warned was dependent on the fickle state of relations between Egypt and Sudan. From Aswan it was fairly easy going to Cairo – depending, of course, on the Muslim fundamentalists deciding not to blow up any tourists that week.

I didn't have any problems buying a train ticket. There weren't any sleeper berths available, but I was able to secure a first class seat without much trouble – as long as you don't count a little RSI from counting out 5000 dinar in 50-dinar notes.

Getting a ticket on the ferry from Wadi Halfa to Aswan proved more problematic. I tracked down the office selling tickets in Khartoum and found people throwing themselves at a window. I joined in and soon found myself face-to-face with a wizened old man with grey hair who looked like he'd had the job – and the uniform – since before the British left.

I told him that I needed to be on the next ferry out of Wadi Halfa and he shook his head. 'All the tickets for that ferry are sold,' he said in a clipped British accent. 'And the ferry the following week is fully booked too. You must go to Wadi Halfa and try there.'

Officially it takes 50 hours for the train to travel from Khartoum to Wadi Halfa. It leaves early Monday morning and arrives Wednesday morning, just in time for the once-a-week ferry to Aswan in Egypt. Of course it rarely arrives on time. Although it was once one of the best railways in Africa, the Sudanese rail system has deteriorated badly, thanks largely to a lack of funds and the government's desire to break the strong union that ran it. The good news is that the ferry doesn't leave until the train arrives. It can't really. Wadi Halfa has a permanent population of about three men and a mangy dog. If the ferry relied on the town for its custom, it would always leave empty.

For my 5000 dinar I got a crusty velour seat in a cramped, dusty compartment and three amiable, well-off travelling companions. One was a silver-haired civil engineer who popped pills from containers marked 'Free Medical Samples'. Another was a professor on his way to a conference in Cairo with a fixation with revising his notes. And the third was a 'doctor' who specialised in herbal medicines. He was the only one of the men who didn't speak English and he sat silently, as if meditating, for most of the trip. They told me their names, but I promptly forgot them and referred to them instead as the Civil Engineer, the Professor and the Witch Doctor.

I was surprised when the train left 20 minutes early but not when it broke down half an hour later and sat on the outskirts of Khartoum.

A team of engineers crawled underneath the carriages, tapping and clanking and trying to fix whatever was wrong. The Civil Engineer told me that a carriage full of engineers travelled with the train along with a full complement of parts and tools. The news both impressed and alarmed me. I was amazed at the forethought – I had not come across the likes of it in my entire time in Africa. But I was disturbed by the fact that mechanical failure was considered such a sure thing by the Sudanese Railway Authority. When I muttered that I should have caught a bus the Civil Engineer pointed out the window at a bus that had crashed into a ditch, its tail sticking in the air. Three hours later we headed off again and into the dry, hot north of Sudan.

The train made quite a number of stops that day, and not all of them at train stations. They were always lengthy stops, too, usually 20 minutes at a time, so I used them as an opportunity to get off the train and stretch my legs. I was the only white person on the train so these impromptu walks often took on the appearance of a royal tour, with whole Sudanese families rushing to their compartment window to wave at me, and me waving back, very much in the manner of the Queen from the back of her official Daimler.

Eventually, even the thrill of seeing a scruffy Australian waned and I was left to ponder the advertisements for Nile Petroleum on the side of the carriages. What the marketing manager of Nile Petroleum was thinking when he commissioned these ads was beyond me. The train wasn't a particularly good advertisement for their products – it spent more time broken down than moving. And the people likely to see it weren't exactly part of the petroleum-purchasing demographic. I couldn't imagine a nomad in the far north leading his camel through the desert, for example, spotting the ad and thinking, 'Hey, I really should get myself a couple of litres of Nile Petroleum premium unleaded.'

When I wasn't despairing the marketing nous of Nile Petroleum I would walk to the front of the train and peer wistfully into the first class-sleepers, startling the passengers luxuriating in the space there. Or I'd buy a glass of cool moya (water) from the girls who sold it from metal jugs, too hot and thirsty to care about the nasty bacteria thriving in it.

On the few occasions that the train was actually moving, the Civil Engineer insisted on showing me photos of the new Customs and Immigration Hall he was building at Wadi Halfa. It was a large white building set below brown dry mountains – modelled on a lotus flower, he said – and although it wasn't open yet, I would see it when I boarded the ferry to Aswan.

The Professor asked me if I had been able to get a cabin ticket on the ferry and I told him that I hadn't been able to buy a ticket at all. He thought he had misheard me and asked if I had a deck ticket at least and looked alarmed when I repeated that I didn't have any sort of ticket. 'Hmmm,' he said, trying to cloak his concern. 'I'm sure they will make an exception for you. You are our guest!'

The Civil Engineer piped up and said that he had a friend that worked for the ferry office, a Mr Razzaz. Maybe he could help me when I arrived. The Professor nodded reassuringly and said yes, that was probably the case, but he didn't look very convinced.

For the first day and some of the next, the train followed the Nile, so although it was unbearably hot there was always a splash of soothing green to our left. Here farmers tilled the alluvial soil as they had always done and periodically we would arrive at towns that were large and relatively prosperous, where hawkers sold gristly snacks and warm soft drinks. At Abu Hamed, however, the Nile took a sharp left and continued on a more circuitous route through the west of the country. The rail track abandoned the river and headed directly north into the Nubian Desert. Now any speck of green was gone and replaced by a flat sandy landscape, dotted only by tiny railway worker camps that were depressingly named after their distance from Wadi Halfa.

Here the train could get up a bit of speed at last and the driver obliged, hoping to make up for the time lost to the numerous breakdowns. I should have been happy – I had spent most of the journey cursing the train's snail pace – but with speed came new problems. Within seconds our compartment was engulfed by a fog of dust. Even with the window and the door to our compartment closed, I could barely see my hand when I held it to my face.

I tried to sleep, hoping that by dozing off the torture would pass more quickly. It didn't, of course. The dust only got thicker, and at one stage I woke, gasping for air. The dust was so solid that I felt like I was drowning. I slapped my hand against the wall, gulping crazily, struggling for air with the wide-eyed panic you get when you're dumped by a wave at the beach or stay a little longer underwater in a pool than you really ought to. I couldn't breath. I was dying. It was as simple as that.

My initial instinct was to rush out of the cabin and jump out of the train. I was convinced it was the only way I'd survive.

It was a strong urge too. It didn't even enter my mind that we were travelling through uninhabitable desert, thousands of miles from any sizable settlement, where temperatures often hit 50 degrees. Nor did the fact that the only way out of that desert would be to walk or catch the same train when it passed by a week later. I just wanted out.

My second idea – a split second later – was to look for an emergency cable, pull it and force the train to stop. The dust only got this thick when the train travelled above a certain speed. I could apologise for pulling the cable, but kindly ask the driver not to exceed that speed again. That cunning plan was foiled by the lack of such an emergency device in our carriage.

The Professor must have seen the panic in my eyes because he reached across and indicated for me to pull up my shirt and breathe through it. I took short, sharp breaths through the fabric and chanted to myself that everything was all right. It worked too. Within ten minutes I was calmer and didn't feel compelled to jump out of the train any more. It also helped that the train slowed down too. I think the engine could only handle short periods of these heady speeds. Every time it picked up speed I tried willing it not to go any faster. But when it did I had my shirt ready.

It was during these oxygen-depleted moments that I questioned the sanity of what I was doing. Why was I putting myself through this torture? Would I *ever* look back fondly on a 50-hour dust storm masquerading as a train trip? And more to the point, was I simply getting too old for this shit? Guys I had gone to school with were buying investment units and cheating on their wives. I was sitting on a train in the north of Sudan choking on dust. I made a vow in the middle of the

Nubian Desert that I would go somewhere nice for my next overseas jaunt.

Depending on ever getting to Wadi Halfa, of course.

Chapter 20

ASWAN, EGYPT

Fuata nyuki, ule asali.
Follow bees, that you may eat honey.

The train limped into Wadi Halfa in the early hours of Wednesday morning six hours before schedule. How this could have even been possible was beyond my meagre powers of comprehension. The train had broken down so many times that I had expected to arrive in Wadi Halfa some time in the New Year. Worse, arriving early meant that I had to find somewhere to stay for the night.

Judging by the very few lights that burned in Wadi Halfa, I figured I wasn't exactly going to be spoilt for choice. I followed the Professor and the Civil Engineer in the darkness across a dusty plain towards one of the town's only two hotels. It was already full, but the manager was madly pulling out extra mats and laying them in the courtyard for us new arrivals to sleep on. It was a chaotic scene, with entire families propped up against their possessions, some women breastfeeding children. It reminded me of the pictures you see of refugee camps on television. Except by the same time the next day we'd all be on the ferry heading for Egypt and the hotel would be empty again. That was why the manager was trying to fit in as many people as he could. It would be the only time he made any money that week.

The next morning I understood why the Civil Engineer was so proud of his Customs building. It would easily be the most impressive thing in Wadi Halfa. The rest of the town was decrepit and dirty. There were a few shacks, and goats hid in the shade they cast. The only real sign of life was at the ferry ticket office, which, it appeared, people were trying to demolish with their bare fists.

The number of people beating down the ticket office suggested that no one on the train had been able to get a ferry ticket in Khartoum. Thankfully, the Civil Engineer's friend Mr Razzaz was a good contact, and by merely mentioning his name I was ushered past a sea of imploring hands and into the ticket office. A ticket was issued quickly, but now that I was inside the ticket office getting back out was a problem.

The ticket office was built from slats. The people outside were pounding it with such ferocity that gaps had opened between the slats, letting in light that lit the dust that the commotion had kicked up. The light was harsh and bright, and from the inside of the hut it looked like there was a UFO hovering above us. The building, it seemed, was struggling against a traction beam, but gallantly holding on.

I moved to the centre of the room with Mr Razzaz and the

ticket clerks and watched the building buckle, waiting for it to collapse under the pressure. A tall metal cabinet leaning against one of the walls started moving towards the centre of the room and hit the ceiling fan. There was a loud clang of metal upon metal, sparks flew and the blades of the fan broke off, careering into the far wall, barely missing the top of Mr Razzaz's head.

Stunned into action by his near-decapitation Mr Razzaz grabbed a rifle from the guard, flung open the door and brandished the gun at the crowd that surged towards him. It was like a cartoon. The crowd stopped mid-lunge, their eyes widening on seeing the gun. An eerie silence fell. The crowd backed off, not sure what would happen next and I used that moment to escape from the office. Mr Razzaz yelled something in Arabic at them before slamming the door shut again. After a moment of silence the people began their pounding and yelling again.

By the time the Sudanese officialdom had stripped me clean of any local currency I had left (I'm still not sure who they were and why I was paying them) it was late in the afternoon and the ferry to Aswan was ready to leave. Most of the passengers sat in the hellish lower decks drawn, it seemed, towards the heat and noise of the big diesel engines. I made my way instead to the upper deck, where a light breeze ruffled my hair and made white caps dance on Lake Nasser, a huge inland sea that stretched before us.

Only 40 years earlier this had all been desert. (The ferry would pass directly over the original town of Wadi Halfa as well as the submerged ruins of Nubian villages and a few antiquities to boot.) A dam was built at Aswan to regulate the Nile in the sixties and the area was flooded. One hundred thousand people, mainly Nubian villagers, were relocated but 800,000 extra acres of land could be irrigated in Egypt.

The only other passengers on the top deck were Sudanese refugees, young men mainly, who were fleeing persecution in the south of Sudan. They said they were being persecuted for their religious beliefs, but their conversations suggested that they were fleeing for more economic reasons. They swapped tips on cheap places to stay in Cairo and the best places to find work. Compared to Sudan, Egypt was an economic power-house. And if Egypt didn't work out, they were a lot closer to their ultimate aim – Europe.

By ten that night the ferry had crossed into Egypt, and shortly after the temple of Abu Simbel appeared on our left. It was floodlit and even from our position on the lake I could see the massive statues of Ramses II staring impassively across the lake. The statues were carved out of the mountain back in 1290 BC as a show of strength, to tell any boat sailing into the land of the pharaohs just who was in charge.

In my exhausted state I had the rather fanciful notion that the statues were greeting me and that Ramses II was forming a sort of honour guard for the final leg of my grand journey. For the first time I got the feeling that my journey was nearly over. I fell asleep on the deck to the hum of the Muslim passengers praying to Mecca, knowing that I was on the home leg. I should have felt happy, but instead I felt anxious.

❖   ❖   ❖

The boat pulled up beside the Aswan Passenger Terminal just after midday. A pair of self-important-looking immigration officials came aboard and spread out their stamps and inkpads on a laminated table in the dining room. As the only Westerner on board I was herded to the head of the queue and the last of my US dollars were exchanged for a 30-day tourist visa.

The formalities over I tried to disembark but a guard stationed at the gangplank told me I couldn't. I had to wait until every one of the other 450 passengers had been processed. When I asked him how long he thought that would take he said six hours.

I was determined to be the first off so I camped near the doorway, resting against my pack and reading. After an hour I looked up from my book and noticed that a well-dressed man with a briefcase was being ushered off the boat by the same guard who had refused to let me off. I strode up to the guard indignantly and asked why that man had been allowed off and I hadn't been.

'He is a businessman,' replied the guard. 'He has important business to attend to in Aswan.'

I told him that I had important business too, struggling to think of a credible explanation should he ask for one. He didn't ask. He just told me to get my bag.

When you've resigned yourself to a very long, very boring wait, it's amazing how exciting such a small victory is. I clambered off the boat like I'd just won the lottery. Rather than being resentful, the Sudanese passengers still queuing to be processed seemed pleased with my good fortune. They waved me goodbye with a smile and wished me luck with my journey. If I'd tried a similar stunt in a bank queue back home, I'd be curled up on the floor fending off kicks to my head and abdomen.

The Aswan Boat Terminal was like an airport in its layout, with metal detectors and x-ray machines and a customs section replete with concrete benches for searching passengers' bags.

It was complete overkill, of course, and my footfall echoed around the huge arrival hall, startling the customs officials from their slumber. They weren't expecting anyone to pass through for another six hours, and they searched my bag half-heartedly, still wiping the sleep from their eyes. Beyond the boat terminal was a train platform with an arched, vaulted ceiling and wrought iron work that wouldn't have looked out of place in an Agatha Christie novel. Finally, I was on Egyptian soil. It was going to get a lot easier from here.

I found a cheap room in a modest hotel just off Sharia-as-Souq, the bustling market area of Aswan. The room had its own bathroom with piping hot water, and as I filled in the registration form I was already fantasising about the moment the water hit my grimy skin. Just as I was giving my hair a mental shampoo I was interrupted from my reverie by a tall Egyptian chap with a pencil-thin moustache. He claimed to be a businessman and wanted to know if I had bought any duty free yet. When I said that I hadn't, he got terribly excited. 'Then you must come with me to the duty free store now!' he said. 'You can buy Johnny Walker. I will call a taxi.'

I looked at him with a squint of incomprehension. I was tired. I was dirty. And a hot shower and a bed with clean sheets were only two flights of stairs away. The last thing I wanted to do was go shopping, duty free or otherwise.

'But if you don't use your allowance within 24 hours you will lose it,' he said with rising alarm.

I told him that I didn't care. I didn't smoke. I didn't really drink that much. And at that moment a hot shower was going to bring me a lot more happiness than a cut-price bottle of Johnny Walker ever would.

'But you must buy alcohol for me!' he exclaimed.

It finally dawned on me that this guy wanted me to use my duty free allowance to buy cut-price alcohol for *him*. 'Okay,' he said, the picture of magnanimity. 'I will pay for the taxi.'

I laughed, and grabbed my room key. 'I don't *think* so!' I said and bolted up the stairs. I'm not sure if he followed to try and reason with me further. I was too busy having the best goddamn hot shower ever to notice if anyone was pounding on my door.

After I had showered I took a stroll along Sharia-as-Souq and through the markets, running the gauntlet of teashops, spice stores, juice stalls and souvenir shops and ignoring the calls of the men that ran them. 'Meester! Meester!' they implored. 'Good price for you!'

I had only been in the country a couple of hours so I was still vulnerable. When I came to Egypt in 1989 I had to buy an extra bag for all the crap I bought on my first day in Cairo. (I had been particularly drawn to the papyrus paintings – so Egyptian, so cheap!) I walked through the markets with my eyes averted, glancing quickly to get the ambience of each place but avoiding the eye of the shopkeeper, who was more than likely waving a tacky, yet strangely desirable, alabaster pyramid at me. I knew that if I showed the slightest bit of interest – a flicker of eye contact would be enough – I'd be dragged into a long and tortuous bargaining routine that would see me emerge from the shop two hours later loaded up with onyx cats, plaster busts of Tutankhamun and a lifetime supply of papyrus paintings.

Eventually the souvenirs gave way to cheap polyester clothing and plastic kitchen utensils and I knew I had passed the worst of it. Yet I wasn't entirely safe. Just because I was a foreigner with no discernible need for a plastic colander wouldn't stop an enterprising Egyptian from spending three quarters of an hour trying to sell one to me. I spotted an orange juice stall ahead and ducked in for refreshment. Egyptian window shopping is extremely thirsty work.

The guy was already serving someone so I took the opportunity to watch him at work. The shop was completely tiled, with a stainless-steel bench. Fresh oranges were piled in pyramid shapes. The guy would pluck half a dozen or so from the pyramids, cut them in half and place them in a metal vice. Then he pulled down the lever, crushing the orange halves and extracting the juice. He was so adept that it only took him a few seconds to fill the glass for the guy ahead of me, and a few seconds more to fill mine.

'Five pounds,' he said, stretching out his hand.

The guy in front of me had only paid 1 pound. When I pointed this out the juice man grudgingly dropped his price to three. I finished my orange juice in one gulp and put a 1-pound note on the counter. He accepted it with a smile. As I walked away he called after me in English, 'Recommend me to your friends!'

It was such a stark difference to Sudan, where I was given the local price without hesitation. It didn't take long, though, before I had discovered a preferred selection of vendors in Aswan from whom I knew I could buy stuff for the same price, or close enough, to what the locals paid. There was the orange juice stall on Sharia Abtal at-Tahrir where I was only charged a pound. The guy who sold ice-cold Cokes down near the Corniche for the proper price. And the felafel guy near the

Nubian Museum who gave me three sandwiches for the same price as one anywhere else.

Still, there was much to like about Aswan. Summer was still a few months way so it was pleasant rather than hellishly hot. An early evening stroll along the Corniche is particularly pleasant, passing rows of low-level French period buildings, tastefully faded and crumbling and overlooking the Nile, lined by palms. I was also quite partial to the grand Old Cataract Hotel. The movie of Agatha Christie's novel *Death on the Nile* was filmed there and on my last trip to Egypt I had spent an agreeable evening at the Old Cataract with a pretty New Zealand girl I had just met.

Her name was Donna and we'd sat on the huge terrace watching feluccas sail by as the sun set over the sandy ridge opposite and drinking ice-cold Stella beers brought to us by waiters in crisp, white uniforms. It was sublime and for a moment we weren't a pair of scruffy antipodean backpackers but members of the 19th-century aristocracy in the middle of a grand Nile adventure. True, we had to walk back to our decrepit hotel along a potholed road prowled by mangy street dogs rather than retiring to a luxurious suite at the Old Cataract. But it was still an incredibly romantic moment and one that contributed heartily to my brief misconception that I was in love.

I tried to visit the Old Cataract Hotel again but it had a dress code and a minimum spend of 25 Egyptian pounds now. Besides, the hotel was full so the terrace was closed to non-residents like me. I stumbled back to my hotel alone, falling into the same potholes, harangued by the progeny of the mutts from ten years before, sober as a judge and without the company of a pretty girl from Wanganui.

One of my greatest regrets on my first visit to Egypt was that I didn't go on a felucca trip. I had hoped to sail up the Nile with Donna but she had to get back to Cairo in a hurry to catch a plane to London. The thought of floating up the Nile on a felucca without her had held no appeal. I knew I'd spend the entire trip wishing she was there to share it with me. In the end I chartered a taxi to Luxor with a group of other backpackers, stopping at the ruins at Kom Ombo and Edfu along the way. Being squeezed into the back of a Peugeot 504 stationwagon under the sweaty armpit of a guy from Birmingham who hadn't showered for a week was as unromantic as you could get. But in my state of mind at the time that was fine.

This time I was determined to felucca it. My problem, however, was finding a reputable felucca captain. In a country where every profession is regarded as disreputable, felucca captains are regarded as the bottom of the barrel. My guidebook was full of tales about backpackers being ripped off by a man saying he had a boat. Some were shown a nice boat and then put on a crappy one. Others complained of running out of food and water after the first day. Girls were molested, people were abandoned, and dope went missing. And everyone, it seemed, was forced to spend the night on an island that had been used as a toilet stop since the time of the pharaohs.

I bit the bullet and organised my trip through a guy called Salaman. He was the most personable of all the felucca captains who accosted me along the Corniche and the only one that hadn't hissed, 'Grass, man! Strong grass!'

The manager at my hotel hated him. 'He's a very bad man,' he said, sounding an awful lot like Baboo out of 'Seinfeld'. 'Not enough food! Not enough water!'

I hoped it was just sour grapes because I'd robbed him of a sizable commission by not using the captain he had recommended.

The felucca trip was a three day, two night cruise north towards Luxor. When I was in Egypt in 1989, you could sail all the way to Luxor. But since Muslim fundamentalist groups in the region had started attacking tourists it was forbidden to go any further north by felucca than Edfu.

I arrived at the docks on the Corniche at the appointed time and discovered that Salaman would not be our captain after all. Instead the captain was a guy called Jimi, who introduced himself as Jimi Hendrix. Nor would we be setting sail at nine. In order to get more passengers, Salaman had told a French couple that the boat sailed at eleven. They had wanted to visit the Nubian Museum before departing Luxor and the rest of us were left cooling our heels.

While the unannounced changes were annoying they weren't critical. Jimi was a happy guy, with a young offsider called Abdul. Despite my hotel manager's dire warnings, his boat was in good condition and judging by the boxes of water and food the offsider lugged on, well stocked. The other passengers seemed okay too. There was a young English couple, Carol and Adam, a Colombian couple, a Japanese girl and the French couple.

We pushed off and floated into the centre of the Nile, a sense of slothfulness washing over the boat immediately. We all kicked back on the mattresses in the shade thrown by the huge sail. The only sounds were the lapping of water and Bob Marley playing on the sound system. Captain Jimi held the rudder, grinning. He must have done this trip a thousand times but he was beaming with the sort of smile people get when they are doing a job they love so much, and can't believe that people are paying them to do it.

Soon Aswan became a speck behind us and we were on the river alone. The only time our solitude was disturbed was when one of the enormous three-storey cruise ships motored past us on their way upriver to Aswan. With their huge turbines they roared past us, just like spaceships do when they pass close by in science fiction movies. One passed by closer than the others and Captain Jimi called me over. 'Aussies usually moon those ships,' he said, laughing.

I smiled weakly. I imagined a bunch of my countrymen, stoned, drunk, lining up in a row and dropping their pants and waving their white arses at a bunch of people who paid thousands of dollars to enjoy a classy Nile river cruise. I just hoped Captain Jimi didn't expect me to keep up the tradition.

'We love Aussies,' he said. 'Very friendly people. They love the ganja.' Then he put on a broad Aussie accent: 'This is good shit, man!'

His offsider, Abdul, laughed, too. I felt like I was going to be a disappointment to them.

Later that afternoon Carol offered me her copy of *Kerrang!* to read. She'd bought it in Cairo, desperate for something to read in English. 'It's probably not your style,' she said. 'And it's about six months old.'

I wanted to let her know that I wasn't some sad bloke out of touch with the metal music scene (although I was), and very nearly name-dropped the only two nu-metal bands that I had heard of – Linken Park and Papa Roach. It was lucky I didn't. One of the first articles I read damned both bands as nu-metal lite, and the metal equivalent of the Backstreet Boys. I read on, chastened, but heartened by the fact that Ozzy Osbourne, who was around when I was at school, was still regarded as cool.

Just as night fell we stopped at an island. It wasn't the island where we would spend the night. That was a little further north. It was Captain Jimi's home island and he had stopped to visit his family.

Carol, the English girl, asked him if there was a toilet. 'My island is your toilet,' he said beaming, without the slightest trace of sarcasm.

Jimi had been promising all afternoon that the island we stayed the night on would be full of people from other boats 'partying, singing, dancing, ganja'. But when we arrived it was dark and the banks were empty. Adam and the Colombian guy clambered ashore to make a half-hearted attempt at starting a bonfire but soon gave up, coming back for one of Jimi's sheeshes. They took it back onto the island to use for smoking dope and the last we heard, they were giggling, then cursing when one of them trod in one of the turds that littered the island.

Captain Jimi retired to his 'cabin', a hole at the front of the felucca, with the Japanese girl, and his offsider, Abdul, sat talking to Carol and the Colombian girl. The French couple were smooching somewhere down the back of the boat. I leant back, my hands behind my head, and watched the stars. I was thinking how pleasant it was and how I would have loved to have someone to share it with when Carol came up and sat beside me. 'It's beautiful, isn't it?' she said, looking up at the stars. 'I can't believe I'm here. I could be back home freezing my tits off.'

I looked up and nodded. Carol was silhouetted against the stars, the moon shining on her upturned face. She had the kind of English accent that melted hearts. I was struck by how beautiful she looked, but then checked my thoughts before they got more explicit. She was young. She had a boyfriend. She was just being friendly. 'Think I'll hit the sack,' I said, fearing I might do something foolish. 'See you in the morning.'

'Oh, all right,' she said, giving me a funny look before crawling back to the other end of the boat.

I woke the next morning to find Carol curled up in the arms of Abdul, the offsider. Adam was just to the right of them, listening to his Walkman, totally unperturbed by the sight.

The Colombian must have noticed my jaw drop. 'I thought they were a couple, too,' he said. 'But Adam told me last night she was just a mate from back home.'

Fuck! I hadn't even seen it. But Abdul the offsider had. I wondered what it was about these guys. They seemed to have a sixth sense about which girls are single and up for it. Despite all the empirical evidence pointing to Adam and Carol being a couple, Abdul the offsider went ahead and seduced her.

Later that morning, an hour out of Kom Ombo, he was giving Carol a massage. She gave me the kind of look that said, 'You had your chance buddy, and you blew it.'

We reached Kom Ombo just before lunchtime. The huge sandstone temple the town is known for sits on a promontory on the bend of the Nile surrounded by a small village of restaurants and souvenir stalls. There was already a fleet of luxury coaches parked out the front and three cruise ships docked against the bank.

The plan was to spend an hour looking at the temple before continuing along the Nile to another island. We'd spend the night there before heading off to Edfu the next morning. Once again Captain Jimi assured us that there would be 'much partying, singing, dancing, ganja'.

I'm afraid the thought of watching Carol and Abdul the offsider canoodling for another 24 hours was a bit too much for me. My time in Africa had helped mend my heart but I wasn't quite ready for any more rejection just yet. I grabbed my bag and caught the first bus heading to Luxor.

Chapter 21

CAIRO, EGYPT

Hapana marefu yasiyo na ncha.
There is no distance that has no end.

The first thing I did when I got to Luxor was to go to the McDonald's on Sharia al-Karnak and have a Big Mac. It was the first Maccas I'd seen since South Africa (the African continent doesn't seem to figure heavily in Maccas' plans for world domination) and it was like every other McDonald's restaurant. There was a fibreglass Ronald McDonald out the front for the kids to play on, the staff asked me if I wanted fries with my order, and when I tried to pull out a single napkin from the napkin dispenser it rewarded me with a fist full of 20.

There were a few Egyptian touches, though. The notice-board for the employee of the month also featured a papyrus painting of Nefertiti with the golden arches beside her. And you had to haggle with the girl behind the cash register over the price of a Big Mac Meal (just joking!). Maccas' customers were largely tourists who alighted from huge coaches, on day trips from the seaside resorts at Hurghada, or from one of the quaint horse and buggies that could be found lined three-deep on the corner opposite Luxor Temple.

Once the ancient city of Thebes, Luxor has always been popular with tourists, even before there was a McDonald's. The splendour of its monumental architecture and its superb state of preservation has meant that since Greco-Roman times people have been using their annual leave to see the temples of Luxor, Karnak, Ramses II and Hatshepsut. The popularity of Nile cruises to the ruins among Europe's wealthy virtually kick-started the Thomas Cook company back in the 1800s. And the incredible archeological discoveries in the Valley of the Kings encouraged millions to follow in the footsteps of famous excavators like Howard Carter, the Englishman who discovered the Tomb of Tutankhamun, not all of them disreputable.

The Valley of the Kings is on the west bank of the Nile, opposite the town of Luxor, in the dry hills about 5 kilometres from the ferry dock. On my first visit to Luxor 12 years before I had thought it would be terribly exotic to ride a donkey out to the Valley of the Kings. Worse, I convinced two lesbian school teachers from Melbourne to come along with me.

I didn't know that they were lesbians at the time. I thought they were just two more Australian women with absolutely no interest in me. It was only as the dramatic events of the day unfolded that their feelings for each other – and towards my gender – became apparent.

The plan was to meet the tout we had arranged the expedition through at the ferry dock on the west bank. He would introduce us to our guide and donkeys and we would ride through villages and farmland to the Colossi of Memnon. From there we would trot over to Queen Hatshepsut's temple, before climbing over the high broken ridge to the Valley of the Kings. After visiting the tombs of our choice, we would return directly to the ferry dock along the main road, a round trip of about 20 kilometres. All the while soaking up the atmosphere with but a mere clip-clop of hooves to distract us.

Well, that was the plan. Our 'guide' turned out to be an illiterate farm boy, barely able to string together a sentence in Arabic let alone English. The donkeys were in poor condition, with knobbly knees and their ribs clearly visible. And they were tiny. I'm not a tall person by anyone's standard, but when I 'mounted' my donkey, my feet could still touch the ground. In fact, if I stood up there was a good 5-centimetre clearance between my crotch and the saddle. We couldn't change the donkeys unless we agreed to treble the price we had negotiated earlier in our hotel foyer. We wouldn't be able to start for another two hours, either, so we decided to stick with our dwarfish donkeys to avoid riding during the hottest part of the day.

We set off towards the Colossi, avoiding the main road by riding through fields of sugar cane. It was lovely. There was a light breeze rustling through the stalks and our donkeys set a fairly respectable pace. We passed through small farming villages where children ran out waving and laughing, amused by the sight of big white people on little brown donkeys. Soon we came upon an irrigation channel and followed it. It was a dirty ditch, full of putrid Nile water, used by villagers as a rubbish dump and toilet. But trees grew along it and we revelled in the shade they gave.

Although we'd only been going for half an hour, our donkeys began to tire. They wheezed like asthmatics, swayed groggily and stumbled on the smallest of pebbles. The tallest lesbian, Christine, had the smallest donkey and it was the first to give up. It let out a sigh before falling to its front knees like an exhausted runner after a marathon. Christine was tossed from her saddle and onto the embankment of the canal, which she promptly rolled down and into the putrid water.

I know I shouldn't have, but I laughed. We were riding single file and I was right behind her, so the whole thing unfolded in front of me like a Marx Brothers' movie. Clare, the other lesbian, had the presence of mind to jump off her donkey and clamber down the embankment to help pull Christine out. Christine was stuck in the mud pretty bad, and in the process of being pulled out she pulled Clare in. Then Clare's boot came off and stayed stuck in the mud after she had struggled out of the canal. Donkey Boy and I simply stood and watched it all happen. In my defence, I was astounded at the slapstick way the whole thing panned out. It wasn't until they were both on the side of the embankment, the rogue boot rescued, that I offered my hand to help them.

'Bit late now,' scolded Clare, storming past my outstretched hand. 'Wouldn't want to muddy those lovely white runners now, would we?'

I should point out in my defence that it was the late eighties and white runners with acid-washed stretch jeans were all the rage. And yes, it would have been a bit of a bugger to get them dirty.

'And they wonder why we don't like men,' said Christine with a humph.

I rode chastened and silent all the way to the Temple of Hatshepsut. I'd met two attractive lesbians and they already hated me.

If anything the ride got worse after Hatshepsut's temple. The girls hadn't paid too much attention to the hieroglyphics that lined the walls there or the stone statues of ancient Egyptian gods scattered in the antechambers. They were looking for water to wash the mud from their clothes and faces and blamed me when they couldn't find any. Their mood darkened when Donkey Boy pointed to a thin dusty path that wove its way up through the barren, craggy hills behind the temple, even though he assured us it was the short cut to the Valley of the Kings.

It was a short cut that demanded we walk most of the way beside our donkeys. It reminded me of a scene from a western, where the cowboys are picking their way along paths in Death Valley, a cliff face on one side, a sheer drop onto jagged rocks on the other. The sun beat down relentlessly. Heat shimmered off the broken rocks and we ran out of drinking water. Soon both the donkeys and we were sucking hard for breath.

We arrived at the Valley of the Kings two hours later, hot, sweaty and exhausted. After visiting one or two tombs we handed the donkeys back to Donkey Boy, paid him the agreed sum and caught a taxi back to the ferry dock. (I don't think he realised what was happening at first. It wasn't until we got into the taxi and drove off that I noticed a look of alarm cross his face.) Christine and Clare were still furious with me for not helping them out of the slime. They sat whispering between themselves, ignoring me. I remember thinking that it was lucky I hadn't been entertaining any lesbian fantasies. I would have ended up a very disappointed man.

This visit I decided to save the donkeys and hire a taxi, choosing the taxi driver who seemed least interested in taking me. I told him that I simply wanted to go to the Temple of Hatshepsut, the Valley of the Kings and back again. We would agree on a price before we set off. And I didn't want to stop at any papyrus museums, soapstone factories or carpet weavers so he could supplement that price with a commission.

He nodded as if what I was asking was perfectly reasonable. 'I already own my car,' he explained. 'So any money you give me is mine. These other men have to rent the cars. Also, I live on this side. It is cheaper.'

His name was Ali and he wore a grubby grey galabayya stretched tight across his fat belly. His chin was flecked with grey stubble and he drove with his arm lazily draped over the steering wheel. I asked him about the massacre at Hatshepsut's temple in 1997. Fifty-eight tourists were killed and I wondered if they had caught the men responsible.

'No,' he said gravely. 'The army scoured the hills. And they raided our villages. But they found nothing. Some say they didn't want to find them.'

When we arrived at Hatshepsut's temple it was as if the massacre had never occurred. Hundreds of sunburnt tourists, bussed in from the coast for the day, walked up the long path to the temple, set majestically against the rugged mountain backdrop. They gathered in groups in what little shade they could find while guides spoke to them in their own language about the statues and hieroglyphics that surrounded them. The only sign that something was amiss was the dozen or so armed tourist police stationed at various high points on the temple. I approached one, and after ascertaining that he spoke English, asked where the massacre took place. He looked at me, startled, before begging off that he didn't understand English, despite being fluent enough moments before to ask me about Australia and kangaroos.

The workmen in dusty galabayyas and turbans didn't know either. They chipped lazily at stones, stopping to pose for photos for tourists and then demanding baksheesh. The water carrier was in particular demand, the shapely terracotta resting lazily on his shoulder adding a certain exotic element to photos. He was in such demand that he forgot about the task at hand. I'm sure he would have kept posing quite happily all afternoon, tucking the crumpled pound notes in his galabayya, but for the fact that the thirsty workers were haranguing him to do his real job.

When I got back in the cab, I told Ali what had happened. 'They try to pretend it never happened,' he said. 'They have even filled in the bullet holes.'

I was astounded. Why wasn't there a plaque of remembrance for the people who lost their lives? There had been a similar massacre at Port Arthur in Tasmania and the authorities there had created a monument commemorating the people killed. Why couldn't they do something similar here?

'That would only remind people of the massacre,' said Ali. 'And maybe it will make people realise that nothing has changed. It is still dangerous.'

A huge asphalt carpark had been built out at the Valley of the Kings since my last visit, so getting to the entrance involved dodging luxury coaches and running the gauntlet of trinket stalls selling crappy souvenirs, cold drinks and film in faded boxes at prices that suggested a roll of Fuji was worth more,

ounce for ounce, than a lump of gold. On reaching the entrance
your dignity is challenged by a twee choo-choo train that takes
visitors the last 1.5 kilometres to the tomb entrances. I decided
to walk – despite the 40-degree heat.

The Valley of the Kings always astounds me by how
unassuming it is. There are no grand entrances to the tombs.
They are just holes in the side of the craggy mountains. If it
wasn't for the network of interconnecting pathways and the
hundreds of tourists crawling over them like ants, it wouldn't
look any different from any other craggy valley in North Africa.

That's what had attracted the pharaohs to the place. Fearing
for the safety of the wealth of riches they were taking with them
to the afterlife, they adopted a new plan of concealing their
tombs in this lonely valley. Almost all the pharaohs of the 18th,
19th, and 20th dynasties (1539–1075 BC), from Tuthmosis I to
Ramses X, are buried here, over 62 tombs all told. Sadly, most
were robbed during antiquity, usually during the lifetimes of
their successors.

Except for the tomb of the young pharaoh Tutankhamun,
of course. It was built in such a rush, tucked under another
larger tomb, that thieves missed it altogether. The fabulous
riches found in it by Howard Carter in 1922 meant that
Tutankhamun became the most famous pharaoh of them all,
even though his treasures were only a fraction of those that
must have been buried with a great pharaoh like Ramses II.
His name is still a drawcard. It costs an extra 40 Egyptian
pounds to visit his tomb, even though it is one of the smallest
and least impressive in the valley. I had seen it on my last visit
to Egypt, so I saved the money and admired the colourful
hieroglyphics in the tombs of Seti I and Amenhotep instead.

That evening I went out to the sound and light show at Karnak Temple. It's a little more interactive than most. Instead of sitting on bleachers and simply watching the pretty lights, you are taken to various nooks and crannies of the massive site and the different temples, sanctuaries, kiosks, obelisks and pylons are explained, along with the varying architectural styles employed. When you consider that the place was added to by different pharaohs over a 2000-year period, it is an eminently sensible approach.

The show began out the front of the massive stone entrance, where I milled with hundreds of other tourists between the lines of mini-sphinxes that guarded the gate. As is my way, I had chosen to stand beside the most ignorant man there, a loud, grey-haired American with a new digital camcorder around his neck. 'Yep,' he said, pursing his mouth into an impressed pucker, and nodding his head towards the towering entrance. 'I can imagine a pretty impressive fortress here!'

Moments later he amazed me again with his ability to state the bleeding obvious when an old European gent fell to the ground clutching his chest. 'I don't think he's feeling too well,' he said, stepping aside to let some guards past to carry the guy to the ticket office.

Can I just say now how much I love light and sound shows? I love the way they try to impose a story on the ruins. I love the purple prose and the big, serious voices. My hope is that in a couple of thousand years people will be watching a sound and light show from the steps of a ruined Sydney Opera House. 'And yeah, verily in nineteen hundred and seventy two,' I imagine the voice booming, 'Premier Robert Askin decreed that there should be a public lottery to pay for the extravagance of the building.'

❖   ❖   ❖

I caught the 8.15 am express from Luxor to Cairo. I was only eight hours away from Cairo, the city I'd set out for over six months before, so I celebrated my last big train ride by lashing out on a first-class ticket. Sadly, all I got for the extra money was a slippery blue vinyl seat and airconditioning set at Arctic levels. But that was an improvement on the same journey 12 years before. The only difference between first and second class then was what you found under the shit on the floor of the toilets. In first class there was linoleum. In second class all you got was bare concrete.

The train followed the Nile for the entire journey, passing through a fertile strip of fields, date palms and mudbrick villages. Donkeys ploughed fields. Women washed clothes in the river. Kids got water from pumps and carried the containers back to their homes on their heads. It was a scene that could have been played out in any number of centuries, except for the fact that the guy sitting opposite me was mucking around with his mobile phone, playing all the different ring tones and trying to decide which annoying tune best reflected his personality.

I took the opportunity on that train ride to reflect back on my trip from Cape Town. It had been a pretty intense six months. I'd spent the night in a South African township and gatecrashed a president's birthday party in Zimbabwe. I'd failed an attempt to climb Mount Kilimanjaro but had taken my first steps towards international film stardom. I'd survived riots in Addis Ababa and managed to get into Sudan. Not too bad for a bloke running away from a few emotional issues. Once I'd reached the Sphinx and had my photo taken, I was convinced that even those would be resolved.

By late afternoon the train had reached the outskirts of Cairo and again I rued my decision to start my journey in Cape Town. If I'd started in Cairo I'd be arriving in Cape Town now, admiring the golden beaches, enjoying a cold Castle lager and tucking into a rump steak. Instead I was in Cairo, a sprawling collection of hovels, crumbling tenements and gridlocked traffic, with nothing more than a felafel roll and a Coke to look forward to.

Having said that, I like Cairo. I like the low-rise buildings from the French days, with grand, sweeping staircases and wrought-iron lifts that creak and groan and work only when they feel like it. I like the way the guesthouses are all named after countries and cities in Europe. And the fact that you can eat from roadside food stalls catering for locals that don't jack up the price just because you're a foreigner. I like the way each neighbourhood has its own personality and that there is a hum and a buzz, even though the strongest thing the locals drink is chai. I even like the squalling Egyptian pop music that wails from every shop, stall and car, reminding you that you could only be in Egypt.

I really, really liked my hotel, the Pensione Roma. For $US5 I got a single room with polished floorboards and a breakfast of breadrolls, jam and little triangles of cheese served in a quaint old dining room. I remembered the triangles of cheese from my last visit to Cairo and I noticed with a smile that they were the same brand – the one with the picture of a cow's face that looks remarkably like the Egyptian president, Hosni Mubarak.

I didn't want to go out to the Pyramids straight away. I'd always thought that the Pyramids would be an emphatic fullstop to my journey, and I wasn't quite ready for it to be over just yet. Instead, I wandered around the dusty lanes of old Islamic Cairo, losing myself among the mudbrick buildings and asking for directions from young boys tending pigeons in cages on the roofs. I visited the Egyptian Museum and pottered around its dusty corners, finding pieces neglected and leant without thought against a mummy case that would have had pride of place anywhere else. One night I saw the Whirling Dervishes perform at the Mausoleum of al-Ghouri.

At other times you'd find me wandering the alleys of the Ali Baba-esque bazaar of Khan al-Khalili, being wilfully difficult with the merchants selling alabaster pyramids and children's bellydancing outfits to tourists.

'I want something cheap and nasty,' I'd say. 'What have you got?'

Most would misunderstand what I was saying and would reach for the same carved cat, inlayed backgammon set or alabaster pyramid that they normally would have.

'Is that the cheapest thing you've got?' I'd ask.

'No sir!' they'd protest. 'This piece is fine craftsmanship.'

'I want to see cheap,' I'd continue, 'and preferably nasty. In fact, the nastier the better.'

They'd continue to show me their most precious items until I begged off, saying that they obviously didn't have what I was looking for. Sometimes I'd even shrug my shoulders and give that open-handed magnanimous look that I hoped would communicate that if they'd had what I wanted I would have spent up big time. Unfortunately one canny guy wearing a fez understood exactly what I was saying and I walked out of his store with half a dozen plaster cast busts of Tutankhamun, three banana leaf 'papyrus' paintings and a couple of tiny leather camels that looked more like donkeys. And I hadn't thought karma was a central tenet of Islam.

The rest of my time in Cairo I visited internet cafes, sorting out a ticket to London and catching up with all the latest news back home. The internet cafes ranged in price and ambience: the cheaper ones had old beat-up computers that even the poorest of schools would reject in Australia, the better ones had brand new computers and fast connections. My favourite was the internet cafe just off Talaat Harb. There was a picture of a duck attacking a computer with an axe stuck above each terminal. 'You usually nervous mee!' the duck screamed. 'Too slowly computer!' I wasn't exactly sure what it meant. But after half an hour on the computers at this place I certainly knew how the duck felt.

On the afternoon of my fifth day in Cairo the manager of the Pensione Roma knocked on my door and told me to pull the shutters closed. 'There is a sand storm coming,' he said. 'If we don't close up, the sand will get into everything.'

I joined a group of hotel guests who had gathered on the staircase to watch the storm through a window there. The storm blew in from the desert and up between the buildings like a river of sand. It was so thick that the sky darkened and the sun became a throbbing ball of red. The wind rattled the windows and sand scratched against the glass like it was trying to get in and consume us.

'This is freaking me out, man,' said a Canadian guy.

I knew what he meant. It was like we were in the middle of

the seven plagues of the Bible. Day had turned to night. The sun had turned to blood. All we needed was a swarm of locusts, a couple of million frogs and everyone to break out in boils and we'd be living in the Old Testament. Then, as quickly as it blew up, the wind dropped and the sky lightened from tangerine to a sepia tone.

I ventured out onto the streets an hour later. The air was still heavy with dust and sand. There was a thick layer of sand on everything – cars, shops, windows, dogs – and the people of Cairo stumbled through the streets with scarves across their mouths, trying to filter the air. It was like being on the train in Sudan again. But rather than a carriage, it was an entire city that was coated with dust.

❖   ❖   ❖

I ventured out to the Pyramids the next day. I'd like to say I went because I realised that it was time to finish the trip and get on with my life. But the simple truth of the matter was that I had run out of English language movies to see.

It only cost a couple of bucks to see a movie in Cairo and as most cinemas were airconditioned they were often the best place to spend the hottest part of the day. I'd seen *Traffic*, *The Mexican*, *Miss Congeniality* – hell, I'd even seen the remake of *Get Carter*, starring Sylvester Stallone. But after I suffered through the dreadful *Dr T and the Women*, there were no more English-language movies to see. It was either start watching Egyptian movies in Arabic or go to the Pyramids. Anyone who has ever seen an Egyptian movie will not be surprised that I chose to visit the Pyramids.

It wasn't my first visit to the Pyramids, of course. I had seen them quite a few times on my last visit to Egypt. Back then you could wander around the Pyramids for free, and I had taken the opportunity to gaze upon them in the morning, in the afternoon and at sunset. I'd seen them from the hump of a camel, the back of a horse and from the shoulders of a man who piggybacked me for 200 metres as part of a bet. I even saw the Sound and Light show – well, the German version – for nothing. I hid behind a sandy ridge with a bunch of Aussies and Kiwis, but unfortunately a guard busted us just as the English show was about to start.

The Pyramids are one of those attractions that hold you in thrall, even though you've seen them a million times on television, in magazines and on postcards or painted on the wall at your local psychic's place. But nothing prepares you for the enormity of them. Or for the fact that Cairo has sprawled right up to the edge of them, and that chances are your first sighting of them will be as they peek out from behind a crumbling apartment block. The benefit of that is you can catch public transport out to Giza, paying as little as 20 cents if you want.

I ignored the touts imploring me to ride their particular flea-bitten beast of burden and made my way onto the Pyramid plain by foot.

It's hard not to be overwhelmed by them. They have stood on this sandy plain in Giza for over 4000 years, changing little over that time and offering little in regard to how or why they were built. I wondered if my grandfather had felt the same way 60 years before when he came here on leave during World War II? Or Herodotus when he visited in the fifth century BC, when the Pyramids were already over 2000 years old? The sprawl of Cairo would not have reached as far. There would have been cartloads of tourists rather than coach loads. But judging by the carved aqua scarab beetles my grandfather sent back to my grandmother after his visit, I'm sure we all came away with the same tricked-up souvenirs.

I wandered among the scattered stones, stopping occasionally to look up at a pyramid, my hands on my hips, probably just like my grandfather had done. Boys with metal buckets filled with bottles of soft drink tugged on my sleeve, quoting prices that I'd have to take out a bank loan to afford. They have been doing this for centuries; in fact, I'm sure this kid's great grandfather tried to flog my grandfather a glass of water and a genuine artefact from a pharaoh's tomb.

I made my way down the hill along the paved road towards the Sphinx. It looked in surprisingly good condition – recent restorations had left its paws smooth as a freshly waxed leg and its face seemed more detailed than I remembered. I picked my way among a gaggle of Germans that had just descended from a tour bus and stood in the same spot my grandfather had stood. Suddenly it seemed right I was finishing my journey here. My girlfriend had dumped me but so what? I was alive and healthy, and had just survived six months in Africa relatively unscathed.

The poor bloody Sphinx hadn't been so lucky. He'd lost his nose when Napoleon's soldier used it for target practice. And what about the hordes of tourists streaming off buses in front of me? This was probably the only time they'd get off work all year. Wandering the four corners of the globe *was* my job.

I asked one of the fat German tourists to take a photo of me. He had a large SLR around his neck so I figured he wouldn't stuff it up. My grandfather was smiling broadly in his photograph and if you look closely at the photo taken of me that day you'll see that I'm smiling too. My smile is a little world-wearier than his. It had to be. After what had happened to my grandfather only months after his photo had been taken I knew how transient these moments were. And how easily they can be snatched away from you.

I guess I also realised the danger of dwelling on the heartbreaks that life throws your way. My grandmother never quite got over my grandfather not coming back from the war. After my mother left home my grandmother spent the rest of her life alone. She clung to her grief and never allowed herself to move on. I wasn't in danger of doing that – I knew that the relationship I'd left had run its course. But standing in front of the Sphinx, after travelling from Cape Town to Cairo, I finally felt I was ready to move on.

Besides, if it all went pear-shaped again, I'm sure I could find another corner of the world where I could lose myself for a while.

THE SWAHILI SLIDE SHOW

Now you can make the journey from Cape Town to Cairo in considerably less time than it took Peter by visiting the *Swahili for the Broken-hearted* web site at **www.petermoore.net**

Just follow the links to the *Swahili for the Broken-hearted* slideshow and before you know it you'll be enjoying Cape Town without the rain, Ethiopia without the riots, Sudan without the dust, and Egypt without the hawkers. And, best of all, you can get from Malawi to Tanzania in the time it takes a single picture to download.

While you're there, check out the web sites for Peter's other books, or subscribe to his on-line newsletter for up-to-date information and your chance to win an autographed copy of one of his books.

See you at **www.petermoore.net**